M000314039

A History of Drugs

Why are some psychoactive substances regarded as 'dangerous drugs', to be controlled by the criminal law within a global prohibition regime, whilst others – from alcohol and tobacco, through to those we call 'medicines' – are seen and regulated very differently? *A History of Drugs* traces a genealogy of the construction and governance of the 'drug problem' over the past 200 years, calling into question some of the most fundamental ideas in this field from 'addiction' to the very concept of 'drugs'. At the heart of the book is the claim that it was with the emergence in the late eighteenth century of modern liberal capitalism, with its distinctive emphasis on freedom, that our concerns about the consumption of some of these substances began to grow. And, indeed, notions of freedom, free will and responsibility remain central to the drug question today. Pursuing an innovative inter-disciplinary approach, *A History of Drugs* provides an informed and insightful account of the origins of contemporary drug policy. It will be essential reading for students and academics working in law, criminology, sociology, social policy, history and political science.

Toby Seddon is Senior Research Fellow in the School of Law at the University of Manchester where he is also Director of the Regulation, Security and Justice Research Centre. He is the author of *Punishment and Madness* (Routledge-Cavendish).

A History of Drugs

Drugs and freedom in the liberal age

Toby Seddon

Routledge
Taylor & Francis Group

a GlassHouse book

First published 201(
by Routledge
2 Park Square, Milton Park, Abingdon, Oxon, OX14 4RN

Simultaneously published in the USA and Canada
by Routledge
270 Madison Avenue, New York, NY 10016

A GlassHouse book

Routledge is an imprint of the Taylor & Francis Group, an informa business

Transferred to Digital Printing 2010

Typeset in Garamond by Taylor & Francis Books

British Library Cataloguing in Publication Data
A catalogue record for this book is available from the British Library

Library of Congress Cataloging in Publication Data
Seddon, Toby
   A history of drugs : drugs and freedom in the liberal age / Toby Seddon.
      p. cm.
   Includes bibliographic references
   ISBN-13: 978-0-415-48027-7 (hdk)
   ISBN-10: 0-415-48027-2 (hdk)
   ISBN-13: 978-0-203-88083-8 (ebk)
   ISBN-10: 0-203-88083-8 (ebk)
   1. Drug abuse–Government policy–Great Britain. 2. Drug abuse–Law and
Legislation–Great Britain. I. Title
   HV5840.G7S43 2010
   362.290941–dc22
                        2009037169

ISBN10: 0-415-48027-2 (hbk)
ISBN10: 0-415-58960-6 (pbk)
ISBN10: 0-203-88083-8 (ebk)

ISBN13: 978-0-415-48027-7 (hbk)
ISBN13: 978-0-415-58960-4 (pbk)
ISBN13: 978-0-203-88083-8 (ebk)

For Poppy, Sam and Molly-Eva, as always, and for my dad in his continuing recovery

Contents

Illustrations

Figure

Tables

Box

Acknowledgements

The first spark of the idea for this book came to me in the summer of 2005, as I was sitting in the university library in Leeds trying to finish the manuscript for my first book, *Punishment and Madness*. Reading an essay by Roy Porter on the contribution of Foucault to the study of madness, I was struck by his argument that *Histoire de la Folie* could best be understood as a history of the relationship between madness and reason. In the margins of my notes, I scribbled an idea: 'Could we say the same thing about addiction and freedom?' A year later, I got round to writing a short article exploring this which was eventually published as 'Drugs and freedom' in the journal *Addiction Research & Theory*. Unusually, I received a small number of emails after this article was published from people who found it intriguing and interesting but too brief a treatment of the matter. This persuaded me that I was on to something important and so I decided to write this book.

I owe thanks to several people who have helped along the way. Virginia Berridge literally made the book possible through her body of primary historical research in this field. Without her work, this book simply would not exist. Whilst I remain (obviously) in thrall to Foucault and especially some of his more constructive interpreters, notably Nikolas Rose and Pat O'Malley, in this book I owe a particular intellectual debt to John Braithwaite. Over the past three or four years, I have become increasingly interested in the regulatory scholarship that John has pioneered, which has transformed my thinking about drug policy and the 'drug question'. I would also like to thank Robin Room for advising me on the origins of the 'problem drinker' concept which helped greatly with a section in Chapter 5. An earlier version of Chapter 6 was presented in Vienna at the 3rd Annual Conference of the International Society for Study of Drug Policy. Thanks to participants for helpful comments and special thanks to Alison Ritter, who acted as a discussant at this session and also read a later written version.

Colleagues here at the Law School in Manchester have provided more general support, especially those involved in the Regulation, Security and Justice Research Centre that I helped to set up in 2008 and which is becoming an exciting and fertile place for doing research like this which cuts across disciplinary boundaries.

On a more personal note, my family have once again been immensely supportive, especially Sally, and I thank them all. During the writing of the book, my dad sadly suffered a stroke and I dedicate this book to his continuing recovery.

Lastly, thanks to Colin Perrin at Routledge for having faith in the original idea and for putting up with my terribly late delivery of this manuscript!

Chapter 1

Introduction

Drugs, freedom and liberalism

Drug misuse wastes lives, destroys families and damages communities.
(Jacqui Smith, British Home Secretary, foreword to the 2008–18 national drug strategy)

To punish the evil drug pushers who poison our children, I want the tough new powers.
(Gordon Brown, British Prime Minister, speech to Labour Party Conference, September 2007)

The scourge of drug abuse spares no country, rich or poor. An estimated three to four per cent of the world's population regularly consumes illegal substances, with devastating effect.
(Kofi Annan, United Nations Secretary-General, message for International Day against Drug Abuse and Drug Trafficking, June 2001)

Introduction

The 'drug problem' has become perhaps the archetypal social problem of our time – cross-cutting, globalized and apparently intractable. Its complexity is daunting, requiring engagement with some of the thorniest domestic and international issues, from poverty and crime through to international development and terrorism. Political leaders line up to talk about the 'scourge' of drugs against which 'society must be defended', from the United Nations, to the European Union, to an array of national presidents and prime ministers. And nor is this just a 'phantom' played up by the political classes – there is public concern and anxiety about drugs too.

In response to this, governments by and large do not seem to have risen to the challenge with much obvious success. The 'war on drugs', as it is often (tellingly) described, is viewed by many as one of the least effective areas of public policy in recent decades. For some, this is a result of a failure to take tough enough action on either supply or demand. For others, more fundamentally, it is the entire system of international prohibition that is unworkable. Even the most ardent 'drug warriors' have some frustrations and dissatisfaction at how things are going. In a speech in late 2007 to an audience of drug law reformers, Antonio Maria Costa, Executive Director of the United Nations Office on Drugs and Crime, in effect the head of the global prohibition regime, made this rather remarkable statement:

> Let me begin with the slogan so many of you have ridiculed: a drug free world. Wait, wait: hold on to the tomatoes – I am not the author of this slogan. While in my lifetime I would certainly like to see a world without drugs, I have never used this slogan. Actually, you will not find it in any of my speeches, nor in any of the official United Nations documents, starting from the most relevant of them: the conventions (of 1961, 1971, and 1988) that created the UN drug control regime, and the General. Assembly resolution about drugs. Yes, of course, several years ago (i.e. BC, before Costa) my Office put out posters with that slogan screaming across the page. While I never used this concept, personally I see nothing wrong with it. Is a drugs free world attainable? Probably not. Is it desirable? Most certainly, yes. Therefore I see this slogan as an aspirational goal, and not as an operational target – in the same way that we all aspire to eliminate poverty, hunger, illiteracy, diseases, even wars.
>
> (Costa, 2007)

Simply put, even viewed in the most positive light, existing approaches to the problem are not working. This book is an attempt to introduce some fresh thinking. I want to challenge the whole way we think about this area, to question some of the taken-for-granted understandings and so to destabilize the 'inevitability' of the present. I will try to show that our contemporary ways of thinking about and dealing with the problem are not natural or self-evident. We can do things differently.

Why, then, write a history if my concern is with the present? Around twenty years ago, two of the most interesting and insightful British commentators on drug issues commented acerbically on the vacuousness of those studies which earnestly declare that psychoactive substances have been consumed by human beings since 'times immemorial' (Dorn and South, 1987: 10). They argued for the need to engage in a more direct and practical way with the here and now. I share their sense of urgency and their prioritization of pragmatic action but I think that to do this in a serious and thoroughgoing way we need to look at the matter from both a *longer* and a *broader* perspective. I will explain briefly what I mean by this.

The long view: a 'history of the present'

Taking the long view of an issue or problem has an obvious attraction – uncovering its historical roots or origin may be seen as the only way to recover the pure, primordial truth or essence of the matter. But Foucault (and others) deny such claims and oppose the search for origins:

History also teaches how to laugh at the solemnities of the origin ... We tend to think that this is the moment of their greatest perfection, when they emerged dazzling from the hands of a creator or in the shadowless light of a first morning ... But historical beginnings are lowly: not in the sense of modest or discreet like the steps of a dove, but derisive and ironic.

(Foucault, 1984: 79)

So why write a history then? Foucault (1977: 31) answers: 'Simply because I am interested in the past? No, if one means by that writing a history of the past in terms of the present. Yes, if one means writing the history of the present.' What does this mean though? Much ink has been spilt on debating the relationship between Foucauldian approaches to the past and more conventional historical scholarship. I will not test my readers' patience so early on by discussing this debate in any great detail. Those who are interested are referred first of all to the collection edited by Goldstein (1994) and then, for the very keen, to Mitchell Dean's excellent book *Critical and Effective Histories* (Dean, 1994). With his usual acuity, Garland (2001: 2) points us to the heart of the matter when he observes that the purpose of a 'history of the present' is 'analytical rather than archival'. In other words, it is not concerned with writing a comprehensive account of the past in the way that a historian would. Rather, it seeks to use the investigation of the past to illuminate and problematize the present. However, there is considerable debate here about what exactly such an approach should involve as a 'mode of reading history' (Castel, 1994). Voruz (2005) nicely captures one perspective on the matter in her critical review of Garland's (2001) *The Culture of Control* where she takes him to task for being insufficiently Foucauldian. For the purposes of my project, I am less concerned than Voruz about 'fidelity' to Foucault's work, although I do not dismiss in any way that her argument may be significant for other projects. At the risk of further annoying Foucauldian scholars for whom this quotation has become something of a cliché, I could pray in aid here his own comments on this matter in an interview in 1974 about his hopes for the publication of *Discipline and Punish*:

I would like my books to be a kind of tool-box which others can rummage through to find a tool which they can use however they wish in their own area ... I would like the little volume that I want to write on disciplinary systems to be useful to an educator, a warden, a magistrate, a conscientious objector. I don't write for an audience, I write for users, not readers.

(Foucault, 1974)

From my perspective, to write a 'history of the present' involves starting with the way the question or problem is formulated today and establishing its *genealogy* (Castel, 1994: 238) or, in more straightforward terms, where it has come from. A genealogy centres on the examination of two things: initial *emergence* and subsequent *descent* (Foucault, 1984: 80–86). In other words it involves tracing the complex and multiple lines of development from first emergence to the present, with the critical purpose of rethinking the present. The distinction between this approach and the more conventional 'search for origins' may seem subtle but it is important. In a nutshell, the latter focuses almost entirely on initial *emergence* and assumes that this is the best place to uncover the real 'truth' of the matter. In contrast, genealogy examines both *emergence* and *descent* and assumes that the place to look is in the complex unfolding over time of the elements which make up the present. Furthermore, rather than clinging to the perhaps rather dubious idea that it is possible to find the absolute 'truth' about things of this kind, it is more concerned with understanding the changing 'regime of truth' (Foucault, 1980a). In other words, how does it become possible to say what is 'true' and what is 'false' about a given matter in any given historical time and place? How could it be, for example, that habitual or frequent use of opiates was considered as a 'bad habit' or vice in 1809 but as the 'disease' of addiction in 1909 and then as something else again in 2009? Does this simply show scientific progress over time in our understanding of drug-taking? Or does it reflect instead that there have been broader paradigm shifts in the past 200 years in how we view and govern social and economic life (what Foucault calls 'governmental rationalities')? The book is premised on the idea that it is these changing paradigms of governance that provide a key to understanding some of the otherwise puzzling directions taken in this area.

In an important historical sense, however, to talk in this way about the 'drug problem' prior to the twentieth century is misleading. As the historian Roy Porter (1996: 3) observed:

> If you'd talked about the 'drugs problem' two hundred years ago, no one would have known what you meant. There was no notion then of 'drugs', in the sense of a small group of substances scientifically believed to be harmful because addictive or personality destroying, the availability of which is restricted by law. The term 'drugs' as a shorthand for a bunch of assorted narcotics is in fact a twentieth-century coinage: if you'd mentioned 'drugs' to anyone in George III's time or in the Victorian era, they'd have thought you were referring to the remedies physicians prescribed and apothecaries made up.

An important part, therefore, of what the 'long view' reveals to us is that the very ideas of 'drugs' and of the 'drug problem', in the sense that we understand them today, are relatively recent creations. As Hammersley (2008: 16–42) notes, even today our usages of the term 'drug' are less than stable and unambiguous and there is considerable room for imprecision and lack of clarity. I will say a little more here about this definitional issue.

As Ruggiero (1999: 123) observes, 'there are no drugs in nature ... "drug" is not a descriptive but an evaluative concept'. In its contemporary usage, it refers most often to two categories: medicinal preparations (whether used by medical professionals or self-administered) and substances taken (at least initially) for the purpose of pleasure. Both categories are largely regulated by law, the second typically by the criminal law. As we will see, some substances have moved between these two categories over time. For example, heroin was initially in the first (it was marketed in 1898 as a 'sedative for coughs') but is now in the second. Even here the picture is, however, a little ambiguous. Going by its chemical name of diamorphine, heroin at the same time is still widely used today in British medical practice, usually as a pain-killer (see Gossop et al., 2005). The term 'psychoactive substances' is sometimes used as an all-encompassing category, seeking to sweep up not only the 'illegal drugs' like heroin and cannabis but also their 'legal' counterparts like alcohol and tobacco (and I am aware, of course, that what falls under the 'legal' and 'illegal' banners is different in some countries). This is more useful as a category in certain respects. But as Sherratt (1995: 2) argues, it perhaps fails to capture the sheer breadth of the 'range of preparations with psychoactive properties that form part of everyday consumption: either as food, or drink ... or as other "habits"'. The simple categories of 'food', 'medicine' and 'mind-altering drug' may obscure more than they illuminate (see also Schivelbusch, 1992). For the purposes of my project in this book, the central point is that 'drugs' is an 'invented' governmental category, in the sense of one actively constructed by human beings for specific governmental purposes, which has arisen relatively recently in the context of the emergence of modern industrial capitalism.

The broad view: a genealogy of regulation

In an extremely insightful review article, John Braithwaite (2003) sets out a rather different criticism of Garland's use of Foucault in *The Culture of Control*. He suggests that one central difficulty with the 'history of the present' approach is that it can tend towards a myopic or truncated view of the issue being investigated. He observes how Garland develops his account of contemporary penal strategies by tracing their genealogy primarily through criminal justice lines of development. Yet, he argues, equally significant are some of the business regulatory branches. Garland's genealogy is thus one in which some of the most important branches are sawn off. He suggests that what is needed is a more integrated analysis of regulation (2003: 24).

Helpfully for my purposes here, he takes drug policy as one example of how fruitful this broader view could potentially be. He refers to a chapter in his earlier joint book with Peter Drahos, *Global Business Regulation* (Braithwaite and Drahos, 2000), which offers what is in my view a highly original but rather overlooked analytical perspective on the drug issue. Braithwaite and

Drahos (2000: 360–98) argue that over time, five separate regulatory regimes have been created for different types of drug:

- a (globalized) illicit drugs regime;
- a (globalizing) prescription drugs regime;
- national non-prescription ('over-the-counter') drugs regimes;
- national alcohol regimes;
- national tobacco regimes.

They argue that no adequate consideration of the illicit drugs regulatory regime can proceed without understanding and contextualizing it as simply one regulatory branch within a much broader domain of drug or pharmaceutical regulation. The explanatory challenge is therefore to understand how these five sub-divisions came into being and how they have developed since then. This involves an 'integrated explanation of both illicit and licit drug regulation' (Braithwaite, 2003: 17). To put it another way, the task is to explore how the term 'drugs' came to take on its contemporary sense, the 'twentieth-century coinage' to which Porter refers.

An integrated account of these five regulatory regimes would be an extremely complex and difficult undertaking and is certainly beyond my capabilities. My focus in this book is more modest, as I am not attempting such a comprehensive and all-encompassing account. Rather, my objective is to trace out a genealogy of how the 'drug problem' is defined, understood and responded to today. Clearly, as Braithwaite's approach implies, this will require reference throughout to this broader context of alcohol, tobacco and other drugs (both prescribed and 'over-the-counter') but they are not the direct object of my study.

This concept of regulation, as used by Braithwaite and others, has a distinctive meaning that is worth clarifying here. There is much definitional wrangling amongst regulatory scholars (see Black, 2002) but for my purposes I adopt a broad definition of regulation as attempts to 'control, direct or influence behaviour and the flow of events' (Crawford, 2006: 452) in desired directions. There is considerable overlap here between this definition and the Foucauldian concept of 'government' as the 'conduct of conduct' (Foucault, 1991a). For example, Rose (1999: 3) defines government as 'all endeavours to shape, guide, direct the conduct of others ... [and] the ways in which one might be urged and educated ... to govern oneself'. Despite their theoretical differences, I agree with Vincent-Jones (2002) that there is merit and value in drawing on both these perspectives and that will be my approach throughout this book. In this, I follow, in particular, in the footsteps of Clifford Shearing who has demonstrated in perhaps the most sustained and imaginative way the fruitfulness of marrying new regulatory scholarship with Foucauldian ideas of governmentality (e.g. Shearing, 2001; Wood and Shearing, 2007).

At this point, some readers may be unconvinced of the value of these notions of 'regulation' and 'government'. Surely definitions of such a broad kind cannot possibly be of much analytical use? In my view, it is precisely its breadth of scope that makes regulation such a powerful intellectual tool. It provides a conceptual framework for viewing activity in diverse fields and at different levels which is not constrained by existing boundaries of knowledge or action. For a cross-cutting issue like drugs, regulation is a particularly appropriate tool as it offers an integrative perspective which can generate new ideas and insights that synthesize and sweep across different intellectual disciplines and policy domains. John Braithwaite has argued that not only are there 'few projects more central to the social sciences than the study of regulation' (Braithwaite and Drahos, 2000: 10) but, further, that regulatory scholarship is in the process of leading a fundamental transformation of the social sciences (Braithwaite, 2000). Accordingly, throughout this book I will be drawing on a wide of range of disciplines and literatures, from history, philosophy and sociology right through to criminology, law and politics.

Internationalism and globalization

Taking a long and broad view in the way described above opens up a further important question about the scope of this book. One of the striking features of the history of drug control is its international nature and indeed, as Berridge (2001) suggests, in certain respects this dimension is more significant than the domestic side. The current drug prohibition regime, for example, is enshrined in United Nations Conventions and its origins can be traced back to an international conference on the opium trade held in Shanghai in 1909. Going back even earlier, the two Anglo-Chinese Opium Wars in the middle of the nineteenth century are an important part of the story. Similarly, the drug situation today cannot be fully understood without setting it in the context of the globalizing processes of the past thirty or forty years (see Seddon, 2008a).

Despite this, my primary focus in this book will be on the British situation. This is partly a pragmatic choice to make the project a manageable one within a single volume. It also allows for an analysis which can provide the empirical specificity and detail required for the 'gray, meticulous and patiently documentary' (Foucault, 1984: 76) genealogical method. It is in this sense what Garland (2001: vii) calls a 'focused case study' rather than a generalized account. Nevertheless, the vital international and global backdrop will be referred to throughout the book.

Although this broader international backdrop will be significant, it is important to clarify that the book is not attempting a *comparative* inquiry in which the British approach is measured up against how things are done in other countries. Rather, it seeks to examine the British experience by understanding how it has been shaped partly by international and globalizing forces and processes. It engages, in other words, in the enterprise of attempting to trace the 'dialectic between national particularity and inter- or trans- or supra-national mobilities' (Newburn and Sparks, 2004: 1) which has become an increasingly pressing task right across the social sciences and in diverse fields of study. This, in turn, requires some consideration of the idea of globalization. Despite its near-ubiquity in both academic and public discourse, conceptual clarity is in short supply here. Perhaps the best definition is offered by Held and colleagues who, starting from the simply stated idea that globalization refers to the 'widening, deepening and speeding up of global interconnectedness' (Held et al., 1999: 14), provide the following helpful encapsulation of the concept:

> A process (or set of processes) which embodies a transformation in the spatial organization of social relations and transactions – assessed in terms of their extensity, intensity, velocity and impact – generating transcontinental or interregional flows and networks of activity, interaction, and the exercise of power.
>
> (Held et al., 1999: 16)

The central point then is that a genealogy of the contemporary British drug problem cannot proceed without considering these transnational 'flows and networks' and attempting to understand how they interact with the exercise of power within the nation-state. A further important point which this genealogy will highlight is that globalizing processes, whilst they may have accelerated sharply in recent decades, have a much longer historical trajectory. The economist Jeffrey Sachs (2000: 579), for example, suggests that the first long phase of globalization started in about 1870 and continued until the outbreak of the Great War in 1914, with the second phase beginning in the early 1950s and continuing to the present. Many accounts of globalization proceed by ignoring the first phase almost entirely. As noted above, and as later chapters of this book will show in more detail, in the sphere of the regulation of drugs and the pharmaceutical industry, that first phase of globalization in the last decades of the nineteenth century is of great significance (see Braithwaite and Drahos, 2000: 360–98).

Drugs, freedom and modern liberal capitalism

At the heart of this book is a thesis about the emergence and development of our contemporary understandings of the 'drug problem'. It will be argued that the ways in which we view and deal with the matter today are rooted in the emergence of modern liberal capitalism a little over 200 years ago. By way of introduction to the chapters that follow, I want to sketch out here the broad contours of this argument.

According to economic historians, modern capitalism was born in Britain in the Industrial Revolution in the late eighteenth century, subsequently spreading across Western Europe and beyond in the early 1800s, but only becoming a truly global phenomenon at the end of the twentieth century (Sachs, 1999). In Britain, the birth of capitalism in the last two or three decades of the eighteenth century had a transformative impact across diverse areas of citizens' everyday life (Hobsbawm, 1962). More fundamentally, it was also accompanied by the emergence of a new framework of politics and government, liberalism, which, although it has undergone various mutations, remains central to contemporary forms of governance. A key blueprint for this new framework was Adam Smith's *The Wealth of Nations*, originally published in 1776, a significant date as it illustrates how industrial capitalism and liberal government emerged in tandem.

At the heart of the liberal imaginary was the idea of individual freedom. Maximizing the liberty of citizens, and placing limits on the power of the state, was seen as one of the principal purposes of liberal government. The liberal subject was, accordingly, understood as a more or less autonomous individual capable of exercising free will. Underlining its significance, Bauman (1988: 7) suggests that what he calls the 'peculiarly modern connotation' of freedom as the ability to master one's own fate is inextricably linked with 'life conditions in the capitalist society'. Similarly, Foucault (2007: 48), in one of his 1978 Collège de France lectures, argued that this 'ideology of freedom really was one of the conditions of development of modern, or if you like, capitalist forms of economy'. The modern concept of freedom, then, is closely bound up with the advent of liberal capitalism.

The core argument of this book is that questions of freedom and autonomy, questions that is about the 'will', also lie at the centre of any genealogy of how we view and understand the 'drug question' today. Mariana Valverde's superb book *Diseases of the Will* makes this clear for alcohol (Valverde, 1998) and others have made similar arguments in relation to legally prohibited drugs (O'Malley and Valverde, 2004; Reith, 2004; Seddon, 2007a). In this book, I aim to take this argument a stage further by suggesting that since the advent of liberalism, there has been a mutually constitutive relation between the two, that is, between how we think about and regulate 'drugs' and our conceptions of freedom. I will say more about what I mean by this below but before that I want to expand a little on the notions of liberalism and freedom.

Liberalism has been conventionally understood as an ideological or economic doctrine or theory, as set out in the canon of classical liberal political economy in works by Adam Smith, David Ricardo, Thomas Malthus, John Stuart Mill and others. Indeed, Smith, Ricardo and Malthus in particular are regarded by many as the founders of modern economics as a discipline. A rather different, and in my view highly productive, perspective on liberalism can be found in Foucault's 1978 and 1979 Collège de France lecture series (titled respectively *Security, Territory, Population* and *The Birth of Biopolitics*). The originality of Foucault's approach revolves in essence around his insight that liberalism should be understood not as a doctrine or ideology but rather as an 'art of government'. In other words, he views liberalism as a novel set of techniques for governing human conduct. This, in turn, casts a different light on the centrality of freedom to the liberal imaginary. From a Foucauldian perspective, the significance of freedom within liberalism is not political and ideological but rather governmental and practical. Hence, Nikolas Rose (1999: 68) states that 'the importance of liberalism ... is that for the first time the arts of government were systematically linked to the practice of freedom'. Government, then, is not to be juxtaposed with freedom, as an interference or limitation on individual liberty, rather we are 'governed *through* freedom' (Rose, 1999: 72, emphasis in original).

Freedom then is not a universal aspect or aspiration of the human condition but rather a 'technique of government' with a particular meaning and prominence within liberalism (Foucault, 2007: 48–49). As Rose (1996: 62) observes, this does not mean that our freedom is a 'sham' but rather that the 'agonistic relation between liberty and government is an intrinsic part of what we have come to know as freedom'. He adds that a 'key task for intellectual engagement with contemporary relations of power is the critical analysis of these practices of freedom' (1996: 62) and that of course is a central part of the project I am undertaking here.

Returning then to this relationship between drugs and freedom, which I suggested above lies at the heart of this book, what exactly do I mean by saying that within liberal governance they exist in a constitutive relation? In essence, the argument is that, at least since the birth of liberalism, there has been an ongoing two-way dialectic between them. How we view 'drugs' simply cannot be properly grasped without seeing it in terms of these integral connections with freedom. The most obvious facet of this argument is that our changing understandings of drugs and addiction reflect and indeed are rooted in historically variable ideas about freedom. The more radical line of argument suggests that the very concept of freedom within liberalism is partly constituted or made up by dividing it from what it is not and that our understandings and ways of thinking about drugs and addiction are created through these acts of division. In this sense, they are the 'inescapable other side' (Rose, 1990: 378) of freedom. As Sedgwick (1994: 133–34) puts it:

> So long as 'free will' has been hypostatized and charged with ethical value, for just so long has an equally hypostatized 'compulsion' had to be available as a counterstructure always internal to it, always requiring to be ejected from it.

This illustrates what Bauman (1988: 9) more generally terms the *relational* nature of freedom:

> Freedom signifies a social relation, an asymmetry of social conditions; essentially it implies social difference – it presumes and implies the

presence of social division. Some can be free only in so far as there is a form of dependence they can aspire to escape.

Bauman is obviously using the term 'dependence' in a more general sense here but it nicely underlines the point. Interestingly, Adam Smith made a similar point using the same term in one of his *Lectures on Jurisprudence* from 1763: 'Nothing tends to corrupt and enervate and debase the mind as dependency, and nothing gives such noble and generous notions of probity as freedom and independency' (Smith, 1978: 333). As will be seen in later chapters, the concept of 'dependence' is highly significant when used in the context of drugs as it brings together in a single word these two facets of the constitutive drugs–freedom relation.

It is perhaps worth noting here that in certain respects this argument parallels that of Foucault in *Histoire de la Folie*, in which he argues that the history of madness should be understood as the history of the ongoing dialectic between Reason and Madness (Porter, 2003: 4). As Rose (1990) argues, the critical power of Foucault's analysis, its 'enduring and disturbing significance', lies partly in the way he shows how madness 'perpetually undergirds the forms of life and reason that make up the history of "l'homme europèen"' (1990: 378). Similarly, the radical and critical purpose of my own argument here is to demonstrate that rather than being merely a subterranean matter of deviance or pathology, the issues of drugs and addiction have for two centuries underpinned one of the most cherished values of modern society, the idea of freedom.

A chronological framework: three phases of liberalism

As I have already noted in passing, liberalism has undergone a series of mutations over the past 200 years. In tracing out the genealogy I have described over this period, I will draw on a broad chronological framework that sees liberal government as going through three phases (see Braithwaite, 2000: 48–50; Rose et al., 2006: 91–92).

1 *Classical liberalism* (late eighteenth century to late nineteenth century). Emerging alongside the transformations accompanying the Industrial Revolution, the central themes of early or classical liberalism were the importance of the free market and free trade, attempts to limit state government (the 'nightwatchman' state) and the valorization of individual freedom and autonomy. The core classical liberal formula was the notion of *laissez-faire*.
2 *Welfare liberalism* (end of the nineteenth century to the 1970s). Developing at the turn of the twentieth century, welfare or social liberalism involved a shift to a more interventionist state which assured citizens a certain minimum level of security and rights, leading to the establishment of the welfare state in the post-war period. In return for these new

rights of citizenship, the state increasingly reserved the power and authority to intervene where necessary in the social and public realm and in the lives of individuals.

3 *Neo-liberalism* (1980s to the present). Stemming from a critique of social liberalism (on the grounds that it had led to over-powerful states, fiscal crisis, inflexibility and a 'dependency' culture), neo-liberalism saw the revival in the last couple of decades of the twentieth century of certain elements of classical liberalism, notably faith in the 'invisible hand' of the free market. Characteristic of the new politics 'after the welfare state' have been strategies of *responsibilization* in which citizens are governed through their own choices.

This tripartite framework has proved highly productive in studies across diverse areas, although it is worth emphasizing that it is a heuristic device rather than anything more formal or rigid. Also, it should not be taken to imply that I will be taking an 'epochal' approach to my historical account. I share Rose's (1999: 173) misgivings about analyses which seek to find neat successions of entirely novel periods or paradigms:

> I am sceptical about approaches of this 'epochal' sort ... It is not a question of claiming that the older ways have been erased or consigned to history, but of identifying something new taking shape within and alongside the old arrangements, something different threatening or promising to be born.

A nice image for the approach Rose advocates, to which I continually return, is offered by Garland (1985: 155) who describes the social realm as:

> A multi-layered mosaic, the product of layer upon layer of organizational forms, techniques and regulatory practices, each one partial in its operation, each one dealing with the residues and traces of previous strategies as well as its contemporary rivals and limitations.

Attempting to describe and understand this 'multi-layered mosaic' is the analytical challenge for historical studies that seek to resist the temptation for clearer but cruder periodizations (see also Hutchinson, 2006). Certainly, in the chapters that follow, residues, traces and continuities will be as much in evidence as new turns and directions.

Overview and structure of the book

The rest of this book is structured in the following way. Chapter 2 provides a conceptual and theoretical introduction to the book, picking out some central ideas concerning the relationships between drugs, addiction, freedom and liberalism which are then elaborated in the three chapters that follow. Chapters 3, 4 and 5 set out the genealogical investigation I have described. They each analyse a specific 'episode' from the past 200 years, taking the form of case studies in order to highlight the profoundly historical nature of the drugs–freedom relationship and its connection with changes in liberal governance. The episodes which have been chosen are particularly significant regulatory turning points. Drawing on this historical genealogical analysis, Chapter 6 then seeks to apply the lens of regulatory theory to consider the thorny question of how these issues might be better approached today in the era of twenty-first-century global regulatory capitalism. Finally, Chapter 7 summarizes the main arc of the book's central thesis and draws together its main arguments.

More specifically, Chapter 2 examines the related concepts of freedom, the 'will' and autonomy and their interconnections with ideas about habitual drug and alcohol consumption, highlighting the closeness of these notions to the 'conceptual heartland of liberalism' (O'Malley, 2004: 81). It seeks to provide the analytical and conceptual resources and tools for the three chapters that follow.

Chapters 3, 4 and 5 then investigate three historical episodes which provide case studies of different regulatory approaches, each of which reflects and is underpinned by different drugs–freedom relations. Chapter 3 focuses on the development of the Pharmacy Act of 1868 and situates this in the context of Victorian liberal government and *laissez-faire* capitalism. Chapter 4 examines the emergence of the Dangerous Drugs Act 1920 which marked the beginning of the great 'regulatory divide' in which certain drugs came under the ambit of a new prohibition regime. This is set against the background of social change at the turn of the twentieth century as the first building blocks of the welfare state started to be assembled. The chapter draws particularly on David Garland's landmark book *Punishment and Welfare* (Garland, 1985). Chapter 5 then brings the picture up to date by looking at the Drugs Act 2005 which contained a series of measures indicative of the distinctive approach to the 'drugs problem' in early twenty-first-century Britain.

In Chapter 6, an attempt is made to pull out and explore some of the implications from the preceding three chapters for alternative ways of framing and regulating the 'drugs problem'. It draws particularly on the theoretical and empirical work of Braithwaite and others on regulation and governance in diverse fields (see Braithwaite, 2008) and especially the nodal governance approach (see Burris et al., 2005, 2008). The chapter does not offer a 'blueprint' for a new policy approach, which would be an excessively ambitious aim requiring the attention of much greater minds than mine, but rather seeks to set out a framework in which some new directions can be developed in the future.

Lastly, Chapter 7 summarizes and brings together the central arguments of the book. It revisits the conceptual and theoretical terrain introduced in

Chapter 2 and considers how this has been advanced in the central chapters of the book. More broadly, it also explores some of the implications of the analysis for understanding how we choose to govern ourselves and others in the twenty-first century.

Criticism, politics and drug policy reform

I want to conclude this introduction by saying a little more about the critical orientation and purpose of this book. It is not a political or policy text, in the sense of one which ends by making recommendations for a new programme of action. Nor, at the other end of the spectrum, is it an exercise in what Bourdieu disparagingly called 'theoretical theory', the type of abstract system-building theorizing that speaks only to other theorists with little or no reference to empirical investigation (see Sparks, 1997: 419–21). It is instead a work of *critical analysis* which seeks to provide a framework in which questions about 'what should be done' can be better understood and addressed (see Garland, 1985: vii).

This is an important point. The 'governmentality' analytic described earlier has been criticized for its lack of a normative basis and its consequent inability to inform progressive change. Famously, or infamously as some would prefer, Foucault (1991b: 84) had this to say about the role of intellectuals in guiding policy reform:

> The necessity of reform mustn't be allowed to become a form of blackmail serving to limit, reduce or halt the exercise of criticism. Under no circumstances should one pay attention to those who tell one: 'Don't criticize, since you're not capable of carrying out a reform.' That's ministerial cabinet talk. Critique doesn't have to be the premise of a deduction which concludes: this then is what needs to be done. It should be an instrument for those who fight, those who resist and refuse what is. Its use should be in processes of conflict and confrontation, essays in refusal. It doesn't have to lay down the law for the law. It isn't a stage in a programming. It is a challenge directed to what is.

This could be, and indeed often has been, taken to mean that Foucauldian approaches are uninterested in changing the way things are done, that they are somehow divorced from the 'real world' of politics and government. But I do not read it that way. Rather, it seems to me that Foucault is saying that critical analysis should proceed in the first instance completely unfettered and unbounded by concerns about 'practicalities' and 'feasibility', open to questioning everything and taking nothing for granted, shaking the 'false self-evidence' (Foucault, 1991b: 75) of our established ways of doing things. Only on the basis of this kind of thoroughgoing, penetrating and fundamental critical investigation can we begin to see different directions for action in the future.

Developing, and indeed testing out, these 'different directions for action' is a hallmark of the new regulatory scholarship which forms the other main theoretical reference point for this book. John Braithwaite's work on peace-building in areas affected by armed conflict (Braithwaite, 2006) and Clifford Shearing's work on the Zwelethemba model of Peace Committees in very poor communities in South Africa (Cartwright and Shearing, 2004; Froestad and Shearing, 2007) are outstanding examples of how sophisticated regulatory theory, empirical research and practical engagement can come together in inspirational ways to tackle some of the most troubling and difficult problems we face in the world today. The critical aim of this book is to provide a starting point for the development of new ways of understanding and dealing with the constellation of issues that we currently call the 'drug problem'. What is set out throughout this book, and drawn together particularly in Chapter 6, is just a beginning but hopefully the first step towards a better approach that can help promote security, justice and well-being rather than undermining them.

A conceptual map

Freedom, the 'will' and addiction

'You can say what you wish. This is a free country'. We use and hear this expression too often to pause and think of its meaning; we take it as obvious, self-explanatory, presenting no problem to our, or to our partner's, understanding. In a sense, freedom is like the air we breathe. We don't ask what this air is, we do not spend time discussing it, arguing about it, thinking of it. That is, unless we are in a stuffy room and find breathing difficult.

(Zygmunt Bauman, sociologist, 1988)

The belief that events are determinately related to the state of things immediately preceding them is now held by all competent thinkers in respect to all kinds of occurrence except human volitions ... Step by step, in successive departments of facts, conflicting modes of thought have receded and faded, until at length they have vanished everywhere, except for the mysterious citadel of the will.

(Henry Sidgwick, moral philosopher, 1874)

The will is at the root of human conduct. It is the basis of moral action. It is the foundation of wisdom. It is the controller of impulse. Without it duty cannot be done ... If it be true that this most authoritative faculty of man is in any way lessened by alcohol, that substance would seem to need no other condemnation.

(Sir Thomas Clouston, physician and asylum superintendent, 1914)

Introduction

This chapter explores in more depth three central concepts used in the book: freedom; the 'will'; and addiction. It aims to build a foundation for the argument that is developed in the rest of the book, providing the analytical and conceptual resources for the chapters that follow. This conceptual and theoretical overview will be elaborated and extended in the analysis of historical material presented in Chapters 3, 4 and 5 and then revisited in the concluding chapter.

I should perhaps clarify my purpose here. What I am doing in this chapter is not a conventional type of conceptual analysis as might be undertaken by an analytic philosopher (see Jackson, 1998). I am not seeking to break these ideas down into their constituent parts in order to deepen or extend our understanding of their meaning. Indeed, to the extent that such an approach would involve attributing a fixed or universal or *a priori* meaning to these concepts, that is entirely contrary to the theoretical orientation I set out in the previous chapter. Rather, my starting point is that concepts of this kind can be usefully viewed as governmental or practical, in the sense implied by the governmentality approach (see Rose, 1999; Rose et al., 2006). The purpose or objective of the conceptual overview presented here is therefore to recognize and then begin to map out the multiple, shifting and overlapping meanings these terms have been given. This involves seeing them as multivocal and polysemic discursive resources utilized within changing regulatory strategies. Milan Kundera puts this idea of multiple meanings rather beautifully in *The Unbearable Lightness of Being*:

> The bowler hat was a motif in the musical composition that was Sabina's life. It returned again and again, each time with a different meaning, and all the meanings flowed through the bowler hat like water through a riverbed. I might call it Heraclitus' ('You can't step twice into the same river') riverbed: the bowler hat was a bed through which each time Sabina saw another river flow, another *semantic river*: each time the same object would give rise to a new meaning, though all former meanings would resonate (like an echo, like a parade of echoes) together with the new one ... Now, perhaps, we are in a better position to understand the abyss separating Sabina and Franz: he listened eagerly to the story of her life and she was equally eager to hear the story of his, but although they had a clear understanding of the logical meaning of the words they exchanged, they failed to hear the semantic susurrus of the river flowing through them.
>
> (Kundera, 1984: 88)

So I am not claiming any privileged access to the 'real' meaning or 'truth' of these concepts. I am simply trying to map out some of the ways in which they are and have been differently understood – I am straining to hear the 'semantic susurrus', as Kundera has it. In the three chapters that follow, using this mapping as a framework, I then attempt to explore how at specific historical moments the semantic river flowing through these terms is connected with, or accompanied by, the invention of new ways of shaping and managing conduct in desired directions. In other words, I plot how the changing meanings of these concepts – 'freedom', the 'will' and 'addiction' – are bound up with changing strategies for the regulation and governance of the 'drug problem'. It is, of course, a central part of this book's argument that the sterility of many of the debates within the drugs field about terms like 'addiction' is rooted fundamentally in a failure to recognize their governmental nature, resulting in different sides of the debate being separated by exactly the type of 'abyss' of misunderstanding that Kundera describes. For British drug specialist readers, I need simply mention the word 'recovery' to underline that point! For North American readers, the long 'debate' about controlled drinking is another good example.

A short dictionary of misunderstood words

> I could compile a long lexicon of their misunderstandings. Let us be content, instead, with a short dictionary.
>
> (Milan Kundera, *The Unbearable Lightness of Being* [1984: 89])

Freedom

Freedom has become an iconic idea. It is the ultimate aspiration for individuals. It is the yardstick against which we judge societies. It is the value we use to critique governments and their interventions in our lives. Who could be 'against' freedom, other than tyrants and dictators?

And yet the universality of freedom, its centrality to the human condition, its necessity or 'naturalness', all begin to unravel in the face of historical (and cultural) perspectives. To put it more simply, freedom itself has a history, a 'long and chequered' one as Bauman (1988: 1) observes. Orlando Patterson's (1991) magisterial history of pre-modern freedom in Western culture offers some important, even jarring, claims and insights about the origins of the concept (see also Pohlenz, 1966; Raaflaub, 2004). His best-known thesis is that the idea of freedom was originally generated from the experience of slavery in ancient Greece:

> Who were the first persons to get the unusual idea that being free was not only a value to be cherished but the most important thing that someone could possess? The answer, in a word: slaves ... [T]he idea of freedom has never been divorced from this, its primordial, servile source.
>
> (Patterson, 1991: 9)

According to Patterson, the pre-modern meaning of freedom was simply the status of no longer being a slave (see also Bauman, 1988: 30–32). Manumission, the formal act of releasing an individual from slavery, was in this sense the generator of freedom, literally creating a 'freedman'.

Patterson argues that from its ancient Greek origins, the spread of freedom across the Western world was linked to two principal developments. First, the emergence of Rome and the spread of its empire across the Mediterranean region and Northern Europe. He suggests that the triumph of freedom was partly a consequence of the cultural influence of Greek ideas on the Roman empire. The Romans admired much about Greek life, thought and culture. But, more than this, he argues that the Greek notion of freedom in particular found especially fertile soil in the Roman world precisely because imperial Rome was itself built on a redeveloped and reconstituted system of large-scale slavery. The dominance of Rome across the Western world then led to the spread of freedom. The second critical development was the rise of Christianity which Patterson argues was the first world religion to place the ideal of freedom 'at the very centre of its theology' (Patterson, 1991: xvi). The 'extraordinary diffusion and growth' of Christianity (1991: 293) thus helped to spread freedom further and wider.

The Middle Ages, the final phase of the pre-modern period, has sometimes been viewed as an era in which freedom was relatively unimportant. Patterson (1991: 347–401) strongly challenges that view. At the heart of his account is an analysis of how the transition in this period from classical slavery to medieval serfdom provided a refigured but still powerful foundation for the continuing primacy of freedom as a cultural value. Partly reflecting this important social transition, he highlights the distinctive character of the medieval notion of freedom which largely revolved around the concepts of privilege and exemption: admittance to exclusive rights (e.g. of a city or estate) and exemption from certain duties (e.g. taxes or tolls) (Bauman, 1988: 9–10, 33–35). In others words, medieval freedom concerned the particular rights attached to persons which granted them either exclusive privileges or else exemptions from duties to which they would otherwise be bound (Patterson, 1991: 363–75). Sometimes these were derived from personal relationships with monarchs or other powerful figures (Innes, 2006). We might say then that freedom during the Middle Ages was characterized by privilege – to be free was to be given 'special' treatment in terms of rights and responsibilities (Patterson, 1991: 364).

In the second half of the eighteenth century, a new meaning of freedom began to emerge, one that we would for the first time recognize clearly today – freedom as the 'ability to master one's own fate' (see Bauman, 1988: 7). This modern notion of freedom was closely bound up with the birth of modern industrial capitalism. As Bauman (1988: 7) observes, it is a concept tethered to 'life conditions in the capitalist society' (1988: 7) and indeed only made possible by the advent of such a society. This is a critical point. The way we view and understand freedom today, the freedom that we valorize so strongly and prominently, is not a universal attribute of the human condition. It is in fact a relatively novel connotation of the term, less than 250 years old.

Why is this important? Or, to put the question in more precise terms, what are the analytical implications of grasping the historicity of the modern notion of freedom? Here, Nikolas Rose provides some help in his book *Powers of Freedom* (Rose, 1999). Using the governmentality lens, he suggests that a focus on understanding 'practices of freedom', that is the practical character of the idea of freedom, casts a rather different light on the concept compared with more philosophical or ideological perspectives. Rather than freedom being the opposite of regulation and governance, in the sense that government places restrictions on our 'natural' state of being free, Rose argues that freedom is actually part of the means through which government is achieved. Hence the now almost clichéd idea that we are 'governed through freedom'.

The significance of this idea lies in the connection with liberalism:

> The importance of liberalism is not that it first recognized, defined or defended freedom as a right of all citizens. Rather, its significance is that for the first time the arts of government were systematically linked to the practice of freedom.
>
> (Rose, 1999: 68)

For Foucault (2007: 48–49), the essence of this modern notion of freedom is the idea of *circulation*:

> The possibility of movement, change of place, and processes of circulation of both people and things. I think it is this freedom of circulation, in the broad sense of the term, it is in terms of this option of circulation, that we should understand the word freedom.

This is clearly connected with the core liberal formula of *laissez-faire*. He argues that this is not simply a matter of stepping back and leaving people alone: 'It will be necessary to arouse, to facilitate ... to ensure that the necessary and natural regulations work, or even to create regulations that enable natural regulations to work' (Foucault, 2007: 353). In other words, *laissez-faire* as a governmental method is not merely a form of 'passive abstentionism' (Gordon, 1991: 17) but also has an active and enabling character. It is a 'way of acting, as well as a way of not acting' (Gordon, 1991: 17), an idea that resonates with Polanyi's famous thesis about the 'planned' nature of *laissez-faire* in *The Great Transformation* (Polanyi, 1944). As Rose (1999: 67) notes, this 'double-edged character of freedom' is also what troubled Isaiah Berlin in his famous 1958 lecture on 'Two concepts of liberty'. Liberal freedom is therefore a 'technique of government' which needs to be understood by situating it 'within the mutations and transformations of technologies of power' (Foucault, 2007: 48). Bauman (1988: 44) puts this differently but makes a broadly similar point in noting the interwining of capitalism and modern freedom: 'Under the capitalist form of economic organization, freedom (economic freedom, at least) may flourish. More than that, freedom becomes a necessity. Without freedom, the aim of economic activity cannot be fulfilled.' Emphasizing the enabling or productive nature of modern freedom, Rose (1999: 69–78) makes the telling point that at the same time as allowing individuals freedom of choice, liberal government sought to deploy a range of technologies of responsibilization, all of which aimed to steer people towards governing themselves in desired directions. Norms and codes of civility, reason and orderliness operated across diverse sites – urban space, schools, the family and so on – to guide how individuals exercised their freedom of choice. He describes these sites as machines for 'assembling civilization' (1999: 72). It is in this sense that I argued in Chapter 1 that 'freedom' and the governance of the drug problem can be seen as mutually constitutive. The latter is another site, another machine, where civilization is assembled.

This connection with liberalism suggests a possible framework that we might use in our mapping of the 'semantic river' flowing through the concept of freedom. As discussed in Chapter 1, in charting the 'mutations and transformations' of liberal government over the past 200 years, three broad phases can be identified: classical liberalism; welfare liberalism; and neo-liberalism. Within the first phase, *classical liberalism*, the notion of freedom is built on two foundational principles. First, the belief that the 'population to be governed consists of individuals endowed naturally with the capacity for autonomous action' (Hindess, 2001: 100). Second, the notion of 'natural liberty', as famously set out by Adam Smith in *The Wealth of Nations*, namely that by placing limits on government and enabling free trade, the 'invisible hand' of the market would lead to prosperity for society as a whole. Assuring individual liberty, in the sense of people being left free to pursue their own interests, becomes the governmental watchword (see Campbell, 1977). Within *welfare liberalism*, it is no longer assumed that the entire population has the capacity for autonomous action. Rather, a central governmental objective is to identify those individuals who lack this capacity in order either to provide the necessary support to (re-)build their capacity to act autonomously or to exclude those whose capacities are too malformed for this to be possible (see Garland, 1985). Within *neo-liberalism*, freedom essentially comes to mean freedom of choice. Indeed, a classic text from this period by the neo-liberal guru Milton Friedman was entitled *Free to Choose* (Friedman and Friedman, 1980), a book based incidentally (and rather astonishingly, to me at least) on a ten-part television series of the same name. Individuals are increasingly 'responsibilized' and empowered in order that they can be governed through their choices as citizen-consumers. In the words of that other guru of neo-liberalism, Friedrich von Hayek, freedom concerns the capacity to 'order our own conduct in the sphere where material circumstances force a choice upon us, and responsibility for the arrangement of our own life according to our own conscience' (Hayek, 1944: 157).

Using this framework, and adapting from Stan Cohen (1985: 16–17), the 'master' changes in modern liberal freedom can be summarized as shown in Table 2.1. This then provides us with a provisional map to guide us through our investigation of freedom in the liberal age. It is, of course, no more than a starting point but nevertheless gives us a useful heuristic device for interpreting the empirical material explored in the chapters that follow.

Table 2.1 'Master' changes of modern freedom in liberal government

	Phase One: *Classical liberalism*	*Phase Two:* *Welfare liberalism*	*Phase Three:* *Neo-liberalism*
1. Type of freedom	Economic freedom	Social freedom	Consumer freedom
2. Conception of subject	Responsible and autonomous actor	Social citizen	Calculating choice-maker and consumer
3. Governmental role	Facilitator of freedom	Securer of freedom	Empowerer of freedom

The will

Closely related to the concept of freedom is the idea of the 'will'. But what exactly does it mean? On the face of it, this is something that we all intuitively 'know'. Is it not a self-evident feature of our own inner life and experience? But this question has in fact preoccupied and troubled philosophers for a very long time. Kant, for example, explored the notion of the autonomous will in several of his works, whilst, according to Hamacher (1986: 123) at least, the will became the 'central category of Nietzsche's late work'. Indeed, the roll-call of philosophers who have grappled with the question of the will is long and distinguished in equal measure, from Descartes to Locke, from Aquinas to Hume.

But as with the notion of freedom, my concern in this chapter is with understanding the 'will' not as a philosophical concept but rather as a governmental one. In other words, I am interested in mapping how changing conceptions of the will are connected with the invention of new ways of governing conduct within liberalism.

A good place to begin is perhaps with Jonathan Edwards' monumental book *A Careful and Strict Inquiry into the Modern Prevailing Notions of that Freedom of Will Which is Supposed to be Essential to Moral Agency, Virtue and Vice, Reward and Punishment, Praise and Blame*, originally published in 1754. Helpfully, it was given the shorter title *Freedom of the Will* when re-published in 1957 as volume one of the Yale University Press series of Edwards' writings! In this remarkable work, Edwards, a New England Puritan theologian and philosopher, set out his views on the nature of free will and agency. He defined the will as the 'mind choosing' what it most desired. He argued that whilst an individual's desires and motivations might be shaped by habits and other external determinations, provided that an individual is able literally to do what they choose then they have 'free will'. In other words, he equated an 'act of will' with an 'act of volition' or 'voluntary action':

> The will (without any metaphysical refining) is plainly, that by which the mind chooses anything. The faculty of the will is that faculty or

power or principle of mind by which it is capable of choosing: an act of the will is the same as an act of choosing or choice.

(Edwards, 1754/1957: 137)

This definition leads Edwards to the view that it is impossible for 'will' and 'desire' to be in conflict, in the sense that humans 'will' or choose actions in order to satisfy their desires (1754/1957: 139). For Edwards, this was a way of resolving an otherwise difficult theological problem: how to reconcile the Calvinist belief in the essential 'fallenness' of human nature with the wish to hold individuals morally responsible for their actions. By separating 'will' from 'desire', it allowed him to argue that human beings choose how to act, and therefore bear full moral responsibility for those choices, but that the indelible taint of Original Sin tends to make us desire to act against God by sinning. This view also resonates strongly with the classical liberal notion of the individual as 'an isolated atom of preference-motivated choice and action' (Burchell, 1991: 130), where 'preference' corresponds to Edwards' 'desire' and 'choice' to his 'will'.

Liberal government, according to Foucault (1991a, 2007), for the first time took as its object the population rather than a territory. The techniques of power associated with governing population were, however, individualizing in the sense that the individual was not just an element within the population but also a crucial relay for its government (Foucault, 2007: 128–29, 104). In other words, to govern the population required the government of individuals within it – governing *omnes et singulatim* as Foucault (1979; 2007: 128) famously put it – which, in turn, required individuals to possess the 'faculty of the will' in Edwards' meaning of the term. The absence of 'will', indicating human behaviour which was determined, would render the population ungovernable within the parameters of liberalism. 'Will' as the 'mind choosing' is thus at the heart of the emergence of classical liberal government; indeed it is a necessary condition for its operation. It is part and parcel of the invention or discovery of the liberal subject, *Homo economicus*, a 'subject of individual preferences and choices' (Gordon, 1991: 21).

Following our chronological framework, our next concern is what becomes of the notion of the 'will' with the transition to *welfare liberalism* at the end of the nineteenth century. The late Victorian period was one in which some far-reaching challenges began to emerge to widely held beliefs about 'free will', perhaps most notably from Darwin's *Origin of Species*, first published in 1859. As Wiener (1990: 161) observes, Darwin's work was 'fundamentally subversive' of the idea of human beings freely exercising their will in order to make choices. At the same time, the new positivist human sciences – criminology, social work, the 'psy' sciences – were also transforming ideas about human nature. Put simply, these emerging bodies of knowledge and their associated programmes claimed to be discovering the 'causal laws' which explained human behaviour. For example, criminology – through the work of Lombroso, Ferri, Garofalo, Goring and others – began to identify the mental, physical and other defects which 'caused' criminality. As Garland (1985: 185–89) notes, in the realm of crime, this conflicted profoundly with the need to maintain the idea of free will, and hence responsibility, in order to justify legal punishment. The resolution of this conflict was achieved through the concept of 'character', an idea which involved a substantial refiguring of the 'will'. The concept was based on a developmental logic, in which 'character' is shaped by the acquisition of habits and discipline as well as by environmental and genetic factors. Whilst a

> normal healthy character, untrammelled by genetic defect or vicious habit, will be able to exercise control and choice ... Alongside these responsible individuals are numerous characters that are either unformed or else malformed ... [who] are pathologically determined by their defective character structures.
>
> (Garland, 1985: 188)

The 'will', in other words, was a fragile faculty, the full development of which 'depends upon the delicate mechanisms of character formation and the vicissitudes of individual and social life' (1985: 188). In this view, the sharp distinction drawn in the previous century by Edwards between 'will' and 'desire' began to break down for those individuals with defective characters.

Within the new welfarist programmes of the early twentieth century – social work, social security, penal reform – the 'will' became a central *locus* of intervention. The overarching governmental strategy, as already noted in the previous section, became focused on identifying individuals with a 'defective will', in order to provide individualized treatment designed to 'repair' their will and hence reinstate their moral responsibility for their actions. Garland's book *Punishment and Welfare* provides numerous examples of this, targeted at a wide range of groups, from 'vagrants' to the 'mentally deficient' to 'juvenile delinquents' (Garland, 1985).

A further significant point is the foregrounding within welfare liberalism of the notion of 'habit' as an element in the process of character formation. In this regard, Valverde (1998) argues that the work of American pragmatist philosophers like William James and John Dewey at the turn of the twentieth century was highly influential in generating a changing image of human nature and of the faculty of the will. She observes, for example, how James argued that the binary opposition between 'free will' and 'necessity' was flawed (Valverde, 1998: 35–37). He highlighted the hybrid zone of habitual action as a vital but neglected area for the understanding of human conduct. For James, habits started out as voluntary actions but gradually became 'second nature'. Valverde (1998: 42) suggests that the notion of 'habit' is a vital conceptual component in the development of a 'genealogy of the free will' (see also Sedgwick, 1994). As we will see in the chapters that follow, it is an equally vital part in our genealogy of the construction and regulation of the 'drug problem'. Indeed, the term 'drug habit', a very familiar and widely used one today, sounds a contemporary echo of this particular branch of the genealogy.

With the transition at the tail end of the twentieth century to *neo-liberalism*, understanding of the 'will' has again mutated. To a certain extent, this has involved a revival of the nineteenth-century figure of *Homo economicus*, characterized as a rational actor motivated by his or her own preferences. More than this though, neo-liberal governmental programmes seek to inculcate autonomy, creating active and entrepreneurial citizens. The 'will' of the neo-liberal citizen-subject is in this sense an invention of government designed to facilitate governmental objectives. As Rose and Miller (1992: 188–89) put it: 'Self regulatory techniques can be installed in citizens that will align their personal choices with the ends of government.' Within neo-liberalism, Edwards' notion of the 'will' as the 'mind choosing' becomes prescription, or even obligation, rather than description. We are no longer just 'free to choose'; we are obliged to choose so that we can be governed through our preferences and choices. The 'will' becomes a central tool of government.

As we did with 'freedom', we can now summarize the 'master' changes in conceptions of the 'will' in liberal government (see Table 2.2), again with the caveat that this framework offers no more than a heuristic device.

Addiction

To many contemporary observers, 'addiction' seems to be an unfortunate but near-universal affliction of the modern world from which few, if any, societies or communities are immune. Yet we struggle to pin down what it 'really' is. It is almost ungraspable. Is addiction a personality disorder? A symptom of a genetic weakness? A psychiatric condition? A failure to cope with life? A result of poverty and disadvantage? A consequence of reckless consumption of dangerous substances? Or is it simply a chimera?

Table 2.2 'Master' changes in conceptions of the 'will' in liberal government

	Phase One: Classical liberalism	*Phase Two: Welfare liberalism*	*Phase Three: Neo-liberalism*
1. Nature of 'will'	Will as volition or capacity to choose how to act	Will as an attribute of 'normal' citizens	Will as mechanism for realizing individual preferences
2. Governmental role	To create conditions in which the will can be exercised	To identify citizens with defective characters and attempt to repair their will	To encourage and facilitate the autonomous will of active citizens

I will not attempt here to adjudicate between the psychologists, psychiatrists, neuroscientists and other self-styled addiction experts. Indeed, I am highly sceptical about the whole enterprise of trying to determine the 'true' essence of addiction. For those interested in learning more about this, I particularly recommend Stanton Peele's *The Meaning of Addiction* (Peele, 1985) and John Davies' *The Myth of Addiction* (Davies, 1992), for two contrasting but stimulating critical commentaries on that enterprise. My interest here, however, is in understanding it as a governmental concept, that is one which has been actively assembled in order to enable particular strategies and practices for the government of human conduct.

In a landmark article, published 30 years ago, the American sociologist Harry Levine (1978: 143) argued that our modern conception of addiction was 'about 175 or 200 years old, but no older' (see also McCormick, 1969). This is a radical argument. It undercuts attempts to identify the 'truth' of addiction. Rather, Levine suggests that the concept was 'invented' in the late eighteenth century. Levine's basic thesis has not gone without challenge by historians – Jessica Warner (1994) and Roy Porter (1985) have offered the most notable and sustained critiques – but, as Ferentzy (2001) in particular has persuasively argued, his broad position largely stands up in historical terms and it is worth examining further here.

Levine makes clear that his argument draws on a Foucauldian perspective – he quotes a passage from *The Birth of the Clinic* at the beginning of his article – but it is a testament to the originality and insight of his own analysis that in many respects it utilizes ideas and concepts that at that time Foucault himself was still developing. Indeed, Levine's article was drafted in 1976, well before the 1978 and 1979 courses of lectures at the Collège de France in which Foucault began to set out more fully and explicitly his ideas on governmentality, biopower and liberalism. There was, in other words, no fully formed Foucauldian conceptual and theoretical blueprint on which Levine could draw at the time, which makes his contribution all the more remarkable.

At the heart of his argument is the contention that at the end of the eighteenth century there was a fundamental shift in conceptions of habitual drunkenness:

> During the 17th century, and for most of the 18th, the assumption was that people drank and got drunk because they wanted to, and not because they 'had' to. In colonial thought, alcohol did not permanently disable the will; it was not addicting and habitual drunkenness was not regarded as a disease. With very few exceptions, colonial Americans did not use a vocabulary of compulsion with regard to alcoholic beverages. At the end of the 18th century and in the early years of the 19th some Americans began to report for the first time that they were addicted to alcohol: They said they experienced overwhelming and irresistible desires

for liquor ... Throughout the 19th century, people associated with the Temperance Movement argued that inebriety, intemperance or habitual drunkenness was a disease, and a natural consequence of the moderate use of alcoholic beverage.

(Levine, 1978: 144)

He argues, in effect, without using the language and vocabulary that Foucault had yet to articulate fully, that the invention of the concept of 'addiction' was fundamentally connected with the emergence of liberal government at the end of the eighteenth century:

The invention of the concept of addiction ... at the end of the 18th and beginning of the 19th century can be best understood not as an independent medical or scientific discovery but as part of a transformation in social thought grounded in fundamental changes in social life – in the structure of society.

(Levine, 1978: 165–66)

This 'transformation in social thought' revolves around the new governmental emphasis on individuals as preference-motivated actors: 'The conditions of a "free society", meaning individual freedom to pursue one's own interests, required shifting social control to the individual level. Social order depended upon self-control' (Levine, 1978: 163). It is in this double sense that O'Malley (2004: 155) describes the modern conception of addiction as a 'peculiarly liberal affliction', its invention coinciding historically with the 'ascendancy of liberal governance' and its formulation grounded within the conceptual heartland of liberalism with its concern for individual freedom.

Although the invention of this new conception of habitual drunkenness as the disease of addiction was undoubtedly of fundamental importance, initially it applied specifically and exclusively to alcohol. Indeed, for much of the nineteenth century, certainly for the first five or so decades, habitual use of opium and opiates, which was widespread and common in Britain during that period (Berridge, 1999), was largely viewed in a rather different light, as a 'bad habit' or 'vice', a matter of over-indulgence rather than a disease (Berridge, 1979: 68–70). And such a view fit well with the classical liberal notion of individuals as free and responsible actors. As we will now see, the coming together of these two sets of understandings – disease and vice – lay at the heart of the rather complex mutation in the concept of addiction that unfolded in the late 1800s.

At the turn of the twentieth century, with the transition to *welfare liberalism*, the notion of addiction shifted somewhat. It came to be viewed as one specific instance or example of a character defect requiring special intervention for affected individuals. Garland (1985: 217–18) describes the establishment of inebriate reformatories under the Inebriates Act of 1898 which enabled a new way of dealing with 'habitual drunkards' by providing for their detention in these new institutions for the specific purpose of treatment and reform (see also Johnstone, 1996). He notes how this model of 'special treatment' for a criminogenic disorder provided a blueprint for subsequent measures targeted at a range of other groups, including vagrants and the 'feeble-minded' (1985: 218).

The scope of addiction during this period expanded too, being applied not only to alcohol but, increasingly, to opium, opiates and cocaine as well. From the perspective of the twenty-first century, this is perhaps a surprising point, as many would not imagine that the idea of addiction originated in relation to alcohol and only just over a century ago began to be applied to the opiates and other drugs to which it is firmly attached today. As Levine (1978: 144) observes: 'The idea that drugs are inherently addicting was first systematically worked out for alcohol and then extended to other substances. Long before opium was popularly accepted as addicting, alcohol was so regarded.' The bringing together of alcohol and other substances was achieved partly through the invention of what turned out to be a relatively short-lived new concept, *inebriety*. As the historian David Courtwright (2005: 107–08) notes, inebriety was the governing idea in the field during the late nineteenth century, not only in Britain but also across most of North America. In essence, the theory of inebriety sought to describe the problems associated with the use of alcohol, opium, opiates and so on within a single unified 'disease' framework. Through the process of unification 'what emerged was a hybrid disease theory incorporating both medical and moral formulations' (Berridge, 1979: 77). In other words, the new notion that it was a medical condition co-existed with the older idea that it was a moral failing:

> Addiction was disease *and* vice; it was 'moral bankruptcy', 'disease of the will', 'a form of moral insanity' … This continuing moral component ensured a disease theory which was individually oriented, where the addict was responsible, through volition, for his own condition. Addiction was 'medicalised', but failure to achieve a cure was a failure of self control, not medical science.
>
> (Berridge, 1979: 77, emphasis in original)

This hybrid notion could be drawn on both by countries establishing more penal governance regimes, such as North America, as well as by those following a more medical direction, like Britain. As I have argued elsewhere (Seddon, 2007b), this idea of hybridity also resonates strongly with Garland's (1985) account in which he coins the term 'penal-welfarism' to describe the accommodation between punishment and welfare that was characteristic of welfare liberalism. In other words, 'welfarist and penal approaches in this field, rather than being antithetical or contradictory tendencies engaged in an ongoing "tug of war", are actually involved in a *liaison* (Seddon, 2007b: 149, emphasis in original). This helps to explain how the 'British System' of heroin control, established in the 1920s (see Chapter 4), much-lauded in some quarters as a humane medical response to 'sick' people, operated within a prohibitionist regulatory framework based on the criminal law.

In the latter decades of the twentieth century, with the transition to *neo-liberalism*, the notion of addiction began to shift ground again. At the most basic level, the very word started to lose its pre-eminence in the field, as new terms like 'dependence', 'problem drinking' and 'problem drug use' started to gain ground. A small flurry of correspondence in 2006 in the *American Journal of Psychiatry* illustrates nicely this increasingly crowded and uncertain linguistic terrain, as various experts make cases for their own preferred label, ranging from 'addiction' to 'dependence' to 'chemical dependence' (Erickson and Wilcox, 2006; Fainsinger et al., 2006; Miller, 2006; O'Brien et al., 2006). This fragmentation, or proliferation, in terminology is significant, I think. In a rather neglected article about the state of criminology as a field of enquiry at the end of the twentieth century, Ericson and Carriere (1994) argue that fragmentation is occurring across the human sciences and that this is connected with the shift to late modernity in which discourses of risk are 'refiguring social organisation' (1994: 102). In other words, and to use a shorthand term, the emergence of a 'risk society' (Giddens, 1990; Beck, 1992), where risks and knowledge about risks cut across traditional boundaries, is fragmenting and refiguring existing bodies and fields of knowledge and expertise. In the drug field, the 'rise of risk' (Garland, 2003) also partly explains the increasing dominance of the notion of 'problem use', where drug-related difficulties are seen primarily in terms of the risks they pose both to consumers and to others. Indeed, it can be argued that the articulation of understandings of habitual drug-taking in terms of risk is now the main template for framing the 'drug problem' and its governance (see Seddon et al., 2008). The cross-cutting and boundary-crossing nature of the 'risk society' perhaps also explains the even broader scope of behaviours to which the addiction label is applied at the beginning of the twentieth century. No longer is it just drinking or drug-taking which can become viewed as compulsive uncontrollable behaviours; now, we can be 'addicted' to shopping, to the internet, to gambling, to watching television, to pornography, to chocolate, to sex and lots of activities in between! We might say that today human beings can potentially be viewed as addicted to any form of habitual consumption that appears to be problematic. In what has become a well-worn phrase, Bauman (1988: 93) has referred to the idea of 'flawed consumers' becoming the new 'outsiders' or 'excluded' within late-modern societies.

Table 2.3 summarizes these 'master' changes in conceptions of 'addiction' since its invention in the late eighteenth century.

Table 2.3 'Master' changes in conceptions of 'addiction' in liberal government

	Phase One: *Classical liberalism*	*Phase Two:* *Welfare liberalism*	*Phase Three:* *Neo-liberalism*
1. Nature of 'addiction'	Addiction as a disease of the will	Addiction as a type of 'defect' or abnormality of character	Addiction as a source of risk
2. Scope and coverage	Alcohol and habitual drunkenness	Extended to non-therapeutic use of opium, opiates and cocaine	Further extended to many other forms of habitual consumption
3. Governmental role	Limited encouragement of temperance	Normalization	Risk management

Freedom–will–addiction

In the previous section, and with some difficulty, I attempted to keep separate my analysis of these three concepts of freedom, the 'will' and addiction. Such a separation is in fact rather artificial as they are so closely bound up together. What I am charting in this book is actually a *series*, in which these three elements are connected within a triangular set of relations. I will say a little more about this here.

First, I should clarify my reference to a triangle of relations. That is not quite precisely right. The direct relation is really between the first and third elements, that is between freedom and addiction. The 'will' is in a sense a mechanism or vehicle for articulating that fundamental relationship. In the previous chapter I outlined the broad argument about that relationship and its significance. Here, I will restrict myself to giving a few specific examples to illustrate in outline the nature of this series.

The first example is from Jonathan Edwards' treatise on *Freedom of the Will*. As Valverde (1998: 14–15) observes (see also Levine, 1978), he uses the example of habitual drunkenness in a number of places in order to develop his argument about the relationship between 'will' and 'desire':

> A drunkard who continues in his drunkenness, being under the power of a love, and violent appetite to strong drink and without any love to virtue; but being also extremely covetous and close, and very much exercised and grieved at the diminution of his estate, and prospect of poverty, may in a sort desire the virtue of temperance; and though his present will is to gratify his extravagant appetite, yet he may wish he had a heart to forbear future acts of intemperance ... but still he goes on with his drunkenness; such a man has no proper, direct, sincere willingness to forsake this vice ... for he acts voluntarily in continuing to drink to excess.
>
> (Edwards, 1754/1957: 313)

In this passage, Edwards is almost tortuous in his efforts to preserve the idea that even the most entrenched drunkard 'acts voluntarily in continuing to drink to excess'. Any protestations or claims to desire to stop drinking cannot be 'sincere' or 'proper' if the drunkard continues to drink as the act of taking a drink is a manifestation of the will or 'mind choosing'. We see the series very clearly here. The idea that human beings are entirely free and responsible actors leads to a particular conception of the nature of habitual drunkenness. At the same time, the case of the drunkard provides a specific instance or example in which the nature of this freedom is illuminated.

Let me give a second example. In the various elaborations of the theory of inebriety at the end of the nineteenth century by Kerr, Clouston, Crothers and others (see Chapter 4), one of the central theoretical difficulties they face is to explain why individuals choose to drink heavily or take morphine or opium on a regular basis in the first place, knowing the potential consequences. Another, perhaps even more fundamental, problem comes from the observation that some people manage to control and moderate their consumption apparently without damaging themselves. What kind of disease could inebriety be? Is it beyond the control of the individual, like, for example, tuberculosis or measles or smallpox, or not? The attempted resolution of these difficulties revolves around a revised understanding of the nature of the 'will' as a faculty which could be weakened, impaired or diseased. Hence, Sir William Collins' famous allusion to Rush's notion of addiction as a 'disease of the will' (Collins, 1916). So, again, charting the *freedom–will–addiction* series is key to understanding developments.

One more recent example further underlines the point. Although theorizing about addiction, or at least the construction of grand theoretical schema, has largely gone out of fashion in the past few decades, particular conceptions of addiction can nevertheless still be seen within specific drug policies and practices. What are we to make, for example, of the 'Tough Choices' project, an initiative from 2005 which seeks to coerce certain groups of drug-using offenders into treatment (see Chapter 5)? In essence, it is predicated on the notion that faced with an effective choice of going to prison or entering drug treatment in the community, most habitual heroin or cocaine users will choose the latter. This is based, in turn, on an understanding of those users as individual actors capable of making more or less rational choices motivated by preferences, that is as capable of exercising consumer freedom. Again, the conception of addiction and the conception of freedom are bound up together.

We can see then the importance and relevance of the series across all three 'phases' of liberalism. But although I agree with O'Malley (2004: 155) that there is a significant and distinctive connection between the birth of liberalism and the emergence of modern conceptions of addiction, and indeed that is the central premise and focus of this book, I also think that some aspects of this *freedom–will–addiction* series have even deeper historical roots.

Take the term 'drug dependence', for example, which was first introduced by the World Health Organization in 1964. We might understand this as a modern concept, connected perhaps with neo-liberal debates in recent decades about 'welfare dependency'. However, as Fraser and Gordon (1994) argue in an imaginative and insightful article, the term 'dependence' has a very long history. In its pre-industrial guise, it referred to a relationship of subordination:

> While the term did not mean precisely *unfree*, its context was a social order in which subjection, not citizenship was the norm. *Independence* connoted unusual privilege and superiority, as in freedom from labor.
> (Fraser and Gordon, 1994: 313, emphases in original)

So buried in the word 'dependence' is this pre-industrial concept of freedom, revolving around what Patterson (1991) would have described as a medieval understanding of freedom as privilege, as discussed above. And we can go back even further with this series. As noted at the beginning of this chapter, in Roman law, the word *manumission* referred to the decision to release an individual from slavery or bondage, literally the creation of a freedman. The opposite action, the act of assigning slave to master, was one of the meanings of the Latin word *addicere* and it has been suggested that this may be the etymological root of the word 'addiction' (Redfield, 1997: 6; Seddon, 2007a: 340). We hear a distant echo of this in contemporary use of the metaphor of 'enslavement' to describe addiction to drugs like heroin. Perhaps then it is not stretching things too far to say that freedom and addiction share the same 'primordial, servile source' (Patterson, 1991: 9) which runs all the way back to Antiquity.

Conclusion

This chapter has attempted the difficult but vital task of a preliminary mapping of these three concepts that are fundamental to my thesis in this book. One of the points that I hope I have managed to convey, and this was the purpose of quoting the passage from Kundera at the start of the chapter, is that these concepts contain traces and echoes of earlier incarnations, sometimes entirely obvious and apparent but more often hidden or buried. Understanding this is essential to our explorations of the present, as Ian Hacking (1991: 184) suggests in relation to his own field(s) of enquiry:

> I toy with the idea that many of what we call philosophical problems are a byproduct of dim 'memories' of our conceptual past ... [C]onceptual incoherence which creates philosophical perplexity is a historical incoherence between prior conditions that made a concept possible, and the concept made possible by those prior conditions ... I do not believe that

exposing the historical ground of a problem makes it go away ... and the result is hardly history at all. It is a use of the past for understanding some of the incoherence in present ideas. It cannot aim at exhausting the historical material, but rather at producing an hypothesis about the relationship between concepts in their historical sites.

This is as good a way as any of describing what I will be doing in the next three chapters: viewing the relationship between these three concepts at three historical points. I shall do this through a version, no doubt a rather impoverished one, of what Foucault (1991b: 76–82) called 'eventalization'. To paraphrase his typically dense description of this 'procedure of analysis' (1991b: 76), I take two key points from the idea. First, that the analysis of certain specific historical 'events' can be fruitful where they are what he calls 'singularities', that is those places or points which 'at a given moment establish what subsequently counts as self-evident, universal and necessary' (1991b: 76). Second, to understand such events involves piecing together or recovering a complex multiplicity of causes and lines of development, rather than searching for grand mono-causal explanations. As Rose (2007: 4) puts it, we should 'try to chart the way in which multiple shifts enable something new to emerge – something that does not stabilize, but continues to mutate'.

The three events I investigate in turn in Chapters 3, 4 and 5 respectively are each legislative: the Pharmacy Act of 1868, the Dangerous Drugs Act of 1920 and the Drugs Act 2005 (selected extracts from these Acts are presented in the Appendices). This focus on legislation reflects my concern with regulatory matters, as set out in the previous chapter. I am not suggesting of course that 'regulation' boils down to nothing more than law – that would be entirely antithetical to the body of regulatory scholarship on which I draw in this book and which was introduced in Chapter 1. Rather, I think that these three pieces of legislation crystallize particular significant turns in the imagination and regulation of the 'drug problem' and that they therefore provide a helpful focus for enquiry. Each represents an instantiation of a distinctive way of thinking about and an associated way of acting upon what we call today the 'drug problem'.

To look forward then in a little more detail to the next chapter, this takes as its focal point the passing of the Pharmacy Act of 1868. This has not been the subject of a great deal of scholarly attention to date but, as I will show, it is of considerable significance within the genealogy I am tracing in this book. It marks, for example, the first real attempt to introduce controls on the sale of substances like opium which up until then had been in effect treated scarcely any differently from any other commodity within the market economy. It signals too the first establishment of what would later prove to be important ideas: that commodities of this kind pose potential 'problems' which may require governmental action; and that medical practitioners (broadly defined) are appropriate people through which this action can be delivered. Prior to the 1850s, these ideas were far from established as self-evident or universal, although they have arguably subsequently come to be seen as such. The event of the enactment of the 1868 legislation in this sense fits the bill as a Foucauldian 'singularity' of the type I described earlier and it is to the task of understanding this event that I now turn in Chapter 3.

Opium, regulation and classical liberalism

The Pharmacy Act 1868

Who was the man who invented laudanum? I thank him from the bottom of my heart ... I have had six delicious hours of oblivion; I have woken up with my mind composed ... Drops, you are darling! If I love nothing else, I love you!

(Wilkie Collins, writer, 1865)

Opium was the aspirin of the time [the early nineteenth century]. Contemporaries, with few exceptions, accepted that it was just like any other commodity. Looking at the day book of a 'chemist and grocer', for instance, one sees entries for ginger beer and half-grain morphia pills, or paint, turpentine and laudanum; the drug was simply part of the everyday stock in trade of a general store.

(Virginia Berridge, historian, 1982)

Introduction

There was no 'drug problem' in nineteenth-century Britain. The idea simply did not exist and would not have been understood by the Victorians. As I noted in Chapter 1, the term 'drugs' did not yet have its modern meaning as a grouping of psychoactive substances subject to criminal law controls. This is not to say that issues of consumption and intoxication were of no concern. On the contrary, in relation to alcohol, for example, habitual public drunkenness was a matter that aroused considerable anxiety in some quarters. But in terms of opium and opiates, it is certainly the case, as Virginia Berridge demonstrated in her groundbreaking book *Opium and the People*, that in the first half of the century there was little or no public or official concern (Berridge, 1999). Indeed, as she expertly charts, the use of opium-based 'pick-me-ups', tonics, medicines and elixirs was so widespread that it was largely viewed as a matter of everyday life (see also Berridge, 1977a, 1982). Often these were used therapeutically, for the easing of a wide range of common ailments and conditions, from toothache to diarrhoea. Sometimes they were used more for pleasure, what we would call today 'recreational' use. And at other times, the distinction between the 'therapeutic' and the 'recreational' was somewhat blurred, as the consumption of opium and opiates was for many people simply a way of attempting to cope with the hardships of the daily grind of working-class life in Victorian Britain. The widespread use of opium-based soothing syrups for infants and babies – *Godfrey's Cordial* and *Mrs Winslow's Soothing Syrup* were amongst the most popular – is perhaps best understood from that perspective (Berridge, 1982: 2–3). It has been estimated that by the 1850s, there were as many as 25,000 separate outlets in England for the sale of opium (Harding, 1988: 8).

This context is important – and those readers who want to know more are directed to Virginia Berridge's exemplary historical work (1977a, 1982, 1999) – as it raises even more sharply the 'singularity' that is the focus of this chapter. If opium was so pervasive and common in the first half of the century, why exactly were controls introduced in 1868 on opium and opiates? And why were these controls established in the form, structure and location that they were? And why were only certain psychoactive substances 'captured' by this regulatory development, whilst others were dealt with differently? As we will see in Chapter 4 in particular, this 1868 'event' proved to be a significant turn in our genealogy of the contemporary imagination and regulation of the 'drug problem'. The main body of this chapter thus considers the 1868 'event' and seeks to identify some of the multiple lines of development from which this new regime of 'pharmaceutical regulation' (Berridge, 2005a) emerged. In conclusion, I attempt to pull together the implications of the analysis for my genealogical project and look forward to Chapter 4 which investigates another momentous 'event' some fifty years later in the early decades of the twentieth century.

The emergence of pharmaceutical regulation

I have previously argued that we can best understand the pre-1868 free market in opium and opiates in terms of the dominance of *laissez-faire* and the ideology of free markets within early liberalism, with opium and opiates treated simply as commodities in the market economy (Seddon, 2007b). I now think that in certain respects this is an over-simplification. Undoubtedly it is one part of the story but it does not really help us to understand fully the 1868 legislative 'event'. Here, we need to broaden out our perspective in the way described in Chapter 1 and situate it in the wider context of a genealogy of regulation. This involves looking both backwards to the pre-industrial era and also forwards to twentieth-century welfarism.

Before doing that, it will be helpful if I briefly summarize here the relevant content of the 1868 Act. Its full title was 'An Act to Regulate the Sale of Poisons and Amend the Pharmacy Act, 1852', giving a good indication of its twin purposes: to regulate 'poison' sales and to regulate further the profession(s) involved. In terms of professional regulation, the Act brought in a series of measures, primarily concerning the requirement for Pharmaceutical Chemists, Chemists and Druggists to be registered, with a printed Register of names and residences published annually. On the regulation of sales of 'poisons', the substances covered by the Act were divided into two groups, those listed in Part 1 of the Act's Poisons Schedule and those in Part 2. The Schedule is reproduced in Box 3.1. For 'poisons' in Part 2, which included 'Opium and all Preparations of Opium or of Poppies', the sole requirement for vendors concerned labelling. Under section 17, such products needed to be 'distinctly labelled with the Name of the Article and the Word Poison, and with the Name and Address of the Seller of the Poison'. Regulations were stricter for Part 1 'poisons' – which included arsenic, cyanide and strychnine – involving, for example, requirements to keep a record of purchasers. Patent medicines, that is, proprietary branded medicines like *Godfrey's Cordial* and *Squire's Elixir*, were expressly excluded from the provisions of the Act and could still be freely sold over-the-counter. This was a major limitation on the Act's practical impact, further compounded by the lack of monitoring and enforcement mechanisms for its regulatory measures (Berridge, 1999: 123–31).

I now turn to the difficult task of attempting to unravel the lines of development from which this emerged. This will involve charting intersecting changes across different fields, rather than identifying any single determining 'master change'. My account therefore does not claim to provide a

---

Box 3.1 Poisons Schedule from Pharmacy Act of 1868

PART 1

Arsenic and its Preparations
Prussic Acid
Cyanides of Potassium and all metallic Cyanides
Strychnine and all poisonous vegetable Alkaloids and their Salts
Aconite and its Preparations
Emetic Tartar
Corrosive Sublimate
Cantharides
Savin and its Oil
Ergot of Rye and its Preparations

PART 2

Oxalic Acid
Chloroform
Belladonna and its Preparations
Essential Oil of Almonds unless deprived of its Prussic Acid
Opium and all Preparations of Opium or of Poppies

full or comprehensive historical picture, in the manner attempted by historians like Berridge, but instead seeks to open up some different and novel perspectives on this 'event'. It is a history which is 'analytical rather than archival', to use Garland's (2001: 2) phrase.

Problematizing opium I: longevity and insurance

One of the first questions to be answered is how opium first began to be viewed as a 'problem'. One place often cited as an early example is the famous Earl of Mar life insurance case in 1828. The best historical account is given by Berridge (1977b). She summarizes the basic circumstances of the case:

> In 1826, the Earl had effected several insurances on his life, including one for £3,000 with the Edinburgh Life Assurance Company. The policy was held by a banking house in Edinburgh, Sir William Forbes and Company, as security for a debt. In 1828 the Earl died of jaundice and dropsy, and his insurance company then learnt that, as well as drinking alcohol and leading a sedentary life, the Earl had for 30 years been in the habit of taking laudanum to excess. He took a tablespoonful on going to bed, and also when going out for a walk, and had, in 1825, confessed to his housekeeper that he was taking 49 grains of solid opium and one ounce of laudanum a day. The Edinburgh Company, horrified that such a habit had not been revealed at the time of their general inquiry into the Earl's health, refused to pay out on the policy.
>
> (Berridge, 1977b: 371)

Expert evidence on the effect of opium consumption on longevity was provided by Professor Robert Christison, then Professor of Medical Jurisprudence at Edinburgh. A subsequent article published in *The Lancet*, based on his investigations for the Mar case, sparked a long-running debate on the matter (Christison, 1832; Mart, 1832; Little, 1850). For Berridge (1977b), the Mar case is the 'domestic' origin of the controversy about the impact of opium on population health which not only lasted for the rest of the century but also ranged widely, from concern about public health at 'home' to discussions about the morality of British imperial adventures in China and India (notably the Opium Wars in the middle of the century). This is undoubtedly so and I will return to both of those areas below. But I think it is also highly significant that this early problematization of opium was in the context of *insurance* (see also Bull, 2008: 21–23). In his classic essay 'Insurance and risk', François Ewald (1991) notes the importance of insurance technologies to liberal government. He coins the useful term 'insurantial imaginaries' to refer to the 'ways in which, in a given social context, profitable, useful and necessary uses can be found for insurance technology' (1991: 198). As O'Malley (1998: 676–78) emphasizes, these 'insurantial imaginaries' are *governmental*, in the sense that they provide particular sets of techniques linked to specific 'practicable projects of government' (1998: 676). The technology of life insurance took on a distinctive new liberal form following the Life Assurance Act of 1774 (also known as the Gaming Act) (O'Malley, 2004: 103–04). Whereas prior to this, life insurance had been in effect a form of *speculative* activity, 'betting on lives' in Clark's (1999) nice phrase, the 1774 Act transformed it into a *prudential* activity based on notions of individual responsibility.

Why, though, is this of any significance to my genealogical project? I think there are three relevant aspects.

First, the particular 'insurantial imaginary' we see in Mar revolves around what Ewald (2002: 273) has called the 'paradigm of responsibility', a paradigm inextricably linked with the advent of liberalism. Whilst the concept of responsibility is a complex and multi-faceted one (see Baker, 2002), one of the central components of classical liberal versions of it is the idea that individuals are autonomous actors who can therefore be held accountable (morally, financially, legally) for their decisions and actions. Hence we see the discussion of the Earl of Mar's opium and laudanum habit is conducted primarily on the basis that his consumption of those substances was entirely freely chosen. His habit may have been seen as 'bad' or as a 'vice' but it was not articulated in terms of compulsion or being uncontrollable. Consequently, the question of whether, or to what extent, he was under a duty to conduct himself in a prudent manner in relation to his health (if he wished to draw the benefit of his insurance) was raised. The location of the Mar case within this particular 'insurantial imaginary' thus firmly roots this early problematization of opium within liberal understandings of freedom and responsibility.

Second, and related to the first point, it also highlights the valorization of individual autonomy and freedom that is so central to early liberalism. As the work of the historian of insurance Geoffrey Clark (1999, 2002) has shown, this was one of the drivers of the transformation in life insurance in the late eighteenth century, from a speculative to a prudential activity, as 'betting on lives' was felt to demean and undermine the dignity of autonomous human subjects. Intriguingly, in making this point, Clark draws a parallel with slavery, reminding us of the discussion in the previous chapter of pre-modern freedom and the deep origins of the freedom–addiction nexus:

> The institution of slavery and unfettered gambling on lives shared an abstract identity. Each entailed the creation of property in human lives, coercively in the case of slavery, gratuitously in the case of speculative life insurance or gambling. Each transposed the profane calculus of the marketplace into the sacred and invaluable sphere of human life. Moreover, by treating … human life itself as an object of commerce, both slavery and gambling on lives denied to their subjects the primary article of ownership assumed in any Lockean political compact: possession of the self. It was therefore to an emerging consciousness of the problematic

relationship between economic and political liberty that the eighteenth-century insurance 'imaginary' owed its demise.

(Clark, 2002: 88)

It was, of course, exactly this valorization within liberal governance of freedom as individual autonomy that at the same time underpinned the historical coincidence of concerns about habitual drug consumption with the emergence of liberalism – leading O'Malley (2004: 155) to describe it as a 'peculiarly liberal affliction'. We can understand then the connection between life insurance and concerns about the effects of opium that we see in the Mar case in this broader context of the constitution of the responsible and prudential liberal subject.

Third, there is an important connection between life insurance and the emergence of the public-health movement which, as I will explore below, is another key line of development in my genealogy. As Baker (2000: 2–3) observes, 'life insurance companies were pioneers in epidemiology and public health' through their attempts to generate mortality and disease statistics in order to feed into the calculation of premiums. This was part of a much wider 'statistical revolution' in the early nineteenth century. Ian Hacking's marvellous book *The Taming of Chance* charts in detail the intertwining of actuarial expertise, insurance and concerns about population health, which accompanied the 'avalanche of printed numbers' during this period (Hacking, 1990). So, for example, medical experts on opium like Professor Christison at Edinburgh contributed to actuarial journals (e.g. Christison, 1854) as well as medical ones.

Problematizing opium II: public health

This rise of public health during the nineteenth century is another important strand of the genealogy, representing perhaps the principal dimension of the problematization of opium. In most historical accounts, the public-health movement has been viewed as a consequence of the process of industrialization in the first decades of the nineteenth century. Dorothy Porter (1999: 112), for example, argues that the creation of an interventionist public-health system was a response to the environmental threats to health posed by the squalor and overcrowding of the new urban centres of population. Similarly, George Rosen in his influential book *A History of Public Health*, first published in 1958, identified industrialization as one of the central motors for these public-health developments:

> The problem of the public health was inherent in the new industrial civilization. The same process that created the market economy, the factory, and the modern urban environment also brought into being the health problems that made necessary new means of disease prevention

and health protection. It is significant that public attention was first attracted to these problems at Manchester, the first industrial city. Here a series of epidemic fevers had brought sharply to the notice of the community the significance of factories and congested dwellings as providing conditions in which such diseases could flourish and spread.

(Rosen, 1958: 201)

As Roy Porter (1993: 53) observes, a series of cholera epidemics – the main outbreaks were in 1831–32, 1848–49, 1854 and 1861 – sharpened these anxieties about the potential impact on health of squalor and overcrowding, although as early as the 1830s an infrastructure of public-health functionaries and institutions was being assembled (1993: 54). The great public-health pioneer, Edwin Chadwick, identified issues such as clean water supply, drainage and sewerage as the fundamentals to be addressed and he proposed ambitious civil-engineering solutions. His 1842 report on the *Sanitary Conditions of the Labouring Population of Great Britain* was a landmark in the development of public health (Chadwick, 1842).

Chadwick did refer to opium use in this report, albeit briefly, but, as Berridge (Berridge and Edwards, 1981: 77–78) suggests, it was primarily the medical profession, and especially doctors, who began to raise the problem of opium poisonings in the 1850s and 1860s. This was also indicative, in part, of the development of public health at this time, as it broadened out from Chadwick's 'sanitary idea' towards including the notion of public health as 'state medicine' (Rosen, 1958; Porter, 1999: 120–21) – the prominent medical spokesman Dr Henry Rumsey, for example, published a set of *Essays on State Medicine* in 1856 (Porter, 1999: 121). Indeed, the relationship between doctors and the state was substantially refigured during this period (Brand, 1965; Osborne, 1993). It was not just opium that was of concern either – anxieties about arsenic poisoning, for example, led to the Arsenic Act of 1851 (Bartrip, 1992) – but opium was the most common drug involved in poisoning deaths, both accidental and suicidal, throughout this period. During the 1860s, for instance, opiates accounted for around one third of all deaths by poisoning (Berridge and Edwards, 1981: 79). The action of different drugs on the body became a growing medical specialism. Professor Christison, the principal expert involved in the Earl of Mar case, was one of the pioneers, his 1829 *Treatise on Poisons* proving to be influential. In this context, we might understand then the Pharmacy Act of 1868 as part of this public-health drive to reduce poisoning, in a similar way to the arsenic legislation in 1851. So, Parssinen (1983: 68), for example, describes the 1868 Act as 'one of the smaller triumphs of the larger [public-health] campaign'.

But how should we understand the emergence of this particular mode of problematizing opium and opiates at this time? Clearly, there were real health problems posed by early industrialization and urbanization but, as

Dorothy Porter (1994: 24) emphasizes, there was nothing 'automatic' or inevitable about the particular system that was assembled from the 1830s onwards. Rather, the distinctive forms taken by public health in different countries were expressions of the 'way different societies addressed questions of social order and nationhood' (1994: 24). I think this is an important point, otherwise we risk writing a history of public health that is far too crude and determined. But how we can develop the idea? I think both Foucauldian and regulatory perspectives are useful here. In his influential essay 'The Politics of Health in the Eighteenth Century', Foucault (1980b) identifies the 'discovery' of the category of 'population' as a critical transition:

> 'Population', with its numerical variables of space and chronology, longevity and health, ... emerge[s] not only as a problem but as an object of surveillance, analysis, intervention, modification etc. [and t]he project of a technology of population begins to be sketched.
>
> (Foucault, 1980b: 171)

This was also one of the themes of his 1978 Collège de France lecture course, *Security, Territory, Population* (Foucault, 2007) in which he identified the 'discovery of population' as central to the transition to liberal forms of government and rule (see also Curtis, 2002; Elden, 2003). Critical to this was the 'avalanche of printed numbers' in the early nineteenth century (Hacking, 1982, 1990, 1991), which led to an array of new statistical information about populations being compiled: mortality rates; disease profiles; age profiles; suicide rates; crime rates; birth rates; and so on. With this new population knowledge, new social 'facts' and 'problems' became visible and therefore governable for the first time. Many of these new administrative and statistical categories related to matters of 'longevity and health' which, in turn, became objectives of political power. The assembling of the public-health apparatus can be seen then as part of this broader project of developing new liberal technologies of population in order to respond to these newly visible population-health problems. In Foucault's formulation of population, it is not possible to act directly upon it, in the way that the sovereign will could act directly upon individual juridical subjects; rather interventions need to be directed at the range of 'complex and modifiable variables' on which the process of population depends (Foucault, 2007: 74). Technologies of population like public health are therefore targeted at a dispersed set of intervention points.

Regulation, police and liberalism

This takes us a little further forward but still begs some questions. To varying extents, drug historians have tempered the emphasis on public health as a driver of regulatory change by pointing also to the importance of professionalization within the (broadly defined) medical field (e.g. Parssinen, 1983; Holloway, 1995; Berridge, 1999). In this vein, they argue that the 1868 Act was partly the result of the developing power and influence of the pharmacy profession. This may be so but I think the matter needs to be set in a much broader regulatory context. In his famous essay *On Liberty* from 1859, John Stuart Mill discussed the question of poisons at some length:

> The sale of poisons, opens a new question; the proper limits of what may be called the functions of police; how far liberty may legitimately be invaded for the prevention of crime, or of accident. It is one of the undisputed functions of government to take precautions against crime before it has been committed, as well as to detect and punish it afterwards. The preventive function of government, however, is far more liable to be abused, to the prejudice of liberty, than the punitory function.
>
> (Mill, 1859/2002: 81)

The reference to the 'functions of police' is critical. Both regulation scholars (Braithwaite, 2003, 2008) and Foucauldians (Gordon, 1991; Pasquino, 1991; Foucault, 2007) have pointed to the importance of examining *Polizeiwissenschaft* or the 'science of police' developed first in Prussia in the late seventeenth and early eighteenth centuries and then subsequently spreading across much of continental Europe (see also Knemeyer, 1980; Rutgers, 1998; Dodsworth, 2008). 'Police' in this context had a meaning quite different from the modern post-Peelian notion of police as criminal-law enforcers and upholders of public order. The older idea encompassed an astonishingly wide range of interventions, united by their aim of maximizing the happiness and prosperity of citizens and furthering the public good – 'everything from being to well-being' (Foucault, 2007: 328) – perhaps best understood from our twenty-first-century perspective as a form of public administration or public policy. As Braithwaite (2003: 9) notes, police had an especially strong focus on the creation of institutions and mechanisms for enhancing trade, commerce and the operation of the economy, including 'weights and measures and other forms of consumer protection, liquor licensing, health and safety, building, road and traffic regulation and early forms of environmental regulation'. The vast literature on the 'science of police' that accumulated through the seventeenth and eighteenth centuries was in this sense a precursor to contemporary regulation scholarship (Braithwaite, 2008: 12).

The police economy that preceded the emergence of modern liberal capitalism was characterized by being 'rather privatized, subject to considerable local control, relying mostly on volunteer constables and watches for implementation, heavily oriented to self-regulation and infrequent (even if sometimes draconian) in its recourse to punishment' (Braithwaite, 2008: 12). In seventeenth-century Britain, chemists, druggists, apothecaries, grocers and other merchants were largely regulated in this way. Leslie Matthews' (1962) superb *History of Pharmacy in Britain* gives a good account of this. He describes a highly localized system of guilds which regulated sellers of a range of goods in specific towns and cities. For example, in Salisbury in 1612, the 'Traders Association, which included Grocers and Apothecaries, issued an order authorizing its members to search and view merchandise and to examine weights and measures' (1962: 39). In Lichfield at around the same time the guild was known as the Mercers' Company and included a wide range of merchants from apothecaries to salters. It too 'had authority to supervise the weights and measures used by its members and to exact penalties' (1962: 39–40). Exactly which categories of merchants were joined together within a guild varied considerably between local areas but it was not uncommon for spicers and apothecaries to belong to the same association, sometimes alongside more general grocers.

The important point here is that in the pre-industrial era, the manufacture and selling of goods and commodities, including what we would now term drugs or medicines, were certainly subject to some degree of regulation, however uneven and patchy it may have been. If we return to the passage from Mill quoted above, what he highlights is the tension that emerges with the transition from a police economy to a liberal industrial one at the end of the eighteenth century. What are the 'proper limits' of the police function? Or, to put it more simply, to what extent should free trade be restricted by regulatory interventions? It was certainly not the case that the earlier notion of police was simply swept away by industrialization and the rise of liberalism, as Dodsworth (2008) clearly demonstrates. Rather, by moving from an 'interpretation of markets [as] constituted by police to laissez-faire markets' (Braithwaite, 2008: 13), there was a consequent reshaping of the institutional framework for the regulation of markets:

> From the mid-nineteenth century, factories inspectorates, health and sanitation, food inspectorates and countless others were created to begin to fill the vacuum left by constables now concentrating only on crime. Business regulation became variegated into many different specialist regulatory branches. The nineteenth-century regulatory growth is more in the number of branches than in their size and power. Laissez-faire ideology underpinned this regulatory weakness.
>
> (Braithwaite, 2008: 13–14)

This is the crucial point: by understanding the regulatory consequences of this transition from a pre-industrial police economy to an industrial liberal one, we can shed further light on both the emergence of the nineteenth-century public-health movement *and* the increasing specialization within the broad medical field (including the rise of the pharmacy profession). I will now try to sketch this out.

Starting with specialization, this was certainly a well-remarked development. Matthews (1962), for example, entitles one of the chapters in his *History* 'The Parting of the Ways – Further Specialisation'. However, it is rather unclear in his account why this occurred. One way to understand it is as an instance of this general pattern of variegation 'into many specialist regulatory branches' (Braithwaite, 2008: 14) that accompanied the transition from a police economy. The development of the Apothecaries' Act of 1815 is a good early example of this (see Holloway, 1966; Lawrence, 1991). As Porter (1993: 46) suggests this was partly about establishing apothecaries on a stronger footing by introducing some firmer regulatory measures, including the confirmation of the Society of Apothecaries which had been founded in 1617 (Matthews, 1962: 112–15). At the same time, clause XXVIII of the Act expressly left the business of other dispensers of medicines alone, stating that nothing in the Act was to hinder or encumber 'in any way the Trade or Business of a Chemist and Druggist, in the buying, preparing, compounding, dispensing and vending of Drugs, Medicines and Medicinable Compounds, wholesale and retail' (quoted in Matthews, 1962: 115). This is a telling point. Matthews (1962: 115) argues that this was recognition that chemists and druggists were well established by this time as suppliers of medicines. That may well be true but it also suggests to me that the 1815 Act was not primarily driven by professionalization, which we might ordinarily expect to be accompanied by attempts to eliminate 'rivals' outside the nascent profession, but rather was part of this distinctive pattern of regulatory growth that Braithwaite observes.

Similarly, if we look at the emergence of public-health functions and their associated administrative machinery, they can also be viewed as part of this pattern. Hennock (2000: 270–71) notes that the early Chadwickian emphasis on sanitary reform was partly driven by the 'discovery that Boards of Guardians lacked the powers to remove nuisances, powers that their predecessors in the parish had possessed'. In other words, it was filling the regulatory 'vacuum' that Braithwaite (2008: 13) describes. This becomes even clearer when we consider the Public Health Act of 1848. As well as directly sanitary matters like water supply and sewerage, it also gave local Boards of Health powers over street cleansing, regulation of slaughterhouses, street paving, playgrounds and public lavatories. The local Medical Officers of Health created by the Act, a move that Porter (1993: 55) sees as critical in the development of public health, were given wide-ranging regulatory powers under a succession of Nuisance Removal Acts in the 1850s and 1860s in relation to food, waste, pollution and so on. Again, this fits with the pattern of regulatory growth that Braithwaite describes. It is telling too that the 1848 Act was superseded ten years later by the Local Government Act. In this respect, the nineteenth-century public-health movement was the origin of modern local government.

This points us to a further significant insight. Historians have noted, for example, the apparent paradox that the early Victorian period from the 1830s actually saw a major expansion of the administrative machinery of government, famously described by Oliver MacDonagh (1958) as the 'nineteenth-century revolution in government' (see also MacLeod, 2003). Indeed, Rosen (1958: 225–27) in his *History of Public Health* notes this contradictory co-existence between liberal economic freedom and the expanding administrative and regulatory machinery of public health. It has been argued that this revolution 'initiated the process of government growth that eventually led to the "quasi-collectivist" welfare state of the twentieth century' (Conway, 1990: 71), an argument first put of course in David Roberts' seminal *Victorian Origins of the British Welfare State* (Roberts, 1960). The bigger regulatory narrative here then is that public health grew partly out of the transition from the pre-industrial police economy to liberal capitalism but it also prefigured, and laid some of the foundations for, the later shift to welfare liberalism at the turn of the twentieth century. This supports Braithwaite's (2008: 14–16) contention that what he calls the 'provider state' of the twentieth century was created partly out of the regulatory failures of *laissez-faire* liberalism We can understand then the Pharmacy Act of 1868 within this context of ongoing mutations within the paradigm of liberalism. In other words, we need to look both backwards and forwards to understand it fully.

Freedom, free trade and regulation

At the heart of these mutations, and their associated regulatory developments such as the Pharmacy Act, was a set of debates in which freedom loomed large. Let me return to Mill's *On Liberty*:

> There are questions relating to interference with trade which are essentially questions of liberty; such as the Maine Law, already touched upon; the prohibition of the importation of opium into China; the restriction of the sale of poisons; all cases, in short, where the object of the interference is to make it impossible or difficult to obtain a particular commodity. These interferences are objectionable, not as infringements on the liberty of the producer or seller, but on that of the buyer.
>
> (Mill, 1859/2002: 80–81)

Here, interestingly for my purposes, his three examples are all relevant to the genealogy I am sketching out: the 'Maine Law' he refers to was one of the earliest alcohol prohibition laws in the United States, whilst the other two point to the international and domestic side respectively of the opium trade. I will return to the question of alcohol below but I will deal with the other two issues here in turn.

First, there is the question of free trade in the domestic sphere and how far it is appropriate to interfere with trade in potentially harmful commodities for the protection of the public. Mill addresses this point in relation to poisons in detail in *On Liberty*:

> If poisons were never bought or used for any purpose except the commission of murder it would be right to prohibit their manufacture and sale. They may, however, be wanted not only for innocent but for useful purposes, and restrictions cannot be imposed in the one case without operating in the other. Again, it is a proper office of public authority to guard against accidents. If either a public officer or any one else saw a person attempting to cross a bridge which had been ascertained to be unsafe, and there were no time to warn him of his danger, they might seize him and turn him back, without any real infringement of his liberty; for liberty consists in doing what one desires, and he does not desire to fall into the river. Nevertheless, when there is not a certainty, but only a danger of mischief, no one but the person himself can judge of the sufficiency of the motive which may prompt him to incur the risk: in this case, therefore (unless he is a child, or delirious, or in some state of excitement or absorption incompatible with the full use of the reflecting faculty), he ought, I conceive, to be only warned of the danger; not forcibly prevented from exposing himself to it. Similar considerations, applied to such a question as the sale of poisons, may enable us to decide which among the possible modes of regulation are or are not contrary to principle. Such a precaution, for example, as that of labelling the drug with some word expressive of its dangerous character, may be enforced without violation of liberty: the buyer cannot wish not to know that the thing he possesses has poisonous qualities. But to require in all cases the certificate of a medical practitioner would make it sometimes impossible, always expensive, to obtain the article for legitimate uses.
>
> (Mill, 1859/2002: 81–82)

This is perhaps all fairly standard and unremarkable libertarian fare. I think a telling part of this passage though is the exception Mill sets out to this freedom to buy poisons – 'unless he is … in some state of excitement or absorption incompatible with the full use of the reflecting faculty'. In other words, for as long as a potential purchaser retains their 'faculty of the will', in the sense of Jonathan Edwards' 'mind choosing', then they ought to be relatively unrestricted in being able to buy opium and other 'poisons'. Conversely, we can infer that such a light-touch regulatory approach is not compatible with concepts of addiction in which habitual use of opium and opiates is seen as to some degree uncontrollable or compulsive. In other words, there is an affinity between the system of pharmaceutical regulation under the 1868 Act, classical liberal conceptions of freedom and notions of habitual opiate use as vice not disease.

The second point made by Mill, concerning the 'prohibition of the importation of opium into China', reminds us of the significance of the international dimension to our genealogy, as noted in Chapter 1. He is referring here to the importing of opium into China by the Dutch and the British and the attempts by the Chinese to prohibit this trade. Opium importation into China had a very long history, even in the nineteenth century, but it reached a particular crunch point in the 1800s. This history, and the specific details of the two Anglo-Chinese Opium Wars in the middle of that century, is too complex to recount here. Those readers who wish to know more are referred first of all to the classic history by Peter Fay (1975), as well as two high-quality journalistic accounts produced at around the same time by Beeching (1975) and Inglis (1976) respectively (see also Waley, 1958; Holt, 1964). Of the more recent contributions to this literature, Frank Dikötter et al.'s book *Narcotic Culture* (2004) is insightful and at times provocative, whilst Carl Trocki's (1999) *Opium, Empire and the Global Political Economy* sets the issue in the broader context of the history of the region. For my purposes here, there are three key issues to note that are relevant to my genealogy. First, the 'problematization' of opium during the middle third of the nineteenth century was not restricted to Britain and had a strong international character. This is an important antidote or corrective to more parochial accounts. Second, in understanding this international opium trade, it is necessary to engage with the history of empires and colonial rule across the globe (see Trocki, 1999; Buxton, 2006: 7–13). The Opium Wars are but one illustration of this. Third, questions of trade were at the heart of this global dimension and, as illustrated by Mill's concern in the passage quoted above from *On Liberty*, the liberal principle of free trade was central.

Indeed, picking up this third point, as will become apparent in subsequent chapters, looking at the 'drug problem' from the perspective of the question of how to regulate and govern global and domestic markets in certain categories of pharmaceutical commodities, is a useful analytical approach. This also highlights an important issue that I will pick up more directly in Chapter 4. I mention it here briefly in order to highlight its origins in the first half of the nineteenth century. The issue concerns the connections between the emergence and regulation of the modern pharmaceutical industry and the genealogy of the illicit drug problem that I am tracing in this book (see Braithwaite and Drahos, 2000: 360–98). A key development in which these connections are rooted is the rapid advancement in laboratory chemistry that took place from the beginning of the nineteenth century. This laid the foundations not only for the modern pharmaceutical industry but also for much of the history of the contemporary 'drug problem'. For example, it was in 1803 that morphine, the principal active alkaloid in opium, was first isolated by German and French chemists (Berridge and Edwards, 1981: 135–36). It began to be commercially manufactured in the 1820s, including by Merck of Darmstadt, a German pharmaceutical company that would later also pioneer the manufacture of cocaine. Further work on creating new esthers of morphine was undertaken in the middle of the century, one of which, diamorphine, would later be marketed as heroin by Bayer and Co., another German pharmaceutical company (Seddon, 2007b). So, without these advancements in chemistry, not only would the modern pharmaceutical industry as we know it not exist, nor would the twin substances at the heart of the contemporary 'drug problem', heroin and cocaine.

Perhaps the best illustration of the intertwining of the nascent pharmaceutical industry with some of the other threads I have explored in this chapter, and indeed with threads that will be picked up in later chapters, is the case of Macfarlan and Company of Edinburgh in Scotland. Founded in 1815 as a pharmacy shop, one regular customer for laudanum in its early years was Thomas De Quincey, author of the famous *Confessions of an English Opium Eater* (Matthews, 1962: 230). It soon expanded into production of pharmaceuticals and in the 1830s began the commercial manufacture of morphine. A decade later, Mr J.F. Macfarlan, the company's founder, became the representative of the North British Branch of the Pharmaceutical Society, which was a key vehicle for the professionalization of the pharmacy profession which, as I have already discussed, led, in part, to the passing of the 1852 and 1868 Pharmacy Acts. By the 1890s, Macfarlan's production of morphine was claimed to have reached an annual peak of 250,000 ounces (Bolton, 1976; Parssinen, 1983: 152). According to Parssinen (Parssinen and Kerner, 1981; Parssinen, 1983: 144–63), much of this output was for export to China rather than domestic use. After 1909, when its importation to China was prohibited, Parssinen argues that much British-manufactured morphine continued to end up there, largely smuggled via Japan. This practice was largely ended, certainly for morphine produced by Macfarlan, with the passage of the Dangerous Drugs Act of 1920 and the establishment of an 'export certificate' system under the auspices of the League of Nations (Parssinen, 1983: 154). After this, Macfarlan continued to produce morphine for domestic use, alongside other opiates. Today, the company is called Macfarlan Smith and has retained its specialism in the manufacture of opiate alkaloids. In 2006, it took over the sole opium poppy cultivation business in the UK. The company is now part of the Johnson Matthey group which made a pre-tax profit in 2008 of £262 million.

Liberalism and the alcohol question

My primary focus in this chapter has been on tracing the lines of development which led to the emergence of the pharmaceutical regulation of opium as enacted by the 1868 legislative event. A subsidiary but important question is about the other major psychoactive substance consumed in the nineteenth century: alcohol. As I explained in Chapter 1, I am not attempting to provide a comprehensive analysis of the entire gamut of these substances and my primary interest is in what are today illicit drugs. Such a wide-ranging undertaking would in any case certainly be beyond my capabilities. Nevertheless, as the brief discussion above of the history of Mr Macfarlan's company illustrates, it is not possible to lay down rigid demarcations between the licit and illicit sides of the story I am telling. And in that respect, the alcohol question during this period cannot be entirely ignored. So how was alcohol consumption viewed and regulated during the first half of the nineteenth century? And in what ways did this differ from what happened to opium?

In the passage quoted above from Mill's essay *On Liberty*, he condemns the Maine Law, prohibiting the sale of alcohol, on the grounds that it constitutes an unwarrantable interference not only in free trade but also in the personal freedom of individuals to buy and consume any commodity they desire. Boire (2002) calls the latter issue 'freedom of inebriation', that is the freedom of individuals to consume intoxicating substances, provided that in doing so they do not cause harm to others. As Ruggiero (1999) astutely notes, that proviso opens up arguments *for* prohibition (if a link with crime or violence is made), as well as *against*. The question of free trade was particularly significant in the governance of alcohol in the Victorian period and I will return to it shortly.

For Berridge (2005b: 10), it was industrialization and the factory system which both exacerbated and accentuated the 'drink problem' during the nineteenth century:

> By the early years of the nineteenth century, the issue of excess consumption of alcohol began to be defined as a social problem. The processes of urbanization and industrialization increased the resort of the working class to alcohol, and drunkenness was more visible in an urban setting than in rural communities. On the other hand, the pub with its warmth and bright lights, its games, newspapers and company, offered a tolerable relief from an otherwise wretched environment. Excessive drinking was, however, incompatible with the more disciplined and regulated nature of a factory-based workforce.

Harrison (1994: 41), in his superb and highly influential book *Drink and the Victorians*, is more equivocal, arguing that 'industrialization's impact on drinking habits is so complex that one cannot say whether it worsened the drink problem'. He suggests that in certain respects, industrialization had the opposite effect and there is some evidence of a fall in consumption at the beginning of the nineteenth century (Bynum, 1968: 160). But for the purposes of my project, I am not sure that trying to understand responses to alcohol in terms of the changing scale or nature of the 'real problem' is that fruitful. I think a more helpful approach is to look at how habitual drinking was viewed and understood during this period. In other words, it is the changing *conceptions* of alcohol, or, to use Foucauldian language, the 'imagination' of the 'alcohol problem' that are most important, and which also bring out the similarities and differences with opium.

There are certainly many similarities that can be drawn. Harrison (1994: 42) notes for example how alcohol was used by the working classes as an all-purpose painkiller and pick-me-up in the 1820s, in much the same way that Berridge describes for opium in *Opium and the People*. Bynum (1968: 160) notes wryly, and exaggerating only a little, that it 'has been supposed at one time or another to cure virtually every disease'. If anything, in the Victorian period alcohol was even more embedded in everyday social and working life than opium (Harrison, 1994: 45). In this regard, we might greet with a slight smile the fact that the Pharmaceutical Society of Great Britain, an influential body in the professionalization of pharmacy and the development of the 1868 legislation, was established at a meeting in the 'Crown and Anchor' Tavern in the Strand in London in 1841 (Matthews, 1962: 124).

So how was alcohol viewed and dealt with by the Victorians? As discussed in Chapter 2, Levine's (1978) classic article demonstrated how the concept of addiction as a disease was first assembled during this period in relation to habitual drinking. The best-developed and most influential elaboration of this idea was by Dr Benjamin Rush, an American physician, who first termed this new condition a 'disease of the will'. According to Levine (1978: 152), his contribution to the new concept was fourfold:

> First, he identified the causal agent – spirituous liquors; second, he clearly described the drunkard's condition as loss of control over drinking behaviour – as compulsive activity; third, he declared the condition to be a disease; and fourth, he prescribed total abstinence as the only way to cure the drunkard.

Thomas Trotter's *Essay on Drunkenness* from 1804 was an early British example of an idea of addiction being applied to alcohol, although, as Harrison (1994: 23) notes, Trotter's description retains strong 'moral overtones'. This ambivalence illustrates well the two different ideas about drink that co-existed as slightly uneasy bedfellows during the first five or six decades of the century. On the one hand, there was the emergent concept of addiction as out-of-control or compulsive behaviour; on the other, the idea of drinking as a freely chosen expression of desire for intoxication.

These two ideas were reflected in the two principal regulatory approaches to alcohol that prevailed during this period. The first idea, of habitual drunkenness as compulsive or addictive behaviour, found partial expression in the temperance and teetotal movements that were prominent at this time. These movements were the result of a convergence of an extremely complex set of social, economic, cultural and religious factors (see Harrison, 1994) and I do not pretend at all to be able to capture this complexity here. They encompassed a spectrum of views, from being 'anti-spirits' right through to calling for total prohibition. The crucial point here, and one which Levine (1978) draws out insightfully, is the affinity between the emerging addiction concept and the temperance movement:

> The core of the disease concept – the idea that habitual drunkards are alcohol addicts, persons who have lost control over their drinking and who must abstain entirely from alcohol – was also, from Rush on, at the heart of temperance ideology during the 19th century.
>
> (Levine, 1978: 158)

And this affinity, as Levine clearly demonstrates, centres on liberal conceptions of individual responsibility and the idea of the 'free' subject as a prudential and independent actor. Behaviour, like habitual drinking, that is seen as 'out-of-control' and 'irresponsible', is thus highly problematic within liberal modes of government. As I noted earlier in this chapter, it was the absence of any significant application of the addiction concept to opium that allowed for a light-touch regulatory approach. In contrast, by the 1850s there were calls for the total prohibition of alcohol on both sides of the Atlantic.

The second idea, of habitual drinking as freely chosen behaviour, was articulated in a particularly interesting way in the free licensing movement that rose to prominence in the early part of the century (see Harrison, 1994: 63–84; Mason, 2001). In essence, this was an experiment in freeing up the gulation. It was premised on the liberal idea that the 'invisible hand' of a free market would provide the best means of promoting prosperity and economic efficiency within the sector. Existing systems of local licensing and regulation were seen as outdated throwbacks to the pre-industrial era and incompatible with *laissez-faire*. The movement developed, in other words, out of the transition from a police to a liberal economy (see Valverde, 2003). It culminated in the Beer Act of 1830 which created a new category of drinking place, the beerhouse or beershop, which was exempt from local magistrates' control. In this sense, the free licensing movement might be viewed as paralleling the pre-1868 lay/commercial regulation of opium (Berridge, 2005a). Indeed it fell out of favour at around the same time – by the 1870s it had been entirely eclipsed, according to Harrison (1994: 338).

The tensions between these two conceptions of alcohol and their associated regulatory technologies were partly accommodated by the distinctions drawn between different types of alcoholic drink, distinctions which may look somewhat odd to contemporary eyes. In the early decades of the century, beer was not seen as alcohol in the same way as wine and spirits (O'Malley and Valverde, 2004: 28). Indeed, many early temperance advocates viewed beer drinking in a positive light. This changed over time, as temperance ideology began to veer towards teetotalism and calls for prohibition of all types of alcohol, including beer. Ironically, in certain respects, the Beer Act seems to have marked a turning point, as it became a focus for concerns about working-class drunkenness (Mason, 2001). Engels, for example, in his famous work *The Condition of the Working Class in England* published in 1844, deprecated the drunkenness he observed in the beershops in the slum areas of Manchester, blaming this 'spread of intemperance' on the legislators who passed the Beer Act (Engels, 1844/1987).

Despite the clear similarities, there were also some differences between the problematizations of alcohol and opium during this period. Whilst questions of freedom were central to both, the 'problem' was in certain respects viewed as different. For opium, it was at heart about its impact on the individual consumer's body (whether in terms of longevity or the risk of poisoning); whilst for alcohol, it was about public disorder, especially in the newly expanding urban areas. I have already attempted to explain how conceptions of opium underwent a transition from it being seen purely as a therapeutic substance (in the broadest sense) to it being viewed as a potentially dangerous poison. In relation to alcohol, the historical origins of the connection with disorder are clearly deep but it has been argued that this linkage became significantly stronger with the 'birth of modern industrial capitalism and the development of modern urban life' (Jayne et al., 2006: 453).

Another way to look at this is in terms of the Foucauldian distinction between *discipline* (targeted at the human body) and *regulatory controls* (targeted at the population) (Foucault, 1984; Rabinow and Rose, 2006). For opium, whilst the problem was primarily located at the level of the human body, many of the responses took the form of regulatory controls aimed at the level of population. For alcohol, both problem and responses were largely positioned in the sphere of population. Hence the drink problem was so often viewed through the lens of the threat of group or communal disorder in urban areas.

These distinctions, however, can be overplayed. As Berridge (1996a: 304) observes, throughout the nineteenth century, responses to opium and alcohol shared much in common (see also Levine and Reinarman, 1991). The sharp regulatory divide that makes up our contemporary experience would take another half-century to emerge after the Pharmacy Act of 1868 and that story is the focus of Chapter 4.

Conclusion

In this chapter, I have attempted to develop some new perspectives on the emergence of the Pharmacy Act of 1868, a legislative 'event' which has an important place in the genealogy of the contemporary drug problem. Its genealogical importance lies primarily in three aspects:

1   It marked the *beginning of the conception of opium and opiates as a 'problem'*. Before the mid-nineteenth century, opium was part and parcel of everyday

life and seen to play a largely positive social and therapeutic role. Public or policy concern about it was minimal, verging on non-existent. This 'problem framework' has become an almost unquestionable feature of how opiates are considered today.

2 It was the *starting point of the idea that medical professionals were the appropriate gatekeepers and dispensers of opium and opium-based products*. Whilst the 1868 Act did not fully achieve a medical monopoly, it was an important first step along this path. Doctors and pharmacists remain extremely important in the contemporary control and management of opiates and opiate users.

3 It marked the *beginning of the idea that legislative regulation of opium supply could be an effective way of dealing with the 'problem'*. The supply side of the 'drug problem', and the struggle to find effective means of controlling supply, have continued to preoccupy policy-makers and administrators. The use of legislative regulation remains the cornerstone of these efforts.

I should emphasize here that although the 1868 Act marked a critical point in the genealogy I am tracing, it was only a first stepping stone towards the present. A key distinction from what would unfold in the twentieth century is that the Act did not bring in a separate regulatory regime for opiates. Rather, they were included within a broader set of arrangements for controlling substances considered as potentially dangerous 'poisons'.

I have claimed to provide some new perspectives on this 'event'. At the heart of this claim is my attempt to position the account of this 'event' in the context of the emergence of modern industrial capitalism and the transition from a police economy to a liberal one. Situating the genealogy squarely in this context of liberal governance opens up some new vantage points on certain aspects detailed in the historical literature, for example the emergence of the public-health movement. I have also attempted to draw on both Foucauldian and regulatory perspectives in my analysis in what I hope is an insightful way. Whilst Foucault's work on liberalism and governmentality is undoubtedly revelatory, I also believe that it can be supplemented by the very different but equally brilliant work of regulation scholars like Braithwaite, and I have tried to do that here.

As I explained in Chapter 2, running throughout this book is the thesis that the freedom–addiction nexus is fundamental to our understanding of the genealogy of the 'imagination' and governance of the contemporary 'drug problem'. This should be evident in the analysis I have developed in this chapter and I will not repeat here the arguments already made. One point I want to draw out is the connection between the notion of addiction as a 'disease of the will' and prohibition as a regulatory strategy. We have seen how in the period covered in this chapter, the disease concept was applied primarily to alcohol. At the same time, it was alcohol rather than opium that was the target of a prohibitionist movement from the 1850s. As I have argued, this was not a coincidence. The weakening of the faculty of the will, and the consequent challenge to the idea of the prudential and responsible liberal subject, is profoundly troubling to liberal mentalities of rule. I will return to this point in Chapter 4.

Looking ahead then to this next chapter, we move forward to the turn of the twentieth century to examine a pivotal 'event', the passing of the Dangerous Drugs Act of 1920. This Act marked the establishment of several ideas that have subsequently come to appear 'self-evident'. Most fundamental of these is the notion that dangerous drugs like heroin and cocaine should be regulated through a criminal law framework of prohibition. As we will now see, the lines of development out of which this came are complex and varied. I will argue that the best way to understand this 'event' is in terms of the transition from classical liberalism to welfare liberalism.

Chapter 4

Drugs, prohibition and welfarism

The Dangerous Drugs Act 1920

Heroin – the sedative for coughs.

(Bayer & Co. advertisement, 1900)

An Act to Regulate the Importation, Exportation, Manufacture, Sale and Use of Opium and Other Dangerous Drugs

(From preamble to the Dangerous Drugs Act 1920)

With few exceptions addiction to morphine and heroin should be regarded as a manifestation of a morbid state, and not as a mere form of vicious indulgence.

(Rolleston Report, 1926)

Introduction

The period at the turn of the twentieth century, and especially the first two decades of that century, was a transformative one in this field, culminating in some landmark legislative 'events', notably the Harrison Narcotic Act in 1914 in North America and the Dangerous Drugs Act in 1920 in Britain. Indeed, it is arguably the single most important period for understanding how we have arrived where we are today. It marks the emergence not only of our contemporary concept of 'drugs' but also of the 'great regulatory divide' out of which today's international drug prohibition system was developed. So within the genealogy I am tracing here, this chapter is absolutely pivotal and in many respects lies at the heart of the whole book. As I will show, this fundamental regulatory shift needs to be understood by setting it in the wider context of social change, that is in relation to mutations in liberal governance. One of my principal guides to these mutations, characterized as the transition from classical liberalism to welfare liberalism, will be David Garland's (1985) book *Punishment and Welfare*.

By way of setting this background scene, I will say a little more here about the nature and characteristics of this governmental transition. Over the course of roughly 50 years starting in the 1870s, the parameters, assumptions and modes of governmental action were all refigured during a significant period of social change. There are several insightful commentaries on this to which interested readers are referred and on which I draw here. As well as Garland's (1985) book which I have already mentioned, Rose (1999: 98–136) offers a highly influential analysis from a governmentality perspective. An excellent cultural history of the period is provided by Wiener (1990). I have also found Braithwaite's (2008: 14–16) brief comments useful.

There are three main dimensions of this transition.

First, the increasing involvement of the state as both a provider and a regulator, as the mode of government became increasingly interventionist in the closing decades of the nineteenth century. Indeed, for this reason, Braithwaite (2008) prefers to describe this as the era of the 'provider state' rather than of welfare liberalism. This interventionism contrasts sharply with the 'nightwatchman state' of classical liberalism which sought to limit the sphere of governmental activities (Braithwaite, 2000). Indeed, as noted in Chapter 2, the initial and arguably foundational problematic of liberal government revolved around the aim of rationalizing and limiting the exercise of political power rather than extending its scope or reach (see Gordon, 1991). The interventionist turn is therefore a highly significant development. And as Braithwaite (2008: 14–16) suggests, it was created partly through recognition of the limitations of *laissez-faire*, the provider state in effect coming into being as a 'solution' to some of the failures of nineteenth-century regulation.

Second, the trend of proliferating regulatory branches that Braithwaite (2008: 13–14) astutely observes, and that was discussed in Chapter 3, continued to accelerate in the latter part of the nineteenth century. There was thus a multiplication of sites of intervention, more than a deepening or intensification of existing activities. As we will see, this is an important point – the new interventionism involved an extension of state activity in to areas which had previously been largely unregulated.

Third, the emergence of welfare liberalism was founded on what Rose (1999), after Donzelot (1984), terms the 'invention of the social', that is the creation of a new 'form of sociality constructed around mass democracy, monopoly capital and an interventionist State' (Garland, 1981: 35). The endeavour was 'to construct a new kind of human being, social citizens taking responsibility for their physical and mental health and that of their family' (Rose, 1999: 131). The corollary of this new social citizenship was the creation of new powers to intervene in the lives of individuals failing to meet those responsibilities in order to effect the 'identification and repair of behavioural "abnormalities"' (Garland, 1981: 29). It is these new 'normalizing' strategies that Garland (1985) charts so expertly. The emergence of these strategies was partly rooted in, and enabled by, the growth of the administrative machinery of government that I noted in the previous chapter and which began as early as the 1830s – MacDonagh's (1958) 'nineteenth-century revolution in government'. There are continuities here, alongside transition and change.

In the main section of this chapter, I describe the emergence of the Dangerous Drugs Act in 1920 and attempt to trace the various intersecting changes out of which it developed, setting these in the context described above of mutations within liberal governance. The puzzle or 'singularity' that I explore here is how a particular grouping of psychoactive substances that had previously been seen as 'therapeutic' came to be viewed as 'dangerous drugs' requiring regulation within a criminal law framework. In conclusion, I set this analysis in the wider context of my genealogical project and anticipate Chapter 5 which examines a more recent legislative 'event', the Drugs Act 2005.

The emergence of criminal law regulation

I want to approach this puzzle by looking at two broad sets of processes that unfolded as the nineteenth century drew to a close: first, the transition from classical to welfare liberalism and the emerging mentalities, strategies and practices associated with this transformation; second, changing patterns of global political and economic power. First of all, though, I will describe the growing 'problematization' of certain psychoactive substances during this period.

Problematizations and the inebriety concept

In the previous chapter, I described how a 'problem' framework began to be applied to opium in the mid-nineteenth century. In the last two or three decades of the century, this 'problematizing' turn began to gather further momentum. In fact, the greatest anxieties at this time revolved around morphine and alcohol, reminding us importantly that at this point the separate regulatory branches for 'drugs' and alcohol had not yet developed. Concerns about public drunkenness were of course long-standing, as discussed in the previous chapter, but in the late nineteenth century the whole Victorian concern with alcohol, and notably the temperance movement in which the first emergence of the idea of 'addiction' was rooted (see Chapters 2 and 3), was reaching a peak (MacLeod, 1967; Johnstone, 1996). This eventually culminated in the Inebriates Act of 1898 which provided powers to commit inebriates to special reformatories (Garland, 1985: 217–18; Harding and Wilkin, 1988; Wiener, 1990: 294–300). The historian Roy MacLeod's classic article from 1967, 'The Edge of Hope', which analyses the development of the inebriates legislation, remains one of the best guides to the problematization of alcohol during this period (MacLeod, 1967). I will return to this legislation later.

Compared with alcohol, morphine was a relatively new source of anxiety. As mentioned in Chapter 3, it had been isolated as the principal active alkaloid of opium at the beginning of the century but its use within medical practice only started to become more widespread from the 1860s, notably with the invention of the hypodermic injecting technique in the 1850s. From this point, the apparently growing prevalence of the self-administration of morphine rapidly began to be a matter of concern. An important article by Dr Thomas Clifford Albutt, published in 1870, first raised the question of whether morphine actually encouraged 'the very pains it pretends to relieve', suggesting that 'if this be so, we are incurring a grave risk in bidding people to inject whenever they need it, and in telling them that morphia can have no ill effects upon them' (Albutt, 1870). Later that decade in 1878, Edward Levinstein's *Die Morphiumsucht* was published in English translation as *The Morbid Craving for Morphia*. Levinstein's work was a landmark as he clearly identified the 'morbid craving' for morphine as a disease, discussing its symptoms, causation, prognosis and prevention as if discussing any other medical pathology (Parssinen, 1983: 86). The significance of this 'diseasing' of habitual morphine-taking lies partly in the opportunity it opened up to make connections with alcohol. Here the concept of inebriety was critical.

As the historian David Courtwright (2005: 107–08) argues, inebriety was the governing idea in the field during the late nineteenth century not only in Britain but also across most of North America. In essence, the theory of inebriety sought to describe the problems associated with the use of alcohol, opium, opiates and other psychoactive substances within a single unified 'disease' framework. Levinstein's work on morphine was drawn on in a series of important works over the following decades which sought to elaborate the idea. For example, Dr Norman Kerr published two books on the subject in the 1880s and 1890s. Kerr was in fact a significant figure in the bringing together of alcohol and opiates within a single 'disease' framework. In 1876, he had formed the Society for Promoting Legislation for the Control and Cure of Habitual Drunkards which subsequently, and tellingly, changed its name in 1884 to the Society for the Study and Cure of Inebriety (the 'Cure' was removed three years later) (Berridge and Edwards, 1981: 152). Other important works in this endeavour included an influential article by Clouston (1890) published in the *Edinburgh Medical Journal* on 'diseased cravings' which ranged across alcohol, chloral, morphine and cocaine and Thomas Crothers' *Morphinism and Narcomanias from Other Drugs* published in 1902. Crothers argued that all these substances affected the nervous system, the effects varying depending on individual susceptibility (which could be environmental or constitutional). He viewed this 'damage' to the nerves as a permanent pathology which could then be worsened by repeated administration of the substance leading to the reckless self-destructiveness of the chronic inebriate. As Courtwright observes, making a point to which I will return, inebriety could become inheritable, with ruinous consequences:

> Once acquired, the trait of inebriety could be passed on as degenerate constitutional tendencies. The process was often one of sinister

transmogrification. The drunkard's child might be an opium addict, his grandchild an epileptic, his great grandchild a congenital idiot. Though inebriate degeneration might assume many forms, its final end was always ruin.

(Courtwright, 2005: 108)

It may perhaps seems a little odd from today's perspective how the inebriety concept has failed to survive. But the fact that it eventually almost disappeared was not a mere matter of linguistic fashion. After the 'great regulatory divide', it of course became increasingly difficult to consider alcohol, heroin and cocaine within a single unified framework. After all, if the problems associated with them were so similar, how could this divide be justified? This question remains part of the policy debate today, particularly for those arguing for reform of the drug laws, and it is still highly controversial. Attempts at reunification invariably come to be seen as being dangerously permissive and 'soft on drugs'. A good recent example of this is the furore caused by the work of David Nutt and colleagues in which they have attempted to rank legal and illegal substances solely in terms of their harmfulness, as measured across a number of domains (Nutt et al., 2007). Some legal drugs, notably alcohol and tobacco, ranked quite high in their 'league table', whilst certain illegal ones, such as ecstasy, were ranked much lower. This destabilizes, of course, the current regulatory framework. A more recent paper in which Nutt compared taking ecstasy with horse riding, and found the latter to be more 'risky', unsurprisingly proved even more controversial (Nutt, 2009)! Despite all this, it is undoubtedly true that unifying frameworks of various kinds, but no longer called inebriety, have seen something of a rebirth in recent years (see Courtwright, 2005: 115). Whether this will lead eventually to any reshaping or reorganization of the various separate regulatory branches remains to be seen.

The significance of the inebriety concept during the late nineteenth century was that it enabled the disease concept to take hold. Its development was critical in forming a bridgehead between opiates and alcohol. The embryonic notion of addiction as disease, first articulated in relation to heavy and habitual drinking, began not only to be more systematically worked out for alcohol but also, crucially, to be extended to a wider range of substances, including opiates. So habitual drunkenness and opiate consumption came increasingly to be viewed not as a 'bad habit' but as a disease (Berridge, 1979; Parssinen and Kerner, 1980; Reinarman, 2005). But as Johnstone (1996) points out, this was not a simple or straightforward 'triumph' for the disease model and there remained considerable ambiguity about the nature of these consumption habits. As we will see, at the heart of this ambiguity lay questions of freedom.

Inebriety, freedom and the transition to welfare liberalism

How might we understand this extension of the problematizing turn and the development of the inebriety concept? Here, Garland's analysis in *Punishment and Welfare* is helpful. He notes how the transition from Victorian penality to what he terms penal-welfarism – welfare liberalism within the terminology I use in this book – involved a related shift in the conception of citizenship and the citizen-subject: the emergence of the social citizen of T.H. Marshall's famous 1949 Oxford lecture (Marshall, 1950; see also Donzelot, 1984; Rose, 1999). Most social citizens were deemed to be free-willed autonomous actors, entirely responsible for their own behaviour and actions. In return for taking on their social responsibilities, they were entitled to a certain level of security assured by the state. The legal, political and social rights associated with this assurance of security were designed to integrate and bind them into society. The other side of this social contract, counterbalancing these new rights of citizenship, were the new powers and authority for the state to intervene in the social and public realm and in the lives of individuals who failed to meet their responsibilities of citizenship.

Unpacking this further, Garland (1985: 185–89) shows how this new citizen-subject was constructed out of a set of compromise positions which centred around debates concerning the notions of 'free will' and 'responsibility'. In brief, the new positivist human sciences, like criminology and the 'psy' sciences (see Rose, 1985), that underpinned the emerging welfarist strategies implied in their strong versions that 'deviant' behaviour was *determined* by individuals' physical and mental defects. This obviously conflicted with the notion of the free and responsible social citizen. Indeed, Garland describes the new positivist human sciences as constituting a 'critique of freedom' which necessitated a 'move from a *philosophy* of freedom to a *psychology* of human behaviour and its determinants' (1985: 91, emphasis in original). The resolution of this conflict was achieved using the notion of 'character' (1985: 185–89). The source of the 'will' and the basis of individual conduct were located in the 'personality' or 'character' of the individual, an entity which was constituted out of a complex blend of biological and social factors. So, whilst generally individual citizens were viewed as free and responsible actors, others were seen to have malformed or 'defective' characters that limited, or in extreme cases entirely effaced, their capacity to exercise control and choice. Those with defective characters then became legitimate objects for state intervention aimed at repairing these abnormalities of character which hampered their capacity to meet their obligations of citizenship. Hence 'normalization' was the principal 'modality of regulation' (Garland, 1981: 29). The new programmes of penal reform, social work and social security were, in this sense, normalization projects.

This compromise between determinist and voluntarist perspectives was paralleled within the new notion of the 'addict' or inebriate (Parssinen and

Kerner, 1980; Stein, 1985: 139–59; Johnstone, 1996). Whilst some figures in the field supported the view that addiction was a physical disease like any other, and hence beyond the control of the individual, many others described it as a mental pathology. As noted in Chapter 2, this raised some difficulties. One key problem was the issue of why individuals would voluntarily begin to consume these substances in the first place. Another difficulty was the observation that some people managed to control their consumption apparently without damaging themselves. The compromise that emerged was encapsulated in the description of addiction as a 'disease of the will', a term which had been formulated originally by Benjamin Rush in relation to alcohol, as discussed in previous chapters. In much the same way as the notion of 'character' resolved the underlying tensions in the new subject of penal-welfarism, so the emerging disease model of addiction managed to accommodate these contradictions between determinism and voluntarism by arguing that it was, at least in part, a condition with a mental or psychological component. As Johnstone discusses, in this respect, the inebriety concept ended up quite some distance away from a somatic notion of disease. Rather, it was more of a moral-psychological idea in which questions of freedom, habit and responsibility were finessed in quite a complex way:

> Moral-psychological understandings and explanations of deviance assume that certain types of deviant conduct were caused by disorders of the moral will, and crucially, imply that while these disorders could be inherited, they usually arose from indiscipline: living in a corrupt environment, failing to regulate one's passions, and being immoderate and intemperate in habit. Within this framework, one could avoid becoming morally disordered by adhering to a balanced, regular and moderate lifestyle. Conversely, once could become disordered by leading an immoral life. *Moral health was therefore one's personal responsibility.* Even though individuals could not control their behaviour once they had deteriorated into moral disorder, they were responsible for letting themselves fall into such a state.
>
> (Johnstone, 1996: 52, emphasis in original)

Berridge (1979: 77) summarizes this nicely: the addiction concept was a hybrid one, in which addiction was both a 'moral failing' *and* a disease. As I observed in Chapter 2, it was precisely through this hybridity that addiction became such a malleable governmental resource, capable of being aligned to diverse programmes and strategies. The analytical lesson here is that it is not enough simply to identify the affinity between the new disease concept and the transition to welfare liberalism, important though that is. The further explanatory job, which I will attempt below, is to look at and try to understand the ways in which the addiction concept came to be deployed within particular political programmes. As O'Malley (1992: 256) astutely notes, such deployments or alignments tend to follow a rather complex pattern of 'articulations and alliances, colonizations and translations, resistances and complicities', rather than unfolding in any 'automatic' way. In other words, actual strategies and practices cannot simply be read off from an abstract concept like 'addiction as disease'.

The development of new responses to inebriety at the tail end of the nineteenth century provides a good illustration of how this shifting addiction concept began to be connected with new welfarist regulatory strategies. North American provision for inebriates had been established some years earlier in 1857 with the New York State Inebriate Asylum in Binghamton, similar institutions later spreading to Boston, Chicago and elsewhere (MacLeod, 1967: 218). In 1869, Dr Donald Dalrymple – a British surgeon and lunatic-asylum proprietor – visited some of the North American institutions and returned to Britain determined to establish similar provision on home soil. He became a Member of Parliament shortly after his return and in the years before his death in 1873 he agitated strongly for the introduction of new provision for inebriates. In 1872, he chaired the Parliamentary Select Committee on 'Habitual Drunkards' which made recommendations for new legislation. His campaign was subsequently taken up by Dr Norman Kerr and others, leading, first of all, to the Habitual Drunkards Act of 1879. This allowed for the voluntary commitment of habitual drunkards to newly created asylums. In practice, this meant that placement in these institutions was restricted to the "few rich enough to afford it and reasonable enough to agree to be committed' (Wiener, 1990: 296). Through the 1880s and into the early 1890s, calls for state provision of institutions for the medical treatment of inebriates began to grow, as the belief hardened that habitual drunkenness was often more symptomatic of disease than criminality. As Wiener (1990: 298–99) observes, the growing volume of these calls was accompanied by a diminishing appetite for the criminal prosecution and punishment of drunkards.

This led eventually to the Inebriates Act of 1898 which gave magistrates the power to commit criminal inebriates to specialist reformatory institutions instead of punishing them. Earlier squeamishness about compulsory commitment had been overcome, although, as MacLeod (1967: 236) observes, there was considerable controversy on this issue during the parliamentary debates prior to the enactment of the legislation. Indeed, he argues that this issue was never completely settled as the 'traditionalist reasoning of economic liberalism lingered long after its social assumptions were found unworkable in the fluctuating conditions of industrial society' (MacLeod, 1967: 241) and inebriate reform ultimately ended in failure, in the sense that the reformatories eventually proved to be unsustainable in practice (see Radzinowicz and Hood, 1986: 307–15). Nevertheless, as Garland (1985: 217–18) suggests, the 1898 Act was an important landmark which provided a model for later measures directed at 'vagrants', 'habitual criminals' and others. It was based squarely on the penal-welfarist logic of normalization: those criminal inebriates whose defective characters weakened their capacity to act responsibly were to be targeted for interventions designed to repair their damaged 'will'. The inebriety concept, and its accommodation of determinist and voluntarist perspectives on freedom and responsibility, provided a set of discursive and conceptual resources for this strategy.

The 1898 Act was clearly primarily targeted at the problem of habitual drunkards, although other substances were covered provided they were ingested in liquid form, for example the opium tincture known as laudanum (Berridge, 2004a: 4). As I have argued, it can be understood partly within the context of the transition to welfare liberalism. Significantly, however, the modern concept of 'drugs' was still not yet in place. There was, for example, no sharp division at this stage between opiates and alcohol. As I noted above, the addiction concept was capable of being aligned with a variety of different programmes and projects.

One project to which it became aligned was the attempt to reverse the perceived problem of national degeneracy. Daniel Pick's superb book *Faces of Degeneration* traces how new discourses of degeneration had a profound social, political and cultural impact across Europe in the second half of the nineteenth century (Pick, 1993; see also Nye, 1984). Pick argues that this was connected in part with emerging evolutionary theory, the focal point of which was, of course, the publication of Darwin's *Origin of Species* in 1859. Garland identifies this broad concern about national degeneracy and inefficiency as an important strand of his thesis in *Punishment and Welfare*. Put simply, for policy-makers, the idea that an expanding 'residuum' of unfit and inadequate individuals was at the root of many of the most pressing social problems of the time became an increasing preoccupation in the late Victorian period (Wiener, 1990). Garland (1985: 142–52) argues that this underpinned the emergence of the eugenics programme at the turn of the twentieth century which aimed in essence to improve the quality of the national character by limiting reproductive activity by the 'unfit'.

The idea of degeneration was a problem posed at the level of population which, as we saw in Chapter 3, was a critical concept within liberal government. With the transition to welfare liberalism, a more interventionist strategy of population management aimed at maintaining its fitness or 'purity' came to the forefront. It is in this broader context that we should understand the growing anxieties during this period about racial purity and inter-racial sexual activity (Bland, 2005). The behaviour and reproductive capacity of women was thus a critical site for interventions, as the point at which population management could be achieved.

How did the emergence of the inebriety concept fit here? As already noted, it was viewed as an inheritable 'weakness' which could be transmitted down the generations. In other words, it was a particular instance or example of the 'master' category of degeneration. Intervening with inebriates was thus one domain of population management designed to address the problem of the weakening of the racial stock and national degeneracy. This helps us to make sense of the ways in which the emerging drug control system was rooted in the politics of race and gender. There was, for example, a considerable furore in the popular press during the early years of the twentieth century concerning Chinese opium dens in Limehouse in East London and their alleged corrupting influence on the white population, especially young women (Parssinen, 1983: 115–28; Kohn, 1992). This picture formed an important part of the shifting cultural sensibilities that made the new drug control system desirable, an important dimension in any explanatory account (Garland, 1990: 213–47). At one level, this can be seen as no more than the commonly observed deployment of 'race' to foment fears about crime and disorder (Hall et al., 1978). At another, it was part of this broader set of anxieties about inter-racial sexual activity and the decline of the national racial stock, as Manderson observes:

> Time and again, we see the Chinese dealer depicted as a trafficker in young white women, and opium as the device by which the sexual inhibition or revulsion of young girls towards the Chinese could be trepanned, weakened, or overborne. Miscegenation was the fear, and the 'Chinaman's' opium was said to play a causal role in bringing it about.
>
> (2005: 39–40)

Whilst the importance of racial politics in this area has often been noted (e.g. Braithwaite and Drahos, 2000: 362–63), Manderson's insight alerts us to the equal significance of the politics of gender in the origins of drug control (see Seddon, 2008b). Marek Kohn's book *Dope Girls* is a superb account of the gendered nature of drugs discourse in the first quarter of the twentieth century (Kohn, 1992). As Kohn (1992: 5) observes, the Great War led to a profound transformation of the position of women in society which was accompanied by anxieties about their growing autonomy. At the heart of these anxieties was a 'fear of unleashing female sexuality' (Smart, 1992: 20). Hence, there was a strong focus on controlling female sexuality. It was the perceived willingness or susceptibility of certain classes of young white women to engage in inter-racial sexual activity that was the fundamental problem because of the potential for damaging racial 'purity'. The public and media fascination with the exploits of the cast of characters that Kohn describes – chorus-girl Billie Carleton, nightclub dancer Freda Kempton, Chinese 'dope king' Brilliant Chang, Jamaican cocaine dealer Edgar Manning – can be understood partly as the playing out of this complex racial and gender politics underpinning the emergence of the new drug control system.

The inebriety concept in this way was aligned during this period with the broader project of tackling national degeneracy. In provocative vein, we might say that drug prohibition and the eugenics programme share a common basis in the revised strategies of population management that arose with the transition to welfare liberalism at the turn of the twentieth century.

To bring together the argument so far, the transition to welfare liberalism was significant in several respects. First, it was characterized by a proliferation of regulatory branches and an increasingly interventionist state. By the end of the nineteenth century, *laissez-faire* liberalism was being trumped more and more by the growth of an administrative state (Braithwaite, 2008: 15). This set the scene for greater regulatory 'interference' in diverse areas and fields which had previously been largely left alone under the Victorian 'nightwatchman' state (Braithwaite, 2000), including the trade in and consumption of psychoactive substances. Second, the new 'social citizen' associated with the rise of welfarism embodied a conception of freedom on to which the developing disease model of inebriety could be mapped. Third, this, in turn, was connected with the emerging welfarist logic of normalization, of which new responses to inebriety were one example.

Yet despite these important developments, as the twentieth century began, the great regulatory divide had still not happened. To understand how this developed, we have to widen out our vision a little at this point and consider matters on a more global scale. To bring these matters into view, I am also at this point going to switch analytical lenses, from the broadly Foucauldian one I have been using so far in this chapter to a more regulatory perspective.

Globalization, global trade and empire

Although globalization is often viewed as a particular feature of 'our times', it has been observed that globalizing processes can be traced back over centuries (Held et al., 1999: 16–20). Sachs (2000: 579) identifies the period from 1870 to 1914 as the first long phase of globalization, in which global flows of commodities, money and people greatly expanded. Indeed, some have argued that in certain domains, notably trade, the extent of globalization during this period outstripped what we see today (see Thompson, 2000: 97–102). John Maynard Keynes famously described this globalized world before the outbreak of the Great War:

> What an extraordinary episode in the economic progress of man that age was which came to an end in August, 1914! ... The inhabitant of London could order by telephone, sipping his morning tea in bed, the various products of the whole earth, in such quantity as he might see fit, and reasonably expect their early delivery upon his doorstep; he could at the same moment and by the same means adventure his wealth in the natural resources and new enterprises of any quarter of the world, and share, without exertion or trouble, in their prospective fruits and advantages; or he could decide to couple the security of his fortunes with

the good faith of the townspeople of any substantial municipality in any continent that fancy or information might recommend. He could secure, forthwith, if he wished it, cheap and comfortable means of transit to any country or climate without passport or other formality, could dispatch his servant to the neighbouring office of a bank for such supply of the precious metals as might seem convenient, and could then proceed abroad to foreign quarters, without knowledge of their religion, language, or customs, bearing coined wealth upon his person, and would consider himself greatly aggrieved and much surprised at the least interference. But, most important of all, he regarded this state of affairs as normal, certain, and permanent, except in the direction of further improvement, and any deviation from it as aberrant, scandalous, and avoidable.

(Keynes, 1920: 11–12)

The picture Keynes describes is perhaps surprising to contemporary eyes convinced of the novelty of today's global marketplace. But however extensive these globalizing processes may have been at the turn of the twentieth century, they were not even in their effects and reach. This is a fundamental point to grasp for our genealogy, as Sachs argues:

Modern economic growth took off in western Europe and its offshoots at the end of the eighteenth century, while not taking off elsewhere for a century or more, thereby creating within a couple of generations an historically unprecedented gap between western Europe and the rest of the world in material well being, industrial power and military force … [A] considerable amount of nineteenth and twentieth century history can be read as the playing out of this profound imbalance in economic and military power.

(Sachs, 1999: 92)

So how is this insight relevant to my concerns here? We can see its significance, first of all, if we look at the distinctively international character of this field during this period. At one level, this is simply symptomatic of the globalizing forces at play at the turn of the twentieth century – in a globalizing world, we might expect policy in many areas to become more international in nature. At another level, the particular contours of this internationalism can be read, precisely as Sachs argues, in terms of these power imbalances. We might note, for example, that the first international agreement about psychoactive substances was actually the Brussels General Act of 1889–90 which concerned not opium but alcohol. The Brussels meeting of European powers was primarily about the slave trade in colonial Africa but it included an agreement about the introduction of 'Restrictive Measures Concerning the Traffic in Spirituous Liquor' in those territories. Lynn Pan's book *Alcohol in Colonial Africa* provides an interesting account of this episode (Pan, 1975). The Brussels Act was later reinforced and extended more widely across the African continent by a Treaty signed at St Germain-en-Laye in 1919 as part of the post-war peace negotiations (Haworth and Acuda, 1998: 28–29).

Colonial interests and power imbalances were also intertwined in the unfolding of internationalized concerns about opium in the late nineteenth century. In Britain, the influential Society for the Suppression of the Opium Trade (SSOT), founded in 1874 by the Quaker Edward Pease, right from the outset focused strongly on British involvement in the opium trade in South Asia (Brown, 1973; Johnson, 1975; Harding, 1988: 17–18). Indeed, it was initially called the Anglo-Oriental Society (Harding, 1988: 25). This international focus contrasted, of course, with the temperance movement for alcohol during the same period which primarily had a domestic outlook, although both shared a strong religious element. For Britain, the difference between opium and alcohol was that the former was important to its trade and imperial interests. The aftershocks from the Anglo-Chinese Opium Wars in the middle of the century were still reverberating, wars described by Sachs (1999: 91) as the 'first conflict of the modern capitalist era ... fought to make the world safe for free trade in narcotics'. The growing influence of the SSOT, and its particular focus on the 'Anglo-Oriental' dimension, can be partly understood then as a refiguring of Britain's colonial relations in the context of the 'profound imbalance' created by the first uneven phase of globalization.

On the global front, arguably a more significant event was America's victory in 1898 in the Spanish American War, which led to the Philippines coming under American control (Buxton, 2006: 30–33). This meant that the extensive opium retail system in the Philippines came under direct control from Washington and so, for the first time, directly raised the question of the opium trade for the American federal government. Their response was to convene the Philippines Opium Commission which reported in 1903, recommending a major curtailment of the import and sale of opium (Buxton, 2006: 32). Stein (1985: 46–49) cautions against overstating the importance of the Philippines situation, preferring to highlight the broader influence of changing Sino-American relations at this time. Either way, we can see the origin here of a new internationalization of the problem which has come to be characteristic of approaches right through to the present. Again, we can understand this partly in terms of changing patterns of economic and military power during this period and America's emerging new imperial interests.

These global trade and imperial interests, and their reshaping by globalizing forces, proved to be highly significant in the first two decades of the twentieth century as the international drug control system was assembled (Bewley-Taylor, 1999; Trocki, 1999; Buxton, 2006). In 1906, American officials sought to solicit support from Britain and other countries for a multi-national commission on the opium trade and opium consumption in the Far East. In Britain, the election of a new Liberal government in that same year added some impetus to British involvement in the commission and in 1907 the Anglo-Chinese Agreement committed Britain to a long-term phasing out of the exporting of opium from British India to China. The commission eventually met in February 1909 in Shanghai, attended by representatives from 13 countries: Austria-Hungary, China, France, Germany, Russia, Great Britain, Italy, Japan, the Netherlands, Portugal, Persia, Siam and the United States (Stein, 1985: 52). Stein (1985: 50–67) provides an illuminating account of the political manoeuvrings there, with imperial and trade interests of participants strongly shaping discussions. Whilst the Shanghai commission reached no clear conclusions or agreements, it marked the opening up of debate about the introduction of international controls on opium.

This debate was picked up in a series of three conferences held at The Hague between 1911 and 1914. The 'International Opium Convention' signed there in 1912 proved to be of lasting importance. Crucially, as well as taking on a global rather than solely Far Eastern dimension, it also broadened the scope from the Shanghai discussions to include cocaine and morphine alongside opium. Its most significant element was the agreement that those drugs should be confined to 'legitimate medical purposes' (Berridge, 1984: 19). In the British context, controls on these drugs had already been tightened four years earlier with a new Pharmacy Act in 1908 (which moved opium to Part 1 of the Poisons Schedule) but the Hague agreement envisaged taking this considerably further. But despite this multi-national agreement, actual domestic implementation of the Hague Convention stalled amongst many signatories in the following years, the notable exception being the US which passed its Harrison Narcotic Act in 1914. Several countries had trade interests to protect: Germany was at that time the world's largest commercial producer of cocaine and Britain that of morphine. This stuttering and uneven domestic implementation was then completely halted by the outbreak of the First World War in 1914 (Berridge, 1980: 12).

War, though, would bring different pressures to bear and had its own impact on drug control. In Britain, a series of wartime scandals – the smuggling of opium on British ships and the use of cocaine by soldiers on leave consorting with prostitutes – led to emergency legislation in 1916 in the form of the Defence of the Realm Act (DORA) Regulation 40B (Berridge, 1978). This placed new restrictions on cocaine and opium, stipulating that they could only be dispensed on prescription. At the end of the war, this emergency legislation lapsed with the signing of the Versailles Peace Treaty in 1919 but Article 295 of the Treaty committed signatories to enacting national controls in accordance with the pre-war Hague Convention. It was this commitment that led to the enactment of the landmark Dangerous Drugs Act of 1920 – in effect, the starting point for drug prohibition in Britain.

We can see then that this legislative 'event' was connected in part with issues of global trade, imperial interests and international relations during this early phase of globalization at the turn of the twentieth century. The new power imbalances created by the uneven diffusion of economic growth and capitalist institutions were crucial influences. As Nadelmann (1990: 511) observes, the dominance of Western Europe and North America during this period led the global drug-prohibition regime to reflect their norms and values over and above those of other nations and regions. On top of this, the 'diseasing' of addiction associated with transitions in liberal governance during this period rendered these psychoactive substances as potentially 'dangerous' because of their destructive effect on the faculty of the will and the consequent ability of 'addicts' to act freely.

This last point about the 'diseasing' of addiction begs a significant question though: exactly why did alcohol not come within the ambit of the 1920 Act given that the addiction concept was originally worked out for alcohol rather than for opium or opiates (see Berridge, 2004b)? The first point to make is that alcohol was indeed prohibited in some countries at around this time. The best-known case is of course the USA between 1920 and 1933. But several other countries experimented with alcohol prohibition in the early twentieth century, including Iceland, Finland, Norway, Canada and the Russian Empire (later the Soviet Union). Nor were these all just very short-run experiments – in Iceland, for example, beer was still prohibited as late as 1989. Several North American states also outlawed tobacco in the first two decades of the century (Studlar, 2008). The prohibition 'impulse' during this period was clearly not just restricted to opiates and cocaine. Even in Britain, there was some tightening of alcohol controls during the war under the Defence of the Realm Act which introduced a range of measures, including the watering down of alcoholic beverages and restrictions on pub opening hours. One might argue, as Courtwright (2005) does, that the unifying project of the inebriety concept was starting to unravel and that it was this that allowed for regulatory diversification. That may be so but whether the demise of the inebriety paradigm was cause or effect of the regulatory divide is rather less clear. A much more telling point in my view is that alcohol was not, by and large, a commodity of any significance in global trade at this time, nor did it particularly affect or impinge upon imperial interests (with the exception of colonial Africa which was dealt with under the regional agreements of Brussels and then St Germain). So there was never much likelihood of attaining international agreement for a global prohibition regime (Nadelmann, 1990: 509–10). Alcohol therefore did not come within the purview of the meetings in Shanghai and The Hague and there was not then any possibility of a global system of alcohol control being established. It was left to individual countries to develop their own national regulatory regimes for alcohol, regimes that were of course strongly shaped by national political and especially cultural forces (see Levine, 1993). In Britain, the temperance movement was simply not strong enough to overpower the sheer embeddedness of alcohol within everyday life. And so the 'great regulatory divide' was established, with alcohol and tobacco coming under entirely separate regulatory branches from the newly minted category of 'dangerous drugs'.

The status of cannabis is interesting and to some extent fits with the above analysis (see Mills, 2003). Although it was not included in the 1920 Act, it had been discussed at the 1912 meeting in The Hague at the insistence of the United States and Italy. Italy's interest was an imperial one, as cannabis was extensively used in Tripolitania and Cyreanica which had both become Italian protectorates following a war with Turkey in 1911 (Lowes, 1966; Zimmer, 1997). Having been discussed once at The Hague, it was returned to at later meetings. International commitment to include cannabis within the new drug-prohibition regime eventually came with the 1925 Geneva Opium Convention. Several countries supported the United States in pushing for this, notably Egypt, South Africa and Canada, each of which had domestic cannabis 'problems', predominantly revolving around its use by particular ethnic groups or social classes (Zimmer, 1997). Unlike the opiates or cocaine, no major countries had global trade interests in cannabis and so there was little or no resistance to its prohibition. In Britain, the Geneva commitment was implemented in 1928. Elsewhere the timing of implementation varied quite significantly – in the USA, for example, federal prohibition did not come until 1937, although many states had outlawed cannabis much earlier than that – but certainly by the outbreak of the Second World War cannabis prohibition had spread across most of the globe.

There is one more line of development behind the 1920 Act that I want to explore a little here. I have described the globalization of the regulation of the 'dangerous drugs', that is opiates and cocaine (Braithwaite and Drahos, 2000: 367) and attempted to explain some of the reasons why this came about. But substances like morphine, heroin and cocaine were of course all initially pharmaceutical products that circulated in what Braithwaite would call 'markets in virtue', rather than the 'markets in vice' to which they would later become attached (Braithwaite, 2005a; Braithwaite and Braithwaite, 2006: 1124). I have written elsewhere about this in relation to heroin, originally marketed as a cough medicine (Seddon, 2007b), but it is equally true for cocaine which was used extensively within dentistry as a local anaesthetic well into the first two decades of the twentieth century (Parssinen, 1983: 134). A significant part of my genealogy therefore involves tracing the developing regulation of the nascent pharmaceutical industry.

The nineteenth century saw a rapid process of industrialization in the area of pharmaceuticals. This was the period in which the modern global pharmaceutical industry was in effect born and, as David Courtwright observes, this profoundly transformed the possibilities for the production and consumption of psychoactive substances:

> If the single most important fact about the early modern world was the expansion of oceangoing commerce, that of its modern successor was industrialization. During the nineteenth century psychoactive discoveries and innovations – the isolation of alkaloids, the invention of hypodermic syringes and safety matches, the creation of synthetic and semisynthetic drugs – were married to new techniques of industrial production and distribution. Factories did for drugs what canning did for vegetables. They democratized them. It became easier, cheaper and faster for the masses to saturate their brains with chemicals.
>
> (Courtwright, 2001: 173)

Braithwaite and Drahos describe how the pharmaceutical trade, and its regulation, had internationalized particularly early in Europe. The first International Medical Congress was held in Paris in 1867 and subsequent meetings helped to establish Europe as the 'centre of epistemic communities on pharmaceutical regulation' (2000: 369). So substances like morphine and cocaine were already subject to a globalizing system of regulation long before they came within the ambit of a globalized system of control as 'dangerous drugs'.

The early history of heroin nicely illustrates the ongoing significance of these connections with the legal pharmaceutical industry and its regulation. Heroin was the product of this rapid period of industrialization when laboratory research led to the discovery of many new drugs. Morphine, which had been isolated as the principal active alkaloid in opium at the beginning of the nineteenth century, had become a staple of medical practice by the middle decades of the century. In 1874, Charles Alder Wright working in St Mary's Hospital in West London synthesized several morphine esters, including diacetylmorphine, later known as diamorphine. In the late 1880s, research scientists at the University of Edinburgh did further work on diacetylmorphine, investigating its effects on frogs and rabbits (Sneader, 1998). It was then rediscovered in 1897 by scientists working in the laboratory at Bayer, apparently unaware of the earlier work by Wright and the Edinburgh team (Sneader, 1998). Bayer registered it under the name heroin in June 1898 and it was launched on the market in September that year for the relief of coughs and respiratory problems alongside Bayer's other new 'wonder drug' aspirin (Scott, 1998; Sneader, 1998). Bayer went on to form part of the conglomerate IG Farben which was formed in 1925 and which Braithwaite and Drahos (2000: 389) have described as 'one of the two greatest industrial cartels in history' (the other being the Standard Oil Trust). Bayer re-emerged as an entity in its own right after the Allies broke up IG Farben in the aftermath of the Second World War and it has gone from strength to strength commercially since then. Today, it is the largest pharmaceutical company in Europe, now known as Bayer AG. It is a breathtakingly large commercial enterprise – in 2006 it had a total revenue of nearly $45 billion, making it one of the leading players globally within 'Big Pharma'.

So, we can also view the 'great regulatory divide' in a broader regulatory perspective. The creation of a centralized state system for regulating pharmaceutical products was in part a response to the weaknesses of regulation within the *laissez-faire* economy. The rapid industrialization of the pharmaceutical industry which led to the discovery and mass manufacture of new and powerful psychoactive substances like morphine and heroin posed new regulatory challenges. As we saw in Chapter 3, the Pharmacy Act of 1868 was an initial response to this. In regulatory terms, the 1920 Act can be seen in part as an extension of this. Indeed, it was accompanied by the assembly of a series of measures that would be very familiar to regulation scholars. A major source for these was the 1921 Dangerous Drugs Regulations, which provided additional detail for the implementation of the 1920 Act. These regulations set in place a system of detailed record-keeping for each transaction in these drugs. Regulation 9, for example, stipulated requirements for all suppliers of relevant substances:

> a) He shall enter or cause to be entered in a book kept for the purpose all supplies of the drug purchased or otherwise obtained by him and all dealings in the drug effected by him (including sale to persons outside the United Kingdom) in the form and containing the particulars shown in the Schedule to these Regulations. b) Separate books shall be kept for (i) cocaine and ecgonine and substances containing them, (ii) morphine and substances containing it, (iii) diamorphine and substances containing it, (iv) medicinal opium.

To monitor compliance with these standards, an inspection system was also established. The Home Office itself had a small inspection capacity, but as Spear (2002: 37) wryly observed, in 1921 when the new Regulations were brought into force, this consisted of just one Inspector and an assistant. The police had been initially authorized to inspect records in 1917 under the DORA 40B wartime regime and they took on an expanded inspection role from 1921 onwards. Ensuring compliance with the record-keeping requirements of Regulation 9 was one of their priorities (Spear, 2002: 37–38). This emphasis on regular inspection of retail pharmacy records by the police continued to be a feature of the British drug control system for many decades, those occupying the role coming to be known as 'chemist officers' (Spear, 2002: 39). Nevertheless, in practice, certainly in its early years, the operation of this inspection system was 'at best haphazard and at worst non-existent' (Spear, 2002: 37). This was partly a capacity issue, compounded by the fact that there were so many retail premises to be visited. But it was also symptomatic of the 'newness' of this type of regulation. As Braithwaite (2008: 14) puts it, the 'inspectorates were only beginning to invent their regulatory technologies for the first time' and so inevitably were patchy in their effectiveness. The more sensitive area of the inspection of record-keeping by doctors was undertaken by Regional Medical Officers of the Ministry of Health who were authorized in 1922 to inspect the records required under the Dangerous Drugs Act and Regulations.

Penal–welfare liaison and the 'British System'

The final key stage of this period of regulatory transformation occurred in the aftermath of the Dangerous Drugs Act 1920. The new control system was built on the idea of restricting opium, opiates and cocaine to 'legitimate' medical use only. This of course begged the question of exactly what this meant. In 1924, a Committee was set up by the Ministry of Health under the Chairmanship of Sir Humphrey Rolleston, President of the Royal College of Physicians, to consider and advise on this question. The resulting report issued in 1926, known as the Rolleston Report (Ministry of Health, 1926), was highly significant (Berridge, 1980; Ashton, 2006). It was founded on acceptance of the disease model of addiction and was overwhelmingly medical in its composition (Berridge, 1980). As well as making several 'regulatory' recommendations for safeguards for the prescription and administration of opiates, the Report also set out an authoritative statement on the appropriate medical use of these drugs in the treatment of addiction:

> There are two groups of persons suffering from addiction to whom the administration of morphine and heroin may be regarded as legitimate medical treatment, namely:

> a) those who are undergoing treatment for cure of addiction by the gradual withdrawal method;
> b) persons for whom, after every effort has been made for the cure of the addiction, the drug cannot be completely withdrawn, either because:

> > (i)   complete withdrawal produces serious symptoms which cannot be satisfactorily treated under the ordinary conditions of private practice; or where
> > (ii) a patient, who while capable of leading a useful and fairly normal life so long as he takes a certain non-progressive quantity, usually small, of the drug of addiction, ceases to be able to do so when the regular allowance is withdrawn.

> (Ministry of Health, 1926)

The medical prescription of drugs to addicts on this twin basis became known as the 'British System' and was to set the framework for policy until the 1960s. Amongst drug historians, one of the key areas of debate about the 'British System' has centred on the nature of this relationship between penal and medical approaches and how an accommodation between the two was reached. Indeed, Berridge (1999: 278) describes the 'British System' as a 'medico-legal alliance'. According to Berridge and others, the Home Office, especially in the figure of senior civil servant Sir Malcolm Delevingne, strongly pushed the penal line that had emerged during the First World War but Rolleston managed to defend doctors' right to prescribe as a medical intervention, albeit within the penal framework of the 1920 Act (Berridge, 1978, 1980, 1984; Parssinen, 1983: 129–43, 183–200; cf. Spear, 2002: 1–32). These accounts describe a 'power struggle' between key individuals and professional interests. This may be so but it is also clear to me that the idea of an accommodation between penal and welfarist approaches resonates very strongly with Garland's analysis of the transition to welfare liberalism (Garland, 1985). In this sense, it might be argued then that the distinctive 'medico-legal alliance' of the 'British System' was to some extent structured by the wider strategic pattern of liaison between penal and welfare elements within the new social realm. So rather than Delevingne and Rolleston being engaged in a 'tug of war' between essentially contradictory or antithetical positions, they might be more fruitfully viewed as actors involved in creating a *liaison* between these tendencies, a liaison which was rooted in deeper structures of governance.

The primacy of doctors within the 'British System' was part of a broader transformation in the public-health sphere, away from the Chadwickian 'sanitary idea' (see Chapter 3) towards a more interventionist and medical form:

> The passage of Lloyd George's Insurance Act [in 1911] demonstrated, as never before, the radical change in public outlook which had taken place in England between 1870 and 1912. Central government compulsion of health and welfare had become acceptable to a degree considered intolerable in the eighteen-seventies. Simultaneously, the scope and direction of public health expanded from sanitary reform to the provision of curative medicine and personal health services.
>
> (Brand, 1965: 232)

For writers like Brand, this is a matter of the refiguring of the relationship between doctors and the state. At one level, this is perhaps so but I think a more fruitful way to look at it is in terms of the late-nineteenth-century transition in liberal governance that I have been describing in this chapter. The administration of the new types of 'normalizing' strategies and 'welfare sanctions' that Garland (1981, 1985) anatomizes involved, *inter alia*, a transformation in the health field and a refocusing of what Foucault famously called the 'clinical gaze' (Foucault, 1973). In other words, the medical 'mode of perception', and hence the role and position of doctors, was itself transformed within the transition to welfare liberalism.

Conclusion

In this chapter, I have explored what was a fundamental 'event' within the genealogy of the contemporary drug problem. The establishment of the international drug-control system, and the passing of the Dangerous Drugs Act of 1920 in Britain, marked the birth of today's drug prohibition system. The regulatory story I have traced has been complex, so it is perhaps useful to summarize here the key areas and dimensions of change out of which this 'event' developed.

As we have seen, this story is not reducible to a single dynamic or set of processes. Rather, it involves a complex braiding together of developments and changes across several domains. Boiling it down to the plainest version, it has two principal strands. First, it is a story about the transition in liberal governance that occurred at the turn of the twentieth century and how this impacted on this area. The transition to welfare liberalism was accompanied by a growing state interventionism and a strategy of normalization targeted at those citizens whose 'defective' character rendered them unable to meet their social obligations. The disease model of addiction and the new drug-prohibition regime can be understood partly in that context. Second, it is an account of how the first phase of globalization within modern industrial capitalism, and the ensuing refiguring of patterns of economic, military and imperial power, also shaped this 'event'. The global trade of particular psychoactive substances, and the playing out of international power politics, had a profound influence on the emerging international drug control system.

At the heart of these two strands are questions of freedom. The first strand tells a story of an emerging new notion of freedom as *social* rather than purely economic. It was no longer assumed that all citizens were capable of acting autonomously in the manner of the *Homo economicus* of classical liberalism. Rather, a central governmental objective was to identify those individuals who lacked this capacity in order to try to help them to (re-)build their capacity for autonomous action. The disease model of addiction and the 'British System' of drug control were instances of this wider transition in the notion of freedom as a governmental concept. Inebriates or addicts were a particular sub-category of people whose 'will', that is their capacity to act autonomously, was damaged or weakened to such an extent that interventions to repair this capacity were justified. We see quite clearly here one of the central arguments of this book: the addiction–freedom relation changes over time as liberal governance itself mutates. In the second strand, my account in this chapter to a great extent revolves around the question of the extent to which free trade should be left entirely unfettered. As will be recalled from Chapter 3, it was this question of interference with free trade that so troubled John Stuart Mill in his essay *On Liberty*. For classical liberals like Mill, measures like the prohibition of psychoactive substances were fundamentally infringements on the liberty of buyers to purchase whatever they wanted. The use of the criminal law to attempt to prevent the circulation of certain commodities was in this sense profoundly troubling. It was this aspect of welfarist politics, and later the Welfare State of the mid-twentieth century, that would of course eventually resurface in the critiques of welfarism which began to appear in the 1970s.

To conclude, the genealogical significance of the story that I have traced in this chapter lies primarily in three areas:

1 It marks the *beginning of the concept of 'dangerous drugs' as a separate and particular category of psychoactive substances*. In this sense, it is the origin of the contemporary 'drug problem'. Prior to this, this concept simply did not exist.
2 It is the *starting point of the deployment of a framework of criminal law for the regulation of these drugs*. Whilst the Pharmacy Act of 1868 had already introduced the idea of legislative regulation of supply as a 'solution' to the opiate 'problem' (see Chapter 3), the notion of using the criminal law as a tool to control the circulation of these psychoactive commodities was new. Today, this is seen by many as a 'self-evident' component of any drug control strategy.
3 It *continued the primacy of medical professionals, and especially doctors, as gate-keepers for these substances*. The 'British System' was to place doctors at the heart of things until at least the 1960s. Arguably, the medical strangle-hold has only been slightly loosened in recent decades, although medical professionals today undoubtedly have to jostle for elbow room with a much wider range of actors.

Looking ahead to the next chapter, we move forward to the turn of the twenty-first century to examine a new phase in the imagination and governance of the drug problem. The Drugs Act 2005 is an exemplar of a new approach that began to be assembled in the final decades of the twentieth century. I will attempt to set this 'event' in the context of the unravelling of welfarist politics from the 1970s and the transition to neo-liberalism.

Chapter 5

Drugs, risk and neo-liberalism

The Drugs Act 2005

Would it be preferable to reduce the incidence of illicit drug use while not promoting safer forms of drug use, or would it be more realistic to give greater priority to the reduction of harm from drug use? ... It is my view, and increasingly the view of others who work with drug users or young people, that it is high time for harm-reduction.

(Russell Newcombe, Researcher, 1987)

The spread of HIV is a greater threat to individual and public health than drug misuse. Accordingly, we believe that services which aim to minimize HIV risk behaviour by all available means should take precedence in development plans.

(Advisory Council on the Misuse of Drugs, 1988)

Problematic drug users ... are most involved in crime... [They] lead extremely chaotic lives, creating a high level of risk to themselves and others.

(Home Office, 2002)

Introduction

The period from the last third of the twentieth century to the present has seen a further significant transformation in the field. In many respects, today's approach appears to be so far away from what was characterized as the 'British System' that it is hard to imagine that they are separated only by a few decades. In the British context, the changes have been dramatic and varied – the curtailment of doctors' 'right to prescribe' in the late 1960s, the establishment of the new 'clinic' system in the 1970s, the rise of harm reduction and HIV prevention in the early 1980s, the emergence of a criminal justice agenda since the 1990s – such that it may seem foolhardy or unhelpful to try to find any pattern within this. Nevertheless, I will be arguing in this chapter that there is indeed a strategic coherence to the past 30 or 40 years in this area which can be best understood by locating developments in the drug field in the wider context of the unravelling of welfarist politics and the rise of neo-liberalism.

I need, first of all, to elaborate a little on the nature of this transition in liberal governance. There is some disagreement about terminology here.

John Braithwaite (2008: 4), for example, one of the surest-footed commentators on these matters on the planet, states baldly that 'those who think we are in an era of neoliberalism are mistaken'. He prefers the term 'regulatory capitalism', which he borrows from the work of Levi-Faur and collaborators (e.g. Levi-Faur, 2005). He argues that this better captures the reality of contemporary governance where the state is very far from being 'hollowed out' and the trend is towards more regulation rather than less (he calls this the 'myth of deregulation'). Amongst governmentality scholars, the other main theoretical reference point for this book, there are two different positions. Foucault himself uses the term 'neo-liberalism' in his influential 1979 Collège de France lecture course *The Birth of Biopolitics* (Foucault, 2008; see also O'Malley, 2004; Read, 2009). Nikolas Rose (1999), on the other hand, prefers the term 'advanced liberalism', partly as a way of downplaying the more 'epochal' connotations implied by the 'neo-' prefix and also to accommodate better the diversity of contemporary liberal governance (see also Rose, 1996). I have been somewhat torn about which term to use in this book, not least because I agree with much of Braithwaite's argument on this. But I have plumped in the end for the label 'neo-liberalism', primarily because it is the most widely understood and used term to describe the contemporary era, utilized not just across different academic disciplines but also in the public sphere. I tend to agree as well with O'Malley (2004: 76) that to the extent that this is mainly about terminology rather than substance, it is not a 'matter over which I want to spill much ink'.

What then are the main contours of this most recent mutation in liberal governance? There is a vast and still growing literature here. Aside from the regulatory and Foucauldian perspectives referred to above, David Harvey's recent book *A Brief History of Neoliberalism* offers an interesting and informative take on it which brings together a lot of this literature and is well worth reading (Harvey, 2007). I draw from this eclectic and diverse body of scholarship five key and inter-related dimensions of neo-liberalism.

First, neo-liberalism involves a revival of certain elements of nineteenth-century liberal capitalism, in particular, the renewed primacy of the idea of the 'free market' as a central mechanism in the effective and efficient operation of a capitalist economy. However, this 'revival' is not simply or solely a 'return to the past'; neo-liberalism has a distinctive and new character (Levi-Faur, 2005: 15). It certainly shares the valorizing of economic activity with its nineteenth-century counterpart, seeing the economic sphere as the dominant realm of society, but takes this considerably further. As Rose (1999: 141) suggests, the economic approach has come to dominate our entire understanding of human behaviour which is now reconceptualized as 'calculative actions undertaken through the universal human faculty of choice'. Garland (2001: 190) calls this the shift from a social to an economic style of reasoning. What is new about neo-liberalism's perspective on economic activity is that it focuses on competition rather than exchange (Foucault,

2008). *Homo economicus* is now recast as a 'creature whose tendency to compete must be fostered' (Read, 2009: 28).

Second, with this new focus on competition, the central liberal formula of '*laissez-faire*' is transformed. The optimal conditions for competition are not achievable simply by a passive strategy of 'leaving markets alone' and allowing Smith's 'invisible hand' to work its magic. Rather, the conditions of the market need to be nurtured and protected by active intervention. Whilst exchange was something that occurred 'naturally' within markets, competition is an 'artificial relation' that has to be created and then sustained (Foucault, 2008; Read, 2009: 28).

Third, this emphasis on competition has spread across diverse areas, including the governmental sphere. Innovations like privatization and marketization have colonized many new areas – from prisons, to health care, to telecommunications, to transport. Contrary to some claims, this has been accompanied by a proliferation of regulatory instruments and technologies, rather than any overall trend towards deregulation (Braithwaite, 2008). This is not as straightforward as just saying that central state oversight and regulation have increased. The picture is a good deal more complex than that. Regulation now also occurs increasingly beyond the state in private-sector and non-governmental agencies, as well as in transnational networks. It is this thickening, extending and spreading of regulation and governance that characterizes contemporary neo-liberal capitalism and which is encapsulated in the idea of 'regulatory capitalism' (Levi-Faur, 2005; Braithwaite, 2008).

Fourth, within neo-liberal capitalism, there has been a shift away from the primacy of production towards a new emphasis on consumption – the rise of the 'consumer society' in shorthand (see Bauman, 1988; Miller and Rose, 1997; Rose, 1999: 85–89). This is connected with the new economic style of reasoning referred to above, as individuals are increasingly obliged 'to understand and enact their lives in terms of choice' (Rose, 1999: 87), with choices about consumption central to the construction of identities. Indeed, consumption has become a site for 'symbolic competition' between individuals about lifestyles and identity (Bauman, 1988: 58).

Fifth, recent decades have also seen the 'rise of risk' (Garland, 2003) or the emergence of a 'risk society' (Beck, 1992), in the sense that risk has become a central organizing principle for life and hence a 'defining characteristic of the world in which we live' (Garland, 2003: 48). Again, there is a connection here with the idea of choice – risk requires the possibility of human choice. The two are thus 'complementary' and 'parallel' notions (O'Malley, 2004: 169). The neo-liberal incarnation of *Homo economicus* is a choice-maker, a consumer, a 'competing creature', required simultaneously to act *responsibly* by minimizing negative risks (O'Malley, 2004: 71–74) and to be *entrepreneurial* in taking risks in order to innovate (Osborne and Gaebler, 1992; O'Malley, 2004: 57–71).

This chapter explores how this transition to neo-liberalism has reshaped and refigured the ways in which we understand and deal with the 'drug problem' today. I will examine in particular a set of provisions within the Drugs Act 2005 and trace the various lines of development out of which this legislative 'event' emerged. The 'puzzle' in this chapter is to unpick how a certain understanding of the notion of 'problem drug use' has taken hold so strongly, leading to a focus on crime above all else.

The emergence of risk-based regulation

I will begin my approach to this 'puzzle' by looking at how the 'problematization' of particular substances has shifted over recent decades and then turn to consider how this has translated into some distinctive forms of response.

Drug problems and the rise of the 'problem drug user'

We have seen in Chapters 3 and 4 that the ways in which the 'drug problem' is 'imagined' have been highly significant elements within the genealogy I am tracing, right from the period that opium first began to be seen from within a 'problem framework' in the nineteenth century. And these changing 'problematizations' have been articulated within the evolving and mutating parameters of liberal governance.

In the last few decades of the twentieth century, an important shift in the imagination of the 'drug problem' began to unfold. In the British context, I think this can be traced back to the 1960s. Use of cannabis, amphetamine and hallucinogens began to increase from the 1950s, a trend which then accelerated more sharply in the 1960s (Bewley, 2005). The idea of an emerging youth drug subculture started to become significantly more prominent in public and media discourse about young people. During the same period, the number of people using heroin and cocaine also appeared to grow (Bewley, 1965, 1966; Spear, 1969), although consumption of both these drugs remained relatively rare and largely confined to London (Pearson, 2001; cf. de Alarcon, 1969). Arguably, then, the 1960s was the point at which Britain's 'slumbering encounter with drugs' (Pearson, 2001: 55) turned into a perception of there being a 'drug problem' about which authorities and policy-makers should be concerned, even if in terms of absolute numbers involved the problem remained very small.

There was a range of responses to this. On amphetamines, for example, concern rapidly gathered pace at the beginning of the 1960s, notably after the publication of Philip Connell's landmark monograph on amphetamine psychosis in 1958 (Connell, 1958). Interestingly, and echoing a theme from earlier chapters, the issue at this time was the diversion of amphetamines from legitimate pharmaceutical manufacturers like Smith, Kline and French.

So, as Spear (2002: 120) recounts, pharmaceutical companies were important voices in the debates about the passing of the Drugs (Prevention of Misuse) Act 1964, which was intended to tighten controls on the availability of amphetamines (in fact, in practice, it largely failed to do so for reasons that Spear (2002: 118–24) outlines).

If the 1964 legislation turned out to be fairly toothless, of more significance were the two interdepartmental committees which were also set up, known as the first and second Brain Committees after their Chairman Sir Russell Brain and reporting in 1961 and 1965 respectively (Ministry of Health, 1961, 1965). Spear (2002) provides a good account of the background to these two reports, as does a short paper by Smart (1984) and readers looking for more detail are directed there. The content of the two reports can be (crudely) summarized as follows: Brain I essentially concluded that there was no problem of any significance requiring policy change; Brain II, in contrast, recommended a significant tightening up of controls on the prescribing of heroin and cocaine in order to curb leakage into a growing illicit drug market.

At the heart of the specific recommendations of the second Brain report was that ordinary doctors, general practitioners, should no longer have the freedom to prescribe heroin and cocaine. This would be limited to doctors granted licences by the Home Office and who would be based at new treatment centres that were to be established. The Dangerous Drugs Act of 1967 set out the relevant legislative provisions concerning prescribing powers, coming into force in April 1968. The new treatment centres, formally known as Drug Dependency Units (DDUs) but which soon came to be termed the 'clinics', were based in the London teaching hospitals and were led primarily by psychiatrists (Spear, 2002). The clinic system, and its underpinning medical model, dominated the 1970s and the start of the 1980s (see Stimson and Oppenheimer, 1982).

The other main set of recommendations in the second Brain report concerned the requirement for 'addicts' to be notified to a central authority. Failure by a doctor to do so was to be a disciplinary matter to be dealt with by the General Medical Council (Spear, 2002: 176–88). The relevant regulation under the 1967 Act came into force in February 1968. Any medical practitioner who came into professional contact with a person known or suspected to be addicted to certain scheduled drugs was required to inform the Chief Medical Officer at the Home Office and supply certain details about that patient (name, date of birth, National Insurance number, drug of addiction, date of contact) (Spear, 2002: 178).

So how should we understand this? At one level, we might see the transition to a system of hospital-based treatment overseen by psychiatrists and the establishment of a notification system as a consolidation of the disease model of addiction for opiates and cocaine. But I think 1968 represents a significant point in our genealogy. Although the problem continued to be seen as a medical one, it was a reshaped medical 'gaze' which focused not so much on individual doctor–patient relations but rather on the medical containment or control of the 'drug problem'. The analogy drawn was with the containment of an infectious disease. The second Brain report, for example, described addiction as a 'socially infectious condition' (Ministry of Health, 1965). The recommendations for compulsory notification can be seen in this light as part a strategy for the surveillance, monitoring and containment of the spread of a contagious disease.

We might see the Brain II approach then as part of the emergence of a public-health problematization of the drug situation. In this, there were parallels with alcohol which, during the 1970s, was strongly influenced by what came to be termed the 'new public health' (see Room, 1984). The rise of epidemiology was significant here, of which perhaps the best example was the landmark work on tobacco by Doll and Hill (1950, 1964) which established the link between smoking and cancer. There were also strong historical resonances from a century earlier when public-health concerns shaped the emergence of the early regulation of opium and opiates, as discussed in Chapter 3 (see also Stimson and Lart, 1991). There are continuities in this genealogy, as well as new departures.

The public-health mode of problematization was strongly connected with the emergence of the notion of 'problem use' which was to become of great significance. As with the disease concept of addiction, the 'problem use' paradigm was first worked out for alcohol. The idea of the 'problem drinker' or 'problem drinking' can in fact be traced as far back as the 1940s, when discomfort with the term 'alcoholism' led people close to the alcohol industry to begin to explore alternative terminology (see Riley and Marden, 1947; Duryea and Hirsh, 1948; Hirsh, 1949). But it was in the late 1960s that the 'problem drinker' concept really took off properly (Clark, 1966; Knupfer, 1967), culminating in Don Cahalan's 1970 book *Problem Drinkers*. A decade later, the idea began to take hold for other substances. In Britain in the early 1980s, the Advisory Council on the Misuse of Drugs, an influential government advisory body, set out a landmark definition of a 'problem drug taker':

> Any person who experiences social, psychological, physical or legal problems related to intoxication and/or regular excessive consumption and/or dependence as a consequence of his own use of drugs or other chemical substances (excluding alcohol and tobacco).
>
> (ACMD, 1982: 34)

Putting to one side the exclusion of alcohol and tobacco, this definition was deliberately meant to be wide, covering anyone from the teenage cannabis user getting into trouble with the police right through to the heroin injector with multiple problems. This signalled a move away from a narrowly conceived medical model. It is clear in the definition that 'problems' are viewed primarily as those experienced by the drug user. More recently, the definition has broadened to include the problems that drug users cause to others. For example, a recent French study uses the following case definition: 'An individual is a "problem drug user" when his [*sic*] consumption of a substance leads to health, social and/or legal problems for himself or others' (Vaissade and Legleye, 2009: 32). In Britain, the emphasis over the past 20 years has shifted increasingly to the problems certain drug users cause for others. In the mid-1980s, the central problem was undoubtedly the threat posed by HIV/AIDS. An ACMD report of the time famously declared that 'the spread of HIV is a greater threat to public and individual health than drug misuse' (ACMD, 1988). During the same period, and in parallel with this, concerns about the impact on communities of 'drug-fuelled' property crime were also emerging (e.g. Parker and Newcombe, 1987). This crime focus has come to dominate over the past decade, leading to some commentators terming this the 'criminalization' of drug policy (Duke, 2006; Stevens, 2007; Seddon et al, 2008). The 'problem drug user' or 'PDU' is now the target of much of contemporary British drug policy.

I should here clarify an important point. I am not arguing that shifts in policy direction were entirely unrelated to 'real' changes in the nature of the problems presented by drug use. Brain II was in part a response to the expansion of the drug-using scene in London (see Spear, 1969), whilst developments in the 1980s were strongly shaped by the heroin 'epidemic' that exploded in many towns and cities across the north of England and Scotland in the first years of that decade (see Pearson et al., 1986; Pearson, 1987; Parker et al, 1988). As several commentators have noted, the changing class profile was significant here in both the 1960s and the 1980s – the middle-class, middle-aged drug taker that Rolleston had considered was being replaced by a younger working-class (or even 'underclass') heroin user. In fact, the relationship between 'problems' and policy responses to them is a little more complex than this. I have dealt with this elsewhere (Seddon et al., 2008) and do not wish to dwell on the point here but a sequence derived from Garland (2001) offers quite a useful way of thinking about this. Broad patterns of social change, like the transition to neo-liberalism, often have an impact on the nature of existing 'problems' as well as throwing up new ones. The same social transformations then also shape the ways in which these 'real' changes to the problem landscape are understood and 'imagined', leading to new 'problematizations' which pose novel 'policy predicaments'. Responses to these predicaments are, in turn, also moulded by this bigger picture of social change. There is thus a complex interactive relationship between problems 'in the real', problematizations and responses.

The claim that I want to examine here is that this focus on the idea of drug-related problems or harms represented a distinctive and new way of framing or 'imagining' the problem that was not simply an inevitable or 'automatic' response to a new drug situation. I think that from the late 1960s we can see a new 'problematization' emerging which is connected with the transition to neo-liberalism that I described at the beginning of this chapter. In viewing drug users as potential sources of harm to themselves but especially to the wider community, we see the notion of risk becoming a key organizing principle in the field. It is notable that at around the same time as Russell Newcombe's pioneering article on harm reduction appeared in 1987, so too commentators were making the first sightings of the rise of risk-based practices more generally across diverse fields – the original German-language version of Ulrich Beck's landmark book *Risk Society* was published in 1986, for example, and a series of highly influential papers appeared between 1986 and 1988 (Reichman, 1986; Simon, 1987, 1988). As we will see, the idea of encouraging or cajoling drug users to engage in responsible choice-making about their drug consumption in order to reduce drug-related risks has become perhaps the central framework for responding to the problem. In this respect, I argue that there is a continuity in the 'imagination' of the drug problem that runs from the second half of the 1960s to the present.

It should be pointed out here that this argument runs counter to the views of many drug-policy commentators who tend to see three quite distinct phases: first of all, the clinic system of the 1970s as a period of policy stagnation in which the 'British System' had been killed off but not clearly replaced; second, the emergence of harm reduction in the 1980s as a major (and largely positive) watershed; and, third, the shift to a crime focus from the 1990s as another significant (but largely negative) transformation (see Stimson, 2000; Hunt and Stevens, 2004). To a certain extent, these commentators undoubtedly have a point – at a particular level of analysis, the differences do loom larger than any similarities. However, it seems to me that when we step back a little and look at these developments in a longer perspective, taking the 'long view' that I described in Chapter 1, there are such strong 'family resemblances' in the various ways of thinking about and acting upon the 'drug problem' during this period as a whole that a 'strategic coherence' starts to become evident (see Rose, 2000: 185). In brief, since the 1960s, the drug user has been recast as potentially posing a threat to the community – whether as a carrier of a metaphorical 'socially infectious disease', as a carrier of a real contagious disease (HIV), or as a criminal predator – which needs to be monitored and controlled. Increasingly, they are urged and enjoined to act prudentially, by making responsible choices about their consumption practices. They are rational actors with the capacity not only to act autonomously but also to utilize available knowledge to do so responsibly. I will now explore this further by looking, first, at the emergence of harm reduction in the 1980s and then, second, at the rise of a crime-focused approach which culminated in certain provisions in the Drugs Act 2005.

Public-health problems, HIV/AIDS and harm reduction

The emergence of harm reduction and the sudden realization that drug users were at particular risk of contracting HIV were inextricably linked. A laboratory test for antibodies to HIV became available in the second half of 1985 and by the end of that year 55 cases amongst injecting drug users in England and Wales had been confirmed, a small number of which dated back to samples taken up to a year earlier; the situation in Scotland was significantly worse (Robertson, 2005: 123). This was a profoundly disturbing discovery which had a major impact in the drug-policy field:

> Since the discovery of the HIV virus among British drug users at the end of 1985, the pace of policy change has been rapid. Two major reports on AIDS and Drug Misuse have followed, together with £17 million for the development of drug services. At least 100 needle exchanges offering new for used syringes are the most tangible public expression of new developments.
>
> (Berridge, 1991: 176)

The advent of HIV/AIDS was certainly a catalytic moment for drug policy, with the period 1986 through to 1988 being one of particularly feverish activity. Those interested in detailed accounts of this era are referred to a useful collection edited by two of the key figures in the British drug field (Strang and Stimson, 1990) and to Virginia Berridge's typically excellent book *AIDS in the UK* (1996b). The two landmark reports by the ACMD (1988, 1989) are also important and useful sources. An essay by Robertson (2005) gives a vivid account of how HIV was able to spread so rapidly amongst injecting drug users in parts of Scotland in the early 1980s.

One story to tell then about this period concerns how the threat of HIV/AIDS led to the development of a pragmatic public-health approach to drug use. Measures to prevent the sharing of injecting equipment were central here and proved controversial initially. Some pioneering and entrepreneurial practitioners in Liverpool in North West England set up the first syringe-exchange scheme (McDermott, 2005) and this was followed swiftly by several government-sponsored pilot projects (Stimson et al., 1988). The concept of harm reduction emerged as the dominant paradigm for British drug policy and practice for a time, as captured in two important edited collections in the early 1990s (O'Hare et al., 1992; Heather et al., 1993), and indeed it has since become an international movement. The 2008 annual conference of the International Harm Reduction Association, a body with roots in the original work in Liverpool in the 1980s, attracted over 1,200 delegates from around 80 countries (www.ihra.net).

The question of the 'newness' or otherwise of the harm-reduction approach is worth considering. A first point to make, although this is little acknowledged in the drugs literature, is that alcohol again to some extent got here first. Ideas about harm and harm reduction were used in relation to alcohol back in the 1970s (Bruun, 1970; Room, 1975; for a retrospective overview see Room, 2004). A paper published in 1970 by the Finnish sociologist Kettil Bruun, for example, set out proposals for a re-orientation of alcohol policy towards the reduction of drink-related harms. The 'newness' of harm reduction in the 1980s has also been challenged by some drug-policy analysts and historians who have noted the connections between the public-health approaches of the 1980s and the 1960s that I have already mentioned (Berridge, 1991; Stimson and Lart, 1991). It has been argued too that many of the structures and services that allowed the harm-reduction approach to take root were in place prior to the HIV threat becoming known (Stimson and Lart, 1991), owing more to the impact of the Central Funding Initiative for the establishment of new treatment services which had been announced in December 1982 (MacGregor et al., 1991; Mold and Berridge, 2007). The work of the Liverpool pioneers was also clearly connected to more general developments in public health in the Mersey region at this time, as captured in John Ashton and Howard Seymour's classic book *The New Public Health* which was published in 1988 (Ashton and Seymour, 1988). So clearly the rise of harm reduction cannot be explained simply in terms of a response to the threat of HIV (see Roe, 2005). How then can we best understand it? I think we can make sense of the multiple interconnections that I have described by seeing them as indicative of a strategic coherence in the field since the 1960s. Whilst this coherence may not be immediately apparent when looking at the level of policy detail, at the level of 'frames of thinking' about drug users and the 'drug problem' it comes more clearly into focus.

We can usefully elaborate on this by looking more closely at the ways in which harm reduction was aligned with a particular vision of the drug user. If we consider the technologies associated with harm reduction, three of the key components were syringe-exchange schemes, the supply of condoms and the provision of information about safer drug-using and related practices to prevent harms. Each of these is based on the notion that if drug users were supplied with the right materials, resources and information, they would tend to make more responsible choices about their consumption practices, that is choices likely to reduce risk. Peter McDermott, one of the early Liverpool harm-reduction pioneers, stated in a recent retrospective interview:

> Giving clean needles to strangers didn't automatically mean they wouldn't share, but if you didn't do it they had no access to the right choices ... People understood the risks they were running. They actively wanted to minimize their risk.
>
> (Quoted in Hölstrom, 2006: 12)

This whole approach is interesting and significant in the way that it conceptualizes the freedom and autonomy of drug users. They are at one and the same time addicted subjects with such severely attenuated free will that their drug-using behaviour is potentially dangerous *and* rational actors able to make responsible choices if given the opportunities to do so. They are viewed in effect as 'calculating risk-takers', as O'Malley (2004: 164) puts it.

O'Malley stresses the centrality of the concept of 'choice' to harm reduction and makes connections with the wider transition to neo-liberalism (1999, 2004: 155–71). The radical departure this represents is worth lingering on for a moment. The classic disease model of addiction is founded on the notion of 'loss of control', that is an impaired capacity to make free choices, and this can be traced all the way from Benjamin Rush's original formulation (see Chapter 3) right through to Jellinek's (1960) famous account in *The Disease Concept of Alcoholism*. To see the addicted subject as exercising choice, or at least as being able to do so, is an entirely different frame of understanding. The emergence over the past 20 or so years of a body of literature on addiction which draws directly on behavioural economics nicely illustrates this new way of thinking (Becker and Murphy, 1988; Vuchinich and Heather, 2003). Furthermore, as these economists helpfully remind us, from this perspective choice should not be equated with unfettered free will. It can be, and usually is, constrained in certain ways. Reading the interesting collection *Choice, Behavioural Economics and Addiction* edited by Rudy Vuchinich and Nick Heather and published in 2003, I am struck by the resonances with Jonathan Edwards' discussion of free will and habitual drinking from the eighteenth century which I discussed in Chapter 2. Edwards highlighted the importance of recognizing the capacity for choice even where this may be highly constrained:

> When a drunkard has his liquor before him, and he has to choose whether to drink it or no; the proper and immediate objects, about which his present volition is conversant, and between which his choice now decides, are his own acts, in drinking the liquor, or letting it alone.
>
> (Edwards, 1754/1957: 143)

Similarly, the twenty-first-century behavioural economists frame their explanatory challenge as 'to explain why a particular level of behavioural allocation towards the addictive behaviour is selected rather than a different level of allocation, and to specify the conditions under which such allocations will be made and the conditions under which they may be changed' (Heather and Vuchinich, 2003: 412). So whilst 'conditions', both internal to the individual and external, may affect or influence what choice is made, they do not *remove* choice – there are always behavioural options to select from. We can see here the lineage of the neo-liberal subject in its classical liberal forebear. I will have more to say about choice in the next section.

Crime problems, 'Tough Choices' and the Drugs Act 2005

The argument that I have developed so far is, on the face of things, severely tested by more recent developments. Indeed, in an extremely influential article from 2000 by one of the central figures in the harm-reduction movement, the following claim is made:

> I have observed the development of British drug policy for the last 30 years and the last 12 months have been the most dismal that I can recall ... This is a crucial juncture in British drug policy. We have lost consensus. We risk losing both a humane vision of how to respond to drug problems, and our respect for human rights.
>
> (Stimson, 2000: 259, 264)

In this epochal account, Stimson argues that we have moved from a 'healthy' policy in the 1980s which was focused on harm reduction and public health, to an 'unhealthy' one that is now centred on crime reduction. How then can my claims of continuity be sustained? At a crude level, Stimson's argument fails in basic chronological terms, certainly for the British case. Harm reduction, initially targeted at HIV prevention, emerged in parallel with new criminal justice initiatives rather than preceding them. In the period 1986–87, for example, when the first needle-exchange pilots and the Liverpool 'experiment' were taking off, so too were pioneering arrest referral schemes being developed for drug users held in police stations (see Dorn, 1994). And by the time the ACMD published its *AIDS and Drug Misuse* update report in 1993 (ACMD, 1993), it had already produced one important report on criminal justice (ACMD, 1991) and was about to complete a second (ACMD, 1994). So Stimson's chronology, in which a criminal justice agenda usurps and succeeds an earlier public health one, is flawed.

But what about his argument that the criminal justice perspective represents a distinctively new way of framing the problem (even if it initially emerged at the same time as the public-health approach that it eventually overpowered)? Here, clearly he has a point – to view the overarching purpose of drug policy as to reduce crime does constitute a significant departure. As I have already suggested, though, there are considerable 'family resemblances' between the two policy 'turns' in terms of how they 'imagine' the problem – drug users as threats to the community who should be urged and empowered to act responsibly in the behavioural choices they make.

Let me develop this a bit further by focusing on some of the provisions in the Drugs Act 2005, especially those that have been brought together under the umbrella of the 'Tough Choices' project. These provisions are the culmination of over two decades of crime-focused drug initiatives, going back to the experimental arrest referral projects of the late 1980s that I have already mentioned. The basic premise of all these initiatives is that the criminal justice system is a good place to find those drug users who are causing the most damage to communities and that it can also be used to channel or push them into drug treatment in order to reduce the threat they pose. So over the past two decades we have seen the expansion of arrest referral schemes throughout the 1990s, the introduction of court-ordered treatment for offenders under probation supervision in the community (first with the section 1A(6) order introduced in 1991 and then the Drug Treatment and Testing Order (DTTO) piloted in 1998) and the establishment of drug testing (in prisons in 1994, as part of DTTOs from 1998 and in police stations from 2001). In 2003, the array of criminal justice interventions was brought together within the Drug Interventions Programme (DIP), an ambitious initiative which aimed to co-ordinate treatment provision more effectively by working across the criminal justice system and providing an 'end-to-end' service for individuals. Under the banner 'out of crime, into treatment', DIP has become a major policy programme.

The 'Tough Choices' project was the name given to a series of provisions within the Drugs Act 2005, designed to expand and strengthen DIP, with a particular focus on coercive measures (see Skodbo et al., 2007). The three key elements of 'Tough Choices' were: the introduction of Testing on Arrest (which had previously been available post-charge only); the introduction of the Required Assessment (in which arrestees with positive tests are required to attend up to two assessments by a drug worker or else face a criminal sanction); and the national roll-out of the Restriction on Bail (in which the usual presumption in favour of court bail is reversed for those with positive tests, unless they agree to attend drug treatment, an agreement which then becomes a bail condition).

If we focus just on the 'Tough Choices' elements of the 2005 legislation, several important points become evident.

First, testing is clearly the foundation, as it is the means of identifying the target 'problem' users – according to Singleton (2008: 4) there are currently over 200,000 tests being carried out each year in police custody suites in England and Wales. As a filtering device, testing is relatively crude in practice and in certain respects quite flawed (see Seddon, 2005), but it is clearly constructed as a means of identifying and selecting those who are believed to offer the greatest potential threat to others. Based on the assumption that the most threatening group consists of heroin and crack users who commit property crime to raise money to buy drugs, the testing regime is 'triggered' by arrests for specified property or drug possession/supply offences and tests for opiates and cocaine only. The evidence for that assumption may be questionable (see Seddon, 2000) but the risk-based logic is impeccable.

Second, both the Required Assessment and the Restriction on Bail involve what Garland (2001: 124–27) calls a strategy of 'responsibilization'. As noted at the beginning of this chapter, this is a distinctive feature of neo-liberalism, where individuals are encouraged and cajoled to act responsibly to minimize risk (O'Malley, 2004: 71–74). This is encapsulated in the very name 'Tough Choices', as explained in a Home Office factsheet: 'Tough Choices was chosen as a name because it was felt to succinctly describe the change in the consequences drug misusers face if they do not take advantage of the opportunities for treatment and support that exist' (Home Office, 2006). Failing to take advantage of opportunities by making the 'correct' choice exposes 'high-risk' individuals to more coercive or punitive measures. So, for example, turning down the 'opportunities' offered by the Restriction on Bail might lead to bail being refused and that person ending up in prison on remand (see Hucklesby et al., 2007). This is a neo-liberal 'form of governing that seeks to govern not through society but through the responsible and prudential choices and actions of individuals on behalf of themselves and those for whom they feel an emotional bond or affinity' (Dean, 1999: 134). It also offers a type of conditional citizenship:

> Those who refuse to become responsible, to govern themselves ethically, have also refused the offer to become members of our moral community. Hence, for them, harsh measures are entirely appropriate. Three strikes and you are out: citizenship becomes conditional upon conduct.
>
> (Rose, 2000: 202)

These ideas of conditionality and responsibilization have proved highly attractive to policy-makers. Analogous proposals have recently been made for the withdrawal of social security benefits for those 'problem drug users' who refuse the offer of treatment (Department for Work and Pensions, 2008). Similar ideas have also taken off in other areas of social policy, for example, in the field of 'anti-social behaviour' (Crawford, 2006) where benefit sanctions were 'pioneered' some years earlier.

The third point, which is related to this idea of responsibilization, concerns the concept of choice. The set of 'Tough Choices' measures is based on the neo-liberal economic style of reasoning that I described in the introduction to this chapter, in which human behaviour is to be understood through the language of choice. The measures operate by establishing a series of rewards and disincentives designed to encourage the desired behavioural choices. Again, this resonates very strongly with a behavioural economic perspective – the Restriction on Bail, for example, can be seen as an intervention attempting to generate conditions under which the 'level of behavioural allocation' may shift away from the undesired selection. Such a perspective embodies the rise of consumer freedom that Bauman (1988) sees as characteristic of what he calls the 'late capitalist' era (see Chapter 2). As Garland (2001: 198) puts it, in describing contemporary crime control strategies: 'Accounts that highlight rational choice and the responsiveness of offenders to rewards and disincentives chime with today's common sense and with the individualistic morality of our consumer culture.'

We can see then that there is a level of strategic fit and coherence between harm-reduction measures like needle-exchange schemes and the type of coercive crime-focused interventions within 'Tough Choices' and DIP. Both are based on a shared problematization (drug users as threats to the community), a shared conception of drug-using subjects (as rational calculating risk-takers and choice-makers) and a shared strategic response (urging and enabling responsible choice-making to reduce risk). As I have already argued, this common ground can be traced back to the late 1960s and the policy and practice developments which followed the second Brain report (Ministry of Health, 1965). This fits also with the idea that the imagination and governance of the 'drug problem' has shifted as liberal governance more broadly has mutated into its neo-liberal form.

Strategic coherence does not mean to say, however, that the two are identical. A potentially important point of difference is the matter of *coercion* (see Seddon, 2007c). Surely the fact that harm-reduction measures do not rely on the use of coercive leverage to engage and retain drug users marks a major distinction from the 'Tough Choices' package in the Drugs Act 2005? Perhaps this is so but, as I have argued elsewhere (Seddon, 2007c), the dividing line between 'voluntary' and 'coerced' entry into drug treatment services is less clear-cut than we might imagine. Several studies have shown that legal pressures to enter treatment operate alongside many other sources of pressure (e.g. family, friends, financial) and may indeed often be of subsidiary importance in individual decision-making (Marlowe et al., 1996, 2001): 'For many people it may be false to assume that the application of criminal justice leverage dramatically increases the level of coercion they feel to enter treatment' (Seddon, 2007c: 273).

Thinking about harm-reduction services for a moment, it is quite easy to imagine that even if criminal justice leverage is absent, there might nevertheless be other quite powerful pressures to engage. For example, an injecting heroin user with a diagnosed blood-borne virus like hepatitis or HIV would likely come under considerable pressure from a long-term sexual partner to engage consistently with a needle-exchange service and to comply with any additional behavioural advice offered to them. But Stevens et al. (2005: 207) argue that the distinctive character of criminal justice coercion is that it constitutes external pressure exerted by the state which has its own 'agencies to deal with those who try to avoid it'. I think this is an important point, although I think it is possible to overstate it. My ambivalence here is partly theoretical – Stevens' argument relies partly on an *analytical* privileging of the state that does not fit well with either governmentality or regulation perspectives (see Chapter 1). For me, it is always an *empirical* question whether the state has a dominant place in any given governmental field, rather than something that can be derived theoretically or simply assumed (Burris et al., 2005). And, as I have already suggested, the empirical evidence here tends to show that the pressures exerted by state criminal

justice agencies are usually not felt to be the most powerful by those individuals on the receiving end (Marlowe et al., 1996, 2001; Seddon, 2007c). It
is interesting though to note that official policy documents have tended to
shy away from use of the term 'coercion', preferring to emphasize the idea
that 'choices' are still available, however constrained or 'tough' they may be.

My argument about the transition from the late 1960s can be further
supported by briefly looking at another set of provisions in the 2005 legislation. Section 1 of the Act, amending section 4 of the Misuse of Drugs Act
1971, creates a new offence of aggravated supply of a controlled drug where
this is committed 'on or in the vicinity of school premises at a relevant time'
('relevant time' covering the period from one hour before the start of the
school day to one hour after its end). This aims to deal with the fear of drug
dealers hanging around schools in order to sell drugs to children, a fear largely
unsubstantiated by any empirical research which tends to suggest that children most commonly obtain illegal drugs from their existing friends and
acquaintances rather than from outside sources (e.g. Parker, 2000). One way
to look at this is in terms of my claim that the drug problem has come to be
viewed in recent decades primarily in terms of risks posed to communities.
The threat of drug dealers 'corrupting' school children is a classic example
of this and section 1 of the 2005 Act can be viewed therefore partly as a
risk-reduction measure.

Others, however, have seen this in more straightforward terms. Quite
simply, the lack of evidence to suggest that there is any need for this new
offence indicated for many that this was simply an instance of 'playing politics' with drug policy. Up to a point, that was no doubt the case – indeed,
the 2005 legislation was rushed through immediately before the General
Election that year and was viewed by some commentators as an exercise in
exactly this type of political populism. Such a view was also felt to apply in
some quarters to the 'Tough Choices' project as well, the use of the word
'tough' consciously echoing Tony Blair's famous (and profoundly 'political')
pledge in the 1990s to be 'tough on crime, tough on the causes of crime' (see
Garside, 2003). But what does 'playing politics' actually mean in the context
of public policy? Here, I draw on Richard Sparks' (2001) creative adaptation
of the work of the great anthropologist Mary Douglas (Douglas, 1986, 1992;
Douglas and Wildavsky, 1982). For Sparks, terms like 'politics' and 'populism' are generally deployed in policy analysis in 'decidedly thin and un-
illuminating' ways which are 'not themselves explanations' but rather 'are
introduced when explanation fails' (2001: 172). In other words, when a
policy development appears not to make 'rational' sense, it is dismissed as
the result of politicians 'playing to the gallery'. A more fruitful approach,
Sparks argues, is to understand 'risk' as an inherently political concept in
which social anxieties and cultural preoccupations are embedded. So instances of the 'politicization' of risks are not only to be expected but also may
tell us much about the organization and values of particular communities or

societies. As I have argued elsewhere, we can understand this focus on risks associated with drug consumption as partly reflective of a profound unease about forms of 'disordered consumption' in a society in which consumer freedom is so highly valued (Seddon et al., 2008). The contemporary concern about 'binge drinking' even better captures this tension: excessive drinking is encouraged and valued for its contribution to the night-time economy whilst at the same time reviled for its connection with crime and disorder (Measham and Brain, 2005). I will return to this 'cultural theory of risk' in the conclusion to this chapter, as it also highlights an important methodological matter.

Reunifying the field and the alcohol question

In Chapter 4, I noted how the demise of the inebriety concept was linked to the emergence of the 'great regulatory divide' in the early twentieth century. The inebriety project, which aimed to provide a unified theory of addiction applicable across the board to all psychoactive substances, sat awkwardly with these new regulatory divisions which implied that some substances were qualitatively and significantly 'different'.

According to the historian David Courtwright (2005), in recent decades there has been a 'long drift back' to treating different substances together or in similar ways – he calls this the 'rebirth of inebriety', whilst noting that 'it doesn't go by that name, or any single name' (Courtwright, 2005: 115; see also White, 1998). Indeed, as I observed in Chapter 2, there has been a proliferation or fragmentation of terminology – chemical dependence, substance misuse and so on. This is an important point that I will return to shortly.

Courtwright locates the drivers of this 'long drift back' in developments in scientific knowledge. First, he points to work on neural reward pathways and, in particular, research from the 1960s onwards on the functioning of the neurotransmitter dopamine. He suggests that scientific explanations which demonstrated how psychoactive substances, whether licit or illicit, shared a common set of mechanisms for their psychoactive effects, encouraged more unifying approaches. Second, he cites the growth of epidemiological research, again from the 1960s, which increasingly identified the serious health risks associated with licit substances like tobacco and alcohol, as well as the synergies and crossovers between use of different substances. This epidemiological evidence, he argues, further reinforced the idea that psychoactive substances had more in common than had been thought.

Although I think Courtwright is correct to identify this trend of a 'long drift back', I am less convinced by his explanation. As Mills (2005) argues in a commentary on Courtwright's article, by privileging scientists and scientific knowledge he presents an almost deterministic account in which the social, cultural and political context for both scientific endeavour and policy-making is largely ignored. In my view, the 'long drift back' can be best understood in terms of the transition to neo-liberalism. There are two points to make here. The first concerns the distinctive place of risk and risk-based thinking within neo-liberal forms of government. As I observed above, the 'new epidemiology' to which Courtwright refers was closely connected with the emergence of a new problematization of the drug situation in which the identification and reduction of drug-related risks becomes paramount. Courtwright (2005: 115) himself alludes to this, albeit briefly and only in passing, when he notes the 'growing western cultural awareness of, and aversion to, health risks of any variety'. It seems to me that a focus on risk will tend to cut across substances and therefore supports and strengthens integrative and unifying perspectives. The second point is more speculative on my part but I see a connection with Nikolas Rose's analysis of the ways in which we are 'becoming neurochemical selves' (Rose, 2003). He argues that in recent decades, we have seen a 'profound transformation in personhood' in which we increasingly view and understand ourselves in bodily terms using the 'language of contemporary biomedicine' (2003: 54). He gives the example of depressed mood: we have relatively recently 'come to think about our sadness as a condition called "depression" caused by a chemical imbalance in the brain and amenable to treatment by drugs that would "rebalance" these chemicals' (2003: 46). I think we might fruitfully situate Courtwright's analysis of the 'long drift back' in the context of the 'transformation of personhood' that Rose describes (see also Rose, 2006).

I return now to the question of terminology that I touched on earlier. At first sight, it might seem odd, contradictory even, that a unifying trend should be accompanied by a fragmentation in terminology. We saw in earlier chapters how the concept of 'addiction' was initially worked out for alcohol, later extending to other substances such as opiates. As I have argued above, a similar process occurred with the notion of 'problem use', which began in the late 1960s as the idea of the 'problem drinker' and was then applied in the early 1980s to the 'problem drug taker'. An idea that travelled in the opposite direction is 'dependence'. This was first coined by the World Health Organization in the 1960s to apply to illegal drugs (WHO, 1964) but was then borrowed a decade later by Edwards and Gross (1976) in their famous paper setting out a new 'alcohol dependence syndrome'. But today, although 'problem use' is the dominant concept for reasons I have already discussed, it co-exists with most of these older terms as well as some other new ones – reading the research and policy literature in the field, an array of different terms are used from 'chemical dependence' to 'substance misuse' and even 'drug addiction' remains common. How can we make sense of this? As I briefly argued in Chapter 2, I think we can understand this partly as a consequence of the epistemological fragmentation that Ericson and Carriere (1994) suggest is characteristic of the 'rise of risk' at the turn of the twenty-first century. Whilst the notions of 'problem drug use' and 'problem drinking' obviously have a particular affinity with risk-based thinking, the proliferation of other terms reflects the fact that risks cut across established fields, knowledges and institutions – it is part, in other words, of 'wider processes of fragmentation ... in the risk society' (Ericson and Carriere, 1994: 105).

What are the practical implications of this re-unifying trend? Are policies for different substances starting to converge? Or might they do so in the future? These are enormous questions which merit extensive study in their own right. There is also obviously a critical comparative dimension here, as the particular dynamic of trends no doubt varies in different parts of the world. I will restrict myself here to a few observations about the British case.

Let me take the example of tobacco, first of all. This appears in certain respects to be travelling in the direction of some regulatory convergence with currently illegal drugs, although I should stress it is still some way off that point. In Britain today, lighting up a cigarette in a pub or railway station, for example, will get you into trouble with those responsible for managing those premises. And if you refuse requests to desist, you might even attract police attention at some stage. What about alcohol? It is now not uncommon to see signs in parts of towns and cities that declare 'you are now entering an Alcohol Control Zone' and warn you that openly carrying or drinking alcohol may result in an on-the-spot fine. In fact, it is arguable that walking down the street in these Zones you are likely to attract more adverse police attention for drinking a can of lager than for smoking a cannabis spliff. The risk-based logic of neo-liberalism is reshaping the regulatory landscape on the ground in ways that cut across existing categories of licit and illicit substances. The policing of public space is undoubtedly an area where the maintenance of sharp distinctions between these categories is being tested to destruction (Lister et al., 2008), as policing more generally is shifting to being more risk-focused (Ericson and Haggerty, 1997).

Perhaps, though, there is a danger of overstating these convergences. There is little sign of substances like heroin or cocaine travelling in the other direction any time soon in most countries, although there are interesting developments in Portugal, for example, where since 2001 personal use of drugs of all types has been decriminalized (Allen et al., 2004; Hughes and Stevens, 2007). At the very least, we can say that the 'return to inebriety' does potentially open up a fault-line underneath the 'great regulatory divide'. Many drug law reformers certainly believe that this is going to lead eventually to the scrapping of the global prohibition regime. I am not so sure – or, more precisely, I tend to see a much longer time frame in that word 'eventually' than do some – but I will return to this question in the next chapter.

It could be argued that the Drugs Act 2005, which I have used in this chapter as a focal point for my exploration of the contemporary imagination and governance of the drug problem, itself indicates the persisting strength of the 'regulatory divide'. It is not, after all, a 'Substance Act' or 'Drug and Alcohol Act'. Yet many of the responsibilizing and coercive strategies in the Act that I have been discussing here are increasingly being applied to alcohol. There are, for example, a growing number of alcohol arrest referral schemes being established in police-custody suites, following the drug-focused model. At the time of writing in April 2009, proposals have been announced to extend to alcohol the initiative to withdraw benefits from those who refuse treatment offers. Perhaps, then, the place to see convergence is not so much at the level of changes in state legislation but rather on the ground in emerging and developing strategies for the shaping and direction of behaviour. This idea fits very well, of course, with the ethos of the governmentality analytic (see Rose, 1999), as well as with the idea that regulation has become increasingly decentred and dispersed (Black, 2001).

Conclusion

In this chapter, I have presented the third and final part of a genealogy of the contemporary governance of the drug problem. It completes the story of how we have arrived where we are today. I will come to some points that follow from this account in due course. But before that, I want to address briefly a question concerning the status of the present by highlighting a famous warning from Foucault:

> One of the most harmful habits of contemporary thought ... is the analysis of the present as being precisely, in history, a present of rupture, of high point, of completion, or of a returning dawn ... the time we live in is not *the* unique or fundamental irruptive point in history where everything is completed and begun again.
>
> (Foucault, 1983: 206)

So whilst my genealogy is 'complete' in the sense that I have arrived at the present, this should not be taken to mean that I have necessarily arrived at a historical point of completion. Whether we are at a high point of neo-liberal governance, or in a period of transition, or even at the beginning of something new, are questions that cannot yet be answered in anything other than a speculative fashion. I will save my own speculations about the future for later chapters!

To conclude this chapter, I want, first of all, to summarize some key aspects of the argument I have put forward. I have suggested that with the unravelling of welfarist politics and the transition to neo-liberalism, the imagination and governance of the drug problem has also been transformed. From the latter half of the 1960s, the idea of certain drug users as threats or sources of risk to the wider community has become increasingly dominant and drug policy has concentrated on developing strategies and interventions to reduce these risks. In this way, we can understand the emergence of harm reduction and then of the current criminal justice focus as manifestations of the same underlying 'problematization'. At the heart of this problematization is a particular conception of drug users as rational calculating risk-takers who should be encouraged and urged to make responsible choices to reduce the risks they pose. Drug users are viewed as having the capacity to act autonomously but must do so prudentially.

We might add also that we can hear certain echoes in this period of earlier sections of the genealogy. I noted this in relation to public health, where the nineteenth-century ghost of Edwin Chadwick could be faintly heard at the tail-end of the twentieth century. Similarly, the criminal justice 'turn' from the 1980s to the present contains echoes of some aspects of the debate a century earlier about what should be done with criminal inebriates (Berridge, 2004a), a debate which culminated in the 1898 Inebriates Act (see Chapter 4). The lines of development behind the Drugs Act 2005 are thus complex, multi-faceted and long-running. This also reminds us of the important methodological point that 'new' strategies do not emerge by entirely effacing all traces of earlier approaches but rather through a messier process of jettisoning some components whilst refiguring and revising others.

Another methodological point I want to make here follows from the earlier discussion of the approach of Sparks and Douglas to a 'cultural theory of risk'. If we accept that the process of risk selection is one informed by, and rooted in, the values of specific cultures at specific points in time, it becomes obvious that this does not tell us what a risk-based drug policy might look like:

> Even if it is true ... that today major political arguments take place *on the terrain of risk*, it in no way follows that we can know in advance how those arguments will turn out, still less that they will turn out identically in different national-political settings ... We can, for this reason, no more deduce the contemporary condition of the penal realm from a totalizing idea such as 'the risk society' than we formerly could from an undifferentiated notion of 'capitalism', though both can be seen as crucial to its analysis.
>
> (Sparks, 2001: 161–62, emphasis in original)

By pointing to the 'strategic coherence' in this field that runs from the late 1960s to the present, I have merely unearthed the underlying generative structure in which the contemporary imagination and governance of the drug problem are based. To go further than this to explain how and why events have unfolded in the particular ways that they have requires a rather different exercise in what Loader and Sparks (2004) have called 'historical recovery'. In other words, that project would involve the detailed excavation of the 'swarming circumstances ... of the struggles, negotiations, actions, and decisions which are undertaken by those involved in the making and implementation of policy' (Garland, 1990: 285). In order to do this adequately, each of the three central 'empirical' chapters I have written here would require (at least) its own full-length book.

In the next chapter, I shift gears somewhat and move forward to a consideration of how we might apply regulation and governance perspectives to the drug problem. As I will explain, the purpose of this is not to set out a policy blueprint but rather to provide some frameworks and conceptual tools for the future development of policy. In doing so, I will also address further the question I raised above of how the potential fault-line underneath the 'great regulatory divide' presented by the 'return to inebriety' might play out in the future.

Chapter 6

Drugs as a regulation and governance problem

Whatever the origin of the UN Drug Treaties, and whatever the official rhetoric about their functions, the best way to look at them now is as religious texts. They have acquired a patina of intrinsic and unquestioned value and they have attracted a clique of true believers and proselytes to promote them. They pursue a version of Humankind for whom abstinence from certain drugs is dogma in the same way as other religious texts might prohibit certain foods or activities. The UN drug treaties thus form the basis of the international Drug Prohibition Church. Belonging to that Church has become an independent source of security, and fighting the Church's enemies has become an automatic source of virtue.

(Peter Cohen, drugs researcher, 2003)

If you are around in 2020, the chances are that you will see drugs prohibition replaced with a system of regulated and controlled markets. If Transform's timeline is right, by 2020 the criminal market will have been forced to relinquish its control of the drug trade and government regulation will be the norm once more. Users will no longer 'score' from unregulated dealers. They will buy their drugs from specialist pharmacists or licensed retailers. Or, for those with a clinical need, via a prescription.

(Transform Drug Policy Foundation, 2006)

I am increasingly convinced countries get the drug problem they deserve. Those that invest political capital – backed by adequate resources – in prevention, treatment and rehabilitation are rewarded with significantly lower rates of drug abuse ... Governments and societies must keep their nerve and avoid being swayed by misguided notions of tolerance. They must not lose sight of the fact that illicit drugs are dangerous – that is why the world agreed to restrict them.

(Antonio Maria Costa, Executive Director UNODC, 2007)

Introduction

This chapter is a departure from the previous three, as I turn to that most thorny of questions: what is to be done? Unlike Lenin when he famously posed the same question just over a century ago, I do not have a direct programme for change to set out here. Nor do I expect the current regime to be swept away by a revolution any time soon. My purpose here is slightly different. I want to explore how viewing this issue as a regulation and governance problem opens up new possibilities and options for change. So it is not a blueprint for action but instead a framework for developing new ideas about the possibilities for action. It is an attempt, in other words, at fresh thinking that goes beyond the debates about legalization, decriminalization and so on that have dominated the discourse of reformers for decades. I will say a bit more about those debates later on but first there is a theoretical and methodological issue to deal with.

When I presented an early version of some of the ideas in this chapter at a drug-policy conference, a colleague there expressed some polite incredulity that I might be talking in any practical way about policy matters in a book that relied in part on Foucauldian analysis. This is a familiar line of criticism, put most trenchantly and authoritatively perhaps by Habermas, notably in his *The Philosophical Discourse of Modernity* (Habermas, 1987; see also Habermas, 1986). What has become known as the Foucault–Habermas debate revolves around some complex issues (see Kelly, 1994) but I think Habermas's primary criticism boils down to this: Foucault's failure to ground his critique in an explicit set of normative values fatally undermines his critical project as it provides no basis for choosing alternative futures. I briefly addressed this argument in Chapter 1, including the well-known quote from Foucault (1991b: 84) in which he urges that 'the necessity of reform mustn't be allowed to become a form of blackmail serving to limit, reduce or halt the exercise of criticism' – indeed, the interview from which that quote is taken, published as 'Questions of Method', is a very useful account of his perspective on the nature and purpose of critical thought and analysis (see also Dean, 1994).

I see things quite differently from those who share Habermas's misgivings. In my view, the disturbing critical power of a Foucauldian approach lies precisely in its lack of anchoring in any particular normative position. It operates on a different plane, challenging and refusing the obviousness or necessity of the present but without having to be tied to any specific set of values. This can be an exhilarating and dazzling perspective when skilfully executed – the impact of work like *Histoire de la Folie* and *Discipline and Punish*, for example, still reverberates across the decades since their first publication in a manner that is exceptionally rare. I have attempted something along these lines in the preceding chapters, albeit in a more modest and limited way than Foucault's peerless *tours de force*, using the governmentality analytic as a tool for clearing the ground, revealing the historical contingency of fundamental concepts and ideas in the field, from 'addiction' through to the very notion of 'drugs'. It seems to me that it is an entirely legitimate and coherent strategy to accompany or follow a ground-clearing exercise of this kind by exploring different ways of thinking about and dealing with the particular matter at hand, a strategy which may or may not involve appeal to a normative position or a set of values. I do not see any inconsistency here. Indeed, in my view, the two are quite neatly complementary. As I explained in Chapter 1, I have adopted exactly this type of twin-track strategy in this book, supplementing the governmentality perspective with a regulatory one, drawing for the latter particularly on the approach to regulation developed by John Braithwaite and colleagues at the Australian National University over the past 20 years. So, to put it another way, having cleared the conceptual ground, I am turning in this chapter to a consideration of options and opportunities for future action.

I want to end these introductory remarks by saying a little more here about what is currently the most pervasive, and indeed most powerful, mode of drug-policy critique. I referred to this above as the arguments for legalization or decriminalization and these are useful shorthand labels for what is a familiar position. It is founded on the idea that the prohibition paradigm lies at the core of our contemporary difficulties in dealing with the 'drug problem'. The solution, from this perspective, is to scrap the drug laws and start afresh with a more rational and humane approach. For those with slightly broader vision, the target is reform not just of national drug laws but of the entire edifice of international drug control administered by the United Nations.

I have a great deal of sympathy for this line of argument. Indeed, it is very difficult to study drug policy for any length of time without coming to the conclusion eventually that the prohibition paradigm is fatally flawed and in fact causes more problems and more suffering than it alleviates or prevents. As I have now been researching in this area for about 15 years, I have certainly seen plenty of evidence for this! Nevertheless, despite this, I have some significant doubts about this approach. At the heart of my concern is a view that this way of identifying or describing the problem does not provide the analytic space necessary for finding and developing a good solution to it. This is somewhat ironic, of course, as most drug-law reform campaigners tend to identify themselves explicitly as focused on policy matters, rather than theoretical or philosophical ones. I think the fundamental difficulty is that the implicit analytical frame is a Hobbesian one which assumes that the solution to the problem must be located within a framework of state institutions (or supra-national institutions like the UN or EU to which states sign up).

I am rather pessimistic about the prospects of finding answers or solutions within this type of frame. And indeed, in my eyes at least, it is telling that one of the weakest parts of the drug-law reformers' case is when it comes to making concrete suggestions or proposals for what should be done after prohibition is dismantled. But I am not in fact pessimistic or nihilistic about the prospects for change and it is here that a regulation perspective comes in. Regulatory scholarship is based on a theoretically and conceptually sophisticated understanding of how regulation and governance actually operate in the real world built up through years of rich empirical research across diverse fields. In this chapter, I want to explore then how far we can get by framing the 'drug problem' as a regulatory and governance challenge and whether this approach may provide new conceptual tools for the construction of new policy directions. Of course, '"governance" is not synonymous with "good governance"' (Burris et al., 2008: 3), nor 'regulation' with 'good regulation'. Simply to identify something as a 'regulatory and governance challenge' does not lead automatically to the 'best' policy solution. Nevertheless, there is good evidence from the work of Braithwaite, Shearing and others to suggest that this type of approach has great potential, both intellectually and practically. As those two scholars, in particular, have demonstrated, the best work here proceeds not by ignoring or evading normative issues but by connecting them with explanatory theory through an ongoing and interactive process of 'iterated adjustment' (Braithwaite, 2000: 64–65).

In the main sections of this chapter, I am going to explore how some related but distinct approaches to regulation and governance might be applied to the analysis of drug policy. As well as the regulatory scholarship from the ANU 'School' led by Braithwaite that I have already mentioned, I will also draw on the closely related nodal governance approach developed by Clifford Shearing, Scott Burris and others. I will look as well at some of the global governance scholarship, including the work on the idea of global administrative law developed by Benedict Kingsbury and colleagues at the New York University School of Law. What all these approaches share in common is that they eschew state-led or state-centric approaches to understanding how politics and government actually work – the Hobbesian frame that I referred to above. This also articulates well with the governmentality perspective and its emphasis on examining 'political power beyond the state' (Rose and Miller, 1992; Rose, 1999), providing a further indication of the coherence within the twin-track analytical strategy I described above.

Regulation

Regulatory scholarship is diverse. Some strands adopt a narrow definition or conceptualization which views regulation primarily as steering through state laws and rules (e.g. Ogus, 1994; Black, 2002). Others take a much broader view, defining regulation as all attempts to steer the flow of events (e.g. Braithwaite, 2008). I incline towards the broader definition, as in my view it is the most fruitful analytically. For some, such a wide and capacious concept is too unwieldy and imprecise an idea to be of any use, either as an explanatory or a normative tool. But I think it is precisely this breadth which renders it such a powerful framework as it allows and encourages us to see the similarities in the task of regulation in diverse fields. So, just to take the work of Braithwaite as an example, he has used his research in areas as wide-ranging as coal mine safety (Braithwaite, 1985), restorative justice with offenders (Braithwaite, 2002) and corporate tax compliance (Braithwaite, 2005a) to develop a theory of responsive regulation applicable across not only these but also other fields. Empirical work in one field has shed light on research in others. It is very difficult to imagine how this might have happened without deploying the cross-cutting regulatory approach. Normally, tax specialists, criminologists and health and safety experts do not talk to each other. For regulation scholars like Braithwaite, such cross-boundary and cross-disciplinary conversations are at the heart of their work. Indeed, one of his more general claims is that regulatory scholarship is part of a new paradigm which is transforming the social sciences by sweeping across existing disciplines (Braithwaite, 2000).

So how might regulatory theory and concepts help us in the area of drug policy? In Chapter 1, I referred to the groundbreaking book *Global Business Regulation* by Braithwaite and Drahos (2000) in which they draw an important and original lesson from the history of regulation in this area. They argue that rather than seeing the regulatory regime for illicit drugs as a 'special' or unique case, it should be viewed instead as simply one regulatory branch that has been created out of a wider system for the regulation of psychoactive and therapeutic substances. In fact, they identify at least five regulatory branches (Braithwaite and Drahos, 2000: 360–98):

- a (globalized) illicit drugs regime;
- a (globalizing) prescription drugs regime;
- national non-prescription ('over-the-counter') drugs regimes;
- national alcohol regimes;
- national tobacco regimes.

They argue that what is required is an 'integrated explanation of both illicit and licit drug regulation' (Braithwaite, 2003: 17). This insight has some radical implications. It invites a much broader and more thoroughgoing rethink of how we deal with the 'drug problem'. Rather than just drawing comparisons with, for example, alcohol or tobacco, as many drug-law reformers and campaigners do, it opens up for consideration and comparison the entire panoply of substances that we consume for more or less therapeutic and/or psychoactive purposes. Pausing for a moment, I am aware that the possibilities and options for change here may seem overwhelmingly large. What does it actually mean to develop an 'integrated explanation' of these different regulatory branches? Can we really produce an account that is able to range so widely without ending up as just a superficial descriptive picture?

One set of answers to these questions involves thinking about how we might redraw the regulatory map with an entirely different structure of branches – starting from scratch, in other words, unconstrained by our contemporary notions about how particular substances 'ought' to be regulated, drawing on our awareness of the historical contingency of the current state of affairs. This broadening out of the vista for reform is significant, as I have already suggested, but nevertheless remains a rather abstract project. How, for example, should we choose the principles to guide such a refiguring of the regulatory branches?

A clue here is to be found in the rather unlikely place of an empirical study of tax avoidance by John Braithwaite (2005a) in which he compares practices of 'aggressive tax planning' in New York and Australia. He situates this research in the wider context of questions about the regulation of competitive markets in a globalized or globalizing economy. The study is relevant here in two respects. First, in substantive terms, the question of taxation is itself of central importance to debates about alternative systems for regulating psychoactive substances, as David Courtwright astutely observes:

> For most of the last five hundred years, officials have regulated drug commodities by means of taxation. (Monopolies on production and sale, run by the government or auctioned to private parties, amounted to indirect taxation.) Governments imposed substantial taxes to raise revenue, and sometimes to limit consumption. US duties on imported smoking opium ran as high as 182 per cent ad valorem; the result was large-scale smuggling. The same thing happened with liquor excises and moonshining. Any controlled legalization regime would entail some degree of criminal activity. The heavier the taxes and the more numerous the controls, the greater the incentives to smuggle, divert, and bribe; the fewer the taxes and controls, the more widespread the drug use. Policy is about these trade-offs.
>
> (Courtwright, 2004: 443–44)

So insights about tax system integrity and the maximization of tax compliance need to be part of the debate here about the construction of new regulatory approaches. An obvious example which illustrates this point is the problem of cigarette smuggling which is partly rooted in the fact that levels of duty levied on cigarettes vary quite significantly between countries (see van Duyne, 2003). For those unfamiliar with tax compliance issues, I have found John Braithwaite's (2005a) book *Markets in Vice, Markets in Virtue*, which I have already mentioned, and the useful collection *Taxing Democracy* edited by Valerie Braithwaite (2003) to be excellent introductions.

But much more significant, in my view, is the second point of relevance of Braithwaite's (2005a) study. With characteristic acuity, he identifies the generic question which his research on the problem of tax avoidance illustrates: how can we develop strategies for flipping 'markets in vice' into 'markets in virtue'? By 'vice' and 'virtue' he means simply those things regarded by large sections of the relevant community or society as 'bads' or 'goods' (Braithwaite, 2005a). He argues that this has become a more general and pressing problem in recent decades, that is in the era of what he calls regulatory capitalism (see Chapter 5), because markets have become more efficient producers of vice: 'Competition in a globally networked economy creates massive problems of markets in vice' (Braithwaite, 2005a: 12). In other words, the extension and intensification of globalizing processes in recent decades has heightened the problems associated with the circulation of illicit commodities (on the impact of globalization on the illegal drug situation, see Seddon, 2008a). He suggests that the most difficult policy domains are those where there is a 'complex tension between the market in virtue and vice' (2005a: 7). In some areas this is not the case – child pornography, for example, is simply a market in vice and therefore more straightforward to deal with in policy terms. If we look at psychoactive and pharmaceutical substances as a single master category, we can see clearly that there are complex tensions between the potential for producing 'bads' and 'goods'. I summarize some examples to illustrate this point in Table 6.1. I should add, as Braithwaite is at pains to point out, that the process of deciding what counts as a 'vice' or 'virtue' is a contested one. Not everyone will agree with all my claims in this table but I am simply using it to illustrate the idea that there are some tensions between 'bads' and 'goods' in this area (even if we cannot easily agree on exactly what these are!). Deciding these matters should, Braithwaite argues, be settled in as deliberative and

Table 6.1 Selected psychoactive substances: vices and virtues

Substance	Vices	Virtues
Cannabis	Distribution can be associated with criminal networks Heavy use linked with mental-health problems for small number of vulnerable individuals. Regular use linked to some physical health problems	Symptomatic relief for sufferers of multiple sclerosis (and other conditions) Recreational pleasure
Heroin	Production linked to problems of poverty, insurgency and insecurity in main source country (Afghanistan) Distribution (in transition and consumer countries) associated with criminal networks Regular use linked to physical health problems (including deaths through overdose) Regular use associated with involvement in property crime	Effective painkiller in medical practice Recreational pleasure for some
Ketamine	Possible health risks, especially if combined with depressants (e.g. alcohol)	Used as an anaesthetic in medical and veterinary practice Recreational pleasure
Rohypnol	Possible links to sexual assault (the 'date rape' drug) Physical dependence and withdrawal difficulties	Used as a tranquillizer to treat sleep disorders

democratic a way as possible. I will return to this issue at the end of this chapter.

So clearly this area represents one of Braithwaite's 'complex policy domains' (2005a: 7) where regulatory strategies need to be crafted to max-imize 'goods' whilst at the same time minimizing 'bads'. This, I suggest, provides a more concrete way forward for thinking about how to redraw our regulatory map. But however radical or imaginative we might be in execut-ing that task, it remains an approach largely fixated on state (or inter-state) systems and regimes. As I argued at the beginning of this chapter, such a perspective fails to grasp the complexity and plurality of contemporary reg-ulation and governance. Here, Braithwaite's study comes into its own. Drawing on his empirical work on tax avoidance, he goes on to set out some general design principles for flipping markets from vice to virtue. A short-ened summary of the principles is presented in Table 6.2, drawing primarily on his later reformulation and recrafting of the principles in his recent book *Regulatory Capitalism*.

Now, it should be emphasized at this point that this is 'no more than a menu of sensible options to be considered for the task of crafting a con-textually attuned integrated strategy' (Braithwaite, 2008: 60) and not all of them will necessarily be relevant to our particular field. Indeed, central to the approach is the idea that specific regulatory strategies need to be devel-oped as part of a detailed and grounded process of empirical research and development activity. What is revelatory, in my view, about this way of proceeding is that it provides in effect a 'theory of transition' which can plausibly explain how we go from where we are now to a radically different

Table 6.2 General design principles for flipping markets in vice to markets in virtue

Design principles
Do not place too much reliance in any single strand of a web of controls
Regulate in a collaborative and conversational way
Organize controls into a responsive regulatory pyramid
Organize regulatory tools in response to problems rather than problems around tools from a standard tool-kit
Enact laws based on principles that technically untrained people can understand
Connect laws to natural systems people use in their lives as opposed to contrived artificial systems created for administrative convenience
Experiment with meta regulation (regulated self-regulation)
Enact heavy penalties for promoters of vice, as opposed to perpetrators of vice
Pay bounties to private detectors of corporate vice
Educate consumers and investors for commission suspicion
Experiment with restorative justice near the base of enforcement pyramids
Redesign competition policy to protect and strengthen standards of professional ethics
Certify large private- and public-sector organizations for continuous improvement in reducing vice and promoting virtue of specified kinds

future. It would involve a process of concrete incremental change conducted in the spirit of Dorf and Sabel's (1998) evidence-based 'democratic experimentalism' (Braithwaite, 2008: 28; see also O'Malley, 2008). Most significantly, it moves us away from the idea that only a 'big bang' revolution in the international drug control system can solve the problem, an idea that I think in practice continually stops the drug-policy reform movement in its tracks.

Some readers may still be sceptical at this point. Can Braithwaite's design principles, developed after all in a very different context, really be translated into practical action? Let me give a couple of examples to persuade the sceptics. One of the options from Braithwaite's menu is to 'experiment with restorative justice near the base of enforcement pyramids'. Restorative justice is closely connected with the theory of responsive regulation that I briefly mentioned earlier (see Ayres and Braithwaite, 1992; Braithwaite, 2002). The basic principle is that 'regulators should be responsive to the conduct of those they seek to regulate in deciding whether a more or less interventionist response is needed' (Braithwaite, 2008: 88). The famous (within regulation circles, at least!) regulatory pyramid summarizes the essence of the model (Ayres and Braithwaite, 1992) – see Figure 6.1 for a basic generic example. The idea is that we begin at the base of the pyramid with the 'most

Figure 6.1 Generic example of a regulatory pyramid.

restorative dialogue-based approach we can craft for securing compliance' (Braithwaite, 2008: 88). Only when these efforts fail should we move, reluctantly, up to the next level of the pyramid. As we progress up the pyramid, interventions become more and more punitive and demanding. At each level, the knowledge that we can escalate up the pyramid is part of what helps to secure compliance. When we reach a level where reform or repair starts to be achieved, we should de-escalate, moving back down towards the base again to reward that positive response. The pyramid is in essence a method for solving the 'puzzle of when to punish and when to persuade' (Braithwaite, 2008: 88). So how might we deploy this approach in relation to drugs? I think there are a number of areas of enforcement where this might be applicable but perhaps one of the most obvious is the policing of cannabis use by young people which, in Britain at least, is currently dogged by uncertainty and a lack of clarity of purpose (see May et al., 2002, 2007). The result is that police practice can often be inconsistent and ineffective – indeed, the legal framework itself has been vacillating as the cannabis question has become a political football in the UK. The crafting of a regulatory pyramid to be applied here could provide a much more constructive strategy, avoiding unnecessary and damaging criminalization but whilst providing a transparent, principled and consistent approach.

My second example takes the principle of 'experimenting with meta regulation' as a starting point. I should first explain the term. In brief, meta regulation arises when direct central regulation becomes too difficult or impossible, often because of limited resources. Instead, meta regulatory strategies focus on encouraging, enhancing and monitoring self-regulation – regulated self-regulation. A superb example of the applicability of the principle to the area of drugs is the study by Peter Grabosky and colleagues of the policing of illicit synthetic drugs (Cherney et al., 2005, 2006). This category refers to substances like ecstasy, amphetamine-type stimulants and methamphetamine which are manufactured through chemical processes rather than relying on harvested crops like opium. One of the distinctive features of the manufacture and distribution of these synthetic drugs is that they have what Grabosky and colleagues term a 'double supply side system' which relies on 'diversions from licit pharmaceutical and chemical trade, as well as illicit manufacture' (Cherney et al., 2006: 373). This poses a major challenge to a traditional direct enforcement approach as 'it is the interface between licit environments and illicit production ... that compounds efforts to control illicit synthetic drugs, given their manufacture is reliant upon the existence of lawful enterprise' (2006: 373). They go on to describe how the mix of policing strategies that have emerged 'epitomize meta-regulation' (2006: 379), relying on a balance of actions which seek to co-opt and enhance the self-regulatory capacity of a range of external agencies, including licit pharmaceutical manufacturers and retailers. Their account also reinforces the importance of an 'integrated explanation of both illicit and licit drug regulation' (Braithwaite, 2003: 17) that I have already discussed and which has been a theme of earlier chapters.

Another key finding from the study is that these emerging policing strategies are increasingly networked, with the police acting as *brokers*, 'co-opting and forming alliances with intermediaries, third parties and non-state orderings by using different instruments of governance' (Cherney et al., 2006: 381). It is to this matter of networked governance that I will shortly turn in the next section. I conclude this brief sketch of regulatory perspectives by underlining what I think is a central point here. Psychoactive and therapeutic substances can be usefully understood as commodities within a global marketplace – the challenge is to develop regulatory strategies which minimize the 'bads' and maximize the 'goods' associated with their production, distribution and consumption. Insights from regulatory scholarship can be applied to address this question.

Nodal governance

Nodal governance is a way of looking at the world, an analytical lens, which has been developed in recent years as part of an attempt to get to grips with some fundamental changes that have taken place in the nature and functioning of governance (Burris et al., 2005, 2008). Put simply, according to this perspective, our conceptual tools for studying and understanding how power and rule are actually exercised in the real world have dramatically failed to keep pace with these transformations in governance. This failure has, in turn, hindered our ability to develop better forms of governance. The contention is that new and different ways of conceptualizing and describing governance can help us to deliver better results and outcomes.

Governance is defined within this approach as 'the management of the course of events in a social system' (Burris et al., 2005: 30). There is a clear overlap here, of course, with the definition of 'regulation' I gave earlier and these two approaches are complementary. Indeed, Braithwaite has accommodated the nodal governance critique of responsive regulation into his more recent work and has gone on to develop notions of networked governance in some imaginative directions (Braithwaite, 2008). This coherence between the two is perhaps unsurprising, as many of the leading nodal governance theorists – notably Clifford Shearing and Peter Drahos – have had strong links with Braithwaite's regulation group at the ANU.

The idea of nodal governance builds on two rather different intellectual sources. First, and most obviously, it draws on Manuel Castells' work on the rise of the 'network society' (Castells, 1996, 2000). Castells' basic thesis is that the network has become the basic unit of contemporary society. He locates this development in the context of the coming of the 'information age', arguing that our key social and economic structures and activities are now increasingly organized around information-based networks. His trilogy of books on *The Information Age* is an inspiring exploration of the way these networks are transforming society (Castells, 1996, 1997, 1998). Second, it builds on ideas developed by the neo-liberal guru Friedrich Hayek in another famous trilogy which explores the creation of order in complex social systems (Hayek, 1944, 1960, 1973–79). The central Hayekian insight that the nodal governance scholars draw on is that particular governance systems are highly complex and generally ungraspable by central state authorities. Hayek uses this, of course, as an argument against socialist state planning which he suggests is doomed to failure because of this fundamental problem of the difficulty of understanding how local social systems work. His analysis provides a brilliant account of the challenges of governance. He goes on to argue, and here is where nodal governance scholars part company with him, that markets provide the best and most effective mechanism for bringing order to complex systems. Hayek's faith in market-based solutions was hugely influential on New Right politicians in the 1980s on both sides of the Atlantic. A famous story has Margaret Thatcher slamming down a copy of his *The Constitution of Liberty* on the table at a late 1970s Conservative policy seminar and announcing 'this is what we believe'!

We live then in an era of networked governance in which the management of the course of events tends to operate through and across networks. At the heart of the accounts of both Castells and Hayek is the idea that knowledge and information are central to these new forms of governance. Social-science research and theorizing on networks largely focuses on the ways in which information and knowledge flow around them but from a governance perspective, this is only part of the story as 'at some point in the network society the flow of information and communication is translated into action' (Burris et al., 2005: 37). It is here that a stronger focus on the nature of nodes is so critical:

> The theory of nodal governance is intended to enrich network theory by focusing attention on and bringing more clarity to the internal characteristics of nodes and thus to the analysis of how power is actually created and exercised within a social system.
>
> (Burris, 2004: 341)

Nodes then are not just relays within networks which serve only to transmit information from one point to the next. Rather, they are institutional sites where knowledge, capacity and resources are mobilized for governance. Nodes have four essential characteristics:

- a way of thinking (*mentalities*) about the matters that the node has emerged to govern;
- a set of methods (*technologies*) for exerting influence over the course of events at issue;

- *resources* to support the operation of the node and the exertion of influence; and
- a structure that enables the directed mobilization of resources, mentalities and technologies over time (*institutions*).

(Burris et al., 2005: 37–38, emphases in original)

Whilst sharing these characteristics, nodes can take on a wide range of forms, from a street gang to a department in a corporate firm (Burris et al., 2005: 38). A node can be part of a single integrated network, or linked to nodes across multiple networks, or it can be what is called a 'superstructural node' which ties together and mobilizes nodes from multiple networks in order to achieve a common goal (2005: 38). Within this framework, state agencies or institutions do not have any privileged analytic or conceptual status. They are not, in other words, a distinct category of node but rather an 'internal characteristic of some nodes' (Burris, 2004: 344). It is an empirical question in any given network of governance whether the 'state' is predominant or not.

So how might we apply the nodal governance approach to the area of drug policy? Following Burris (2004: 344–53), I think there are two principal ways in which we can do this that I will briefly explore here: first, through nodal mapping of system governance; second, by experimentation with microgovernance strategies for 'weak' actors. A good way to illustrate the first of these is the story of TRIPS that Burris et al. (2005) describe. TRIPS was a multilateral agreement made in the 1990s on minimum standards of intellectual property protection which is binding on all WTO members. The details of this are not relevant here but TRIPS was an agreement which greatly favoured the US and especially its pharmaceutical industry. But rather than seeing the achievement of TRIPS as simply a story of US hegemonic power coercing weaker countries into agreement, Burris and colleagues provide a nuanced and sophisticated account of how companies like Pfizer acted as governing nodes in the TRIPS story in order to achieve their objectives. Pfizer mobilized networks and created superstructural nodes in order to steer events towards the TRIPS agreement. State agencies were not the dominant influences in this process at all, although they were critical nodes within the assemblages and networks involved. In effect, Burris and colleagues account of the TRIPS story is an exercise in mapping the complex nodal arrangements involved in this field. The nodal governance lens brings into focus not just the actors involved in governance, as in more conventional approaches which emphasize forms and institutions, but rather a more precise and detailed view of exactly how power is exercised. As a heuristic device, it raises a series of questions. What are the governing nodes? How are they connected and networked with other nodes? How do the internal characteristics of different governing nodes (mentalities, technologies, resources, institutions) affect their governing efficacy? Through such a mapping, and the insights that flow from it, we can begin to think about innovative ways of reconfiguring the governance system. It provides a starting point, in other words, for radically rethinking governance. Methods for nodal mapping have started to be developed, notably by Dupont (2006) and Dupont and Wood (2006).

Nodal mapping is a tool that can potentially be applied right across the drug regulatory system. For example, the recent Political Declaration on Drugs from the UN Commission on Narcotic Drugs, which has set the general direction for the next decade of international drug policy, was the product of months of international negotiation and diplomacy culminating in ten days of intensive activity at UN headquarters in Vienna in March 2009. A detailed mapping of exactly how power was exercised during this complex process might enhance drug-law reformers' understanding of how they could more effectively exert influence to shape the course of events. By viewing themselves as governing nodes, that is as sites for mobilizing relevant knowledge, capacity and resources, campaigning and advocacy strategies could then be focused on networking with other nodes, creating superstructural nodes, connecting networks together and so on. No doubt supranational bodies (like UNODC) and national governments would be critical nodes within these networks but not sitting at the top of a 'pyramid of power and influence' (Burris et al., 2005: 47). Equally, the nodal mapping tool could be deployed to generate a picture of how particular local drug-control policies and practices operate, or, rather, how power is exercised within local governance systems. What are the governing nodes? How are they networked to other nodes? How do the internal characteristics of different nodes shape the functioning of the network(s) of governance? Valverde (1998: 10) gives a brief but interesting example of this kind of local mapping in relation to the governance of alcohol in a specific setting (an American urban hospital). She describes the multiple regimes operating in one site as indicative of what she terms 'regulatory anarchy'. I see this instead as illustrating the nodal and polycentric nature of governance.

So nodal mapping is an important heuristic device. It can document precisely and clearly how power is distributed and exercised in specific systems of governance. And it does so in ways that do not rely on hierarchical or state-centred models or on the maintenance of distinctions between the public and private realms. By mapping in this way and understanding better how governance really works, the opportunities for change and reform can become much clearer.

The second potential application of the nodal governance approach is quite different and involves what has been called microgovernance (Burris, 2004). This starts from the premise that one of the problems faced by 'weak' actors is often that they experience a 'governance deficit' linked to their limited access to effective governing nodes. 'Strong' actors, in contrast, are much more likely to be able to access multiple nodes through which they can achieve governance objectives. Accordingly, one strategy for empowering 'weak' actors is to help them to create and sustain new nodal arrangements through which their collective knowledge, capacity and resources can be mobilized. A key assumption here is that such groups possess the capacity to govern but lack a 'node in which this diffused capacity could be coordinated and mobilised' (Burris et al., 2005: 50).

Drawing on this theoretical argument, Clifford Shearing and colleagues have been developing over the past dozen or so years a pioneering model of local security governance in very poor communities in South Africa known as the Zwelethemba model. Zwelethemba – a Xhosa word meaning place of hope – was the name of the site where the model was first developed in 1997. My description of the model draws on the various accounts Shearing and his collaborators have published (e.g. Shearing and Wood, 2003; Cartwright and Shearing, 2004; Burris et al., 2005; Froestad and Shearing, 2007). In essence, the Zwelethemba experiment was an attempt to build new nodal arrangements that might bring together and harness local community capacity to articulate common interests and to promote more effective governance of security and justice. This was in a context in which the governance gap or deficit for the poor was exceptionally stark. These new nodal arrangements, known as Peace Committees, shared the four characteristics of governing nodes that I described above:

- *Mentalities.* Participants were required to sign up to a Code of Good Practice which included renouncing violence and agreeing to operate within the boundaries of South African law. They also shared the basic idea that the primary purpose of the Peace Committees was to work co-operatively in order to 'create a better tomorrow', rather than looking backwards and assigning blame.
- *Technologies.* At the heart of the model was the simple technology of the community gathering, a form which had a particular cultural resonance. Gatherings focused on two aims: peace-making (solving local disputes in ways that allow disputants to move forward amicably) and peace-building (the broader goal of community development in order to prevent future disputes and problems).
- *Resources.* Initially, Peace Committees relied on public or philanthropic funding. Each gathering attracted a payment, part of which was divided amongst participants and organizers and part of which was assigned to a local development fund controlled by the Committee (a small amount is also set aside to cover administrative running costs). Some Committees have gone on to earn public funding on the basis that they are delivering important public goods.
- *Institutions.* The Peace Committee provided the institutional framework within which the model could operate. Committees were also linked up to an NGO called the Community Peace Programme which provided administrative and other support.

The Zwelethemba model has subsequently spread to a number of other sites in South Africa and has also been tested out in Rosario in Argentina. How might innovative microgovernance strategies of this kind be relevant to our concerns with the 'drug problem'? I think there is considerable scope here for experimenting with adapting the Zwelethemba model as a means of empowering local communities facing neighbourhood drug (and related) problems. Like the communities in Zwelethemba and elsewhere in South Africa, there are localities in Britain where residents can feel very unsafe and insecure, feelings to which drug dealing, drug-using behaviour and other drug-related activities can contribute significantly. Establishing in places like this a version of a Peace Committee, developed and run following the Zwelethemba design principles, could be a fruitful line of 'democratic experimentalism' (Dorf and Sabel, 1998). Another possible experimental site could be focused on the various 'vulnerable groups' (street drinkers, rough sleepers, drug users, people who beg) that often occupy public space in places such as city centres. Such groups can suffer high levels of victimization, ranging from serious violence to low-level harassment and hassle. They often participate in a 'street culture' which is usually seen by welfare professionals as a barrier to helping them. But perhaps it contains a kernel of something much more positive – if these weak informal networks could be focused into a governing node, the collective capacity of such groups might be harnessed for the more effective governance of security. The creation in a city or town centre of an institution like a Peace Committee for these groups could potentially be an effective mechanism for the re-ordering of nodal arrangements along Zwelethemba lines. There are no doubt also many other possibilities for experiments with microgovernance strategies in this area, limited only by the imaginations of researchers and community activists.

The nodal governance perspective has a great deal to offer then, both as a framework for better understanding how the governance of drug problems operates, from the local to the global, and also as a tool for constructing innovative new approaches. As an analytical lens, it opens up two main lines of direction and possibility in connection with drugs: i) nodal mapping as a method to help describe the complex polycentric systems of governance operating across different levels and sites; ii) experimentation with micro-governance strategies for the empowerment of 'weak' actors suffering from governance deficits. I now turn to another set of perspectives on governance.

Global governance

One of the distinctive features of the drug-control system is that not only is it international but this has been so for around 100 years, going back to that famous meeting in Shanghai in 1909 (see Chapter 4). The global character of this system means that we can potentially consider it through the lens of the growing literature on the nature of global governance. There are lots of different strands within this literature and I am going to focus here primarily on one only. There are other lines of enquiry that might be fruitful too. But first I should define what is meant by the idea of global governance. My starting point is a useful contribution by Dingwerth and Pattberg (2006). Building on Rosenau's (1995: 13) influential definition ('systems of rule at all levels of human activity – from the family to the international organization – in which the pursuit of goals through the exercise of control has transnational repercussions'), they identify four central features of the concept of global governance:

1 It does not privilege analytically the place of nation-states but rather recognizes the range of non-state actors that may be involved (*global governance as multi-actor*).
2 It sees global governance as something which operates at, and across, multiple levels, from the local up to the global (*global governance as multi-level*).
3 It rejects the notion that any single logic or driving force lies behind it (*global governance as plural and multi-purpose*).
4 It does not locate the source of authority and legitimacy solely in nation-states (*global governance as based on plural and multiple sources of authority*).

A key idea in this literature is that the emergence of the concept of global governance has been driven by fundamental changes in the nature of world politics and governance, as the expansion and intensification of global interconnectedness more generally ('globalization') has transformed the world in which we live. Traditional approaches within the discipline of International Relations are no longer fit for purpose as tools for describing contemporary transnational governance regimes. So rather than looking solely at how states relate to each other and the role of supra-national bodies, the global governance perspective provides a framework which can better describe and explain how power actually operates. A general implication here for the drug field is that we need to move beyond simply looking at the United Nations and the three international drug-control treaties of 1961, 1971 and 1988 which provide the architecture for the global prohibition regime. Nor can we just look at the domestic drug laws enacted by the 150 or more nation-state signatories to these treaties. Instead, we need to understand global drug governance as *multi-actor, multi-level, multi-purpose* and *multi-source*. In other words, the global character of drug control needs to be grasped as a complex global governance phenomenon rather than simply as a matter of international relations in which the sovereign nation-state is the basic unit of analysis.

How then can we begin to get to grips with this complexity in relation to drugs? There are a series of questions we might ask that are prompted by the global governance framework, questions about actors, institutions, interactions and so on (see Biermann and Pattberg, 2008). And in answering these questions we need to be prepared to sweep across levels (from the local to the global) and to look beyond the nation-state. This is, in other words, a mapping exercise, similar in certain respects to the idea of nodal mapping described above, but using a different lens for viewing the governance terrain which brings different features into focus.

In an attempt to concretize all this a little further, I will turn now to one specific strand within the global governance literature that I think has some particularly useful lessons for us here. Benedict Kingsbury and colleagues at the New York University School of Law have been exploring in recent years how globalizing processes and the emergence of global governance are transforming international and public law (see Kingsbury et al., 2005; Krisch and Kingsbury, 2006; Kingsbury, 2009). Their central thesis is that:

> We are witnessing the emergence of a 'global administrative space': a space in which the strict dichotomy between domestic and international has largely broken down, in which administrative functions are performed in often complex interplays between officials and institutions on different levels, and in which regulation may be highly effective despite its predominantly non-binding forms.
>
> (Krisch and Kingsbury, 2006: 1)

They argue that this transformation is raising important new questions about accountability, not least because of the prominent roles for non-state actors in many areas. If the ideas of 'administration' and 'administrative space' seem a little obscure to some readers, Krisch and Kingsbury (2006: 2) helpfully clarify by referring to the 'regulatory governance of global markets'. This of course is at the heart of the governance challenge presented by the drug problem. So what is this emerging 'global administrative space'? Kingsbury's account is rich, complex and sophisticated – the website of the Global Administrative Law project based at NYU Law School contains dozens of working papers, articles and reports – but I draw three key ideas from it:

- much global regulatory governance can be viewed as administration;
- this administrative activity does not take place at neatly separated levels (private, local, national, inter-state);
- by operating at multiple sites and across multiple levels, it can be understood as forming a 'global administrative space' in which the generation, interpretation and application of rules are conducted through a complex array of networks, partnerships and institutions.

So how might we use this approach in our study and analysis of drug policy? In terms of basic descriptive work, it provides a framework for holding in view at the same time the entire drug-control edifice, from UN conventions, to domestic laws at national level, to local enforcement practices. We can develop an analytical description of the operation of the system which can sweep across levels as required. The pioneering collection edited by Dorn (1999), entitled *Regulating European Drug Problems*, which has been rather neglected by drug researchers to date, attempted something of this kind in its account of an emerging new regulatory space for addressing drug problems in European states. The contributors map what they term a new 'control space' in which administrative, civil law and criminal law measures intertwine and cut across local, municipal, member-state and EU levels. Drawing on the conceptual and theoretical tools of the global administrative law approach, the preliminary mapping work contained in Dorn's collection could be considerably extended and refined.

One of the interesting aspects of this approach is that it includes the examination of the ways in which *non-criminal* measures in particular can be used in drug control. It offers some potential in this way for extending their deployment and for the minimizing of the use of criminal law in this sphere. In other words, it may provide a rigorous, technical and detailed step-by-step route to the creation of strategies and practices for global drug governance that are not rooted in criminalization. In the concluding chapter of the Dorn collection mentioned above, he explores (with Simone White) how this might be undertaken. A selective summary is provided in Table 6.3 to illustrate this.

Dorn and White (1999: 278–87) also pay particular attention to the development of appropriate safeguards and standards applicable to administrative action, identifying four key principles:

(i)   the right to a fair and public procedure, at least on appeal;
(ii) the appropriate standards of evidence required for administrative decision-making, when contested;
(iii) proportionality, especially in relation to outcomes of administrative determinations (e.g. suspensions of rights, administrative sanctions);
(iv) avoidance of the prospect of double or triple jeopardy.

(Dorn and White, 1999: 278)

This is a real strength of the global administrative law approach which focuses sharply on such issues in the emerging 'global administrative space', reminding us of the need to ensure that any transformations in the drug-control system are compatible with, and indeed enhance, human rights and justice. Global administrative law scholars have devoted considerable attention to this question and to the elaboration of tools and mechanisms for ensuring this (see, for example, Krisch and Kingsbury, 2006: 3–5). Specific attention has been paid to matters of accountability (Krisch, 2006; Ferejohn, 2007; Dyzenhaus, 2008) and transparency (Hale, 2008) which are essential components of 'good' governance.

Table 6.3 Selected administrative measures to tackle drug problems

Level	Measures
Manufacture, distribution	• Withdrawal of commercial licences for commercial activities that are 'cover' for trafficking-related activities
	• Requirements to know trading partners and customers (record-keeping, reporting suspicious transactions)
	• Including all income in income tax assessments, regardless of source (illegal, 'grey', etc.)
	• Obligations for transport companies (airlines, railways, ferries)
	• Regulations for chemical manufacturers (in relation to potential precursors)
	• Information exchange between administrative agencies and with criminal law agencies
Nuisance	• Urban planning and licensing of premises
	• Controls on use of residential housing
	• Powers to suspend commercial rights for owners/managers of premises (commercial and residential) which permit nuisances
	• Controls over use of public space

Source: Dorn and White (1999)

So global governance perspectives can help us to grasp the global character of the drug trade and of the drug-control system. They provide a set of concepts and a framework for mapping this complexity. The growing body of scholarship on the idea of global administrative law offers some particularly useful analytical tools, not only for this mapping but also for the development of new practical approaches which emphasize civil and administrative measures rather than reliance on the criminal law.

Conclusions

In the introduction to this chapter, I was at pains to stress that I do not have ready answers to the question of what is to be done about the drug problem. Some readers no doubt took this as weasel words designed to avoid admitting that in fact I have nothing of practical import to say. I hope that in the main body of this chapter I have begun to persuade my more sceptical readers that that is not the case. In setting out a framework for developing new ideas, I have in effect outlined an agenda for research and development rather than a programme for action. But I do believe that this agenda has the potential to contribute to radical change in this area.

Let me bring together here the main contours of my argument. My central foundational thesis has been that there is much to be gained by viewing the 'drug problem' as a regulatory and governance problem. In making that case, I have considered how three particular approaches to understanding regulation and governance might be utilized in such a project. I think that this offers the most productive route to the future development of better approaches and strategies for dealing with the 'drug problem'. As I argued in the introduction, existing modes of drug-policy critique are flawed in their framing of the problem and consequently in the way they go about creating solutions.

The three approaches to regulation and governance that I have examined in this chapter share three key ideas:

- we need to look 'beyond the state', decentring it both in our analyses and in our prescriptions for action;
- we need to look 'beyond the law', as managing the course of events requires a much wider range of tools than just legal instruments;
- we need to understand governance as networked and polycentric, operating in multiple sites and across different levels.

So how should my research and development agenda be progressed? I suggest that the way forward needs to be both *incremental* and *experimental*. It needs to be *incremental* because we are talking about the transformation of a complex global system of governance – it cannot simply be replaced wholesale with a new system all at once. This, as I argued in the introduction to this chapter, is one of the weaknesses of much of the drug-law reform movement. Step-by-step changes may feel less heroic but they can accumulate eventually into radical transformation. It needs to be *experimental* because there are no ready-made off-the-shelf solutions. At each step, new ideas need to be tested out in a strategy of evidence-based 'democratic experimentalism' (Dorf and Sabel, 1998), or 'experiments in government' as O'Malley (2008) puts it (for a drug policy example, see Savary et al., 2009). O'Malley's (2008) recent paper is particularly interesting here as it attempts to construct an argument for using the governmentality analytic to pursue a strategy of experimentalism, tying together the two components of my analytical approach in this book. For O'Malley, the key here is the idea of 'strategic knowledge' which he takes from Foucault:

> Strategic knowledge in this sense I interpret to be the building up of a knowledge – a diagnosis – of the ways in which existing government formulates its truths, and links these truths to specific programs of government whereby problems are to be named and resolved. It also involves an understanding of the governmental techniques whereby these effects are to be achieved, of the kinds of subjects that are to be formed, of what will be a 'successful outcome' of the program, and so on.
>
> (O'Malley, 2008: 455)

He argues that we can build up and utilize strategic knowledge of this kind not just in the analysis of existing governmental programmes but also in appraising potential alternative futures: 'If governmentality provides a technique for the diagnosis of existing government, then it can become an analytical resource for the development of alternative forms of governance that minimize domination' (O'Malley, 2008: 456). I think this is an important argument for my purposes as it not only draws together regulatory and governmentality frameworks but also supports both incrementalism and experimentalism as fruitful strategies for change. At this point, a significant question raised earlier resurfaces. To what purposes or goals should 'good' governance aim? What values should it promote or embody? What yardstick should we use for measuring and evaluating governance processes, institutions and outcomes? O'Malley refers in the quotation above to minimizing domination, a notion which contains an echo of Braithwaite and Pettit's (1990) famous argument for the maximization of dominion as the proper goal of government. For my own part, I favour the promotion of social justice, the upholding of human rights and the enhancement of aspects of well-being and human security as the essence of what we should be aiming for. But I happily acknowledge that others may want to make different choices about the values and goals they would prioritize. We therefore need to build into any process of change or reform, a public democratic discussion about what we are trying to achieve – it is not, in my view, for researchers or policy-makers or campaigners to seek to impose their beliefs on this unilaterally, although they should certainly be noisy voices in such debates. The theoretical and analytical tools I have drawn on in this (and earlier) chapters will allow us: i) to gain a much more penetrating and clear-sighted idea of the costs associated with present ways of doing things as well as with alternatives for the future; and ii) to develop more effective strategies and practices for achieving whatever objectives we decide collectively that we wish to prioritize. Neither the present nor the future is inevitable – and in inventing the latter, we are limited only by our imagination.

In the next and final chapter, I bring together the arguments developed in previous chapters and present my overall thesis. I also revisit some of the central themes and ideas that I have been exploring here and consider some wider implications for how we choose to live and to govern ourselves and others in the twenty-first century.

Chapter 7

Conclusion

Drugs and freedom in the liberal age

For almost 14 years addiction took control of my life. I was trapped in a cycle of drug use, crime and despair. In 2005, I ended up in prison yet again, but this time it was different! Something changed inside me, I had had enough. I knew I could have a better life and I was no longer willing to sell myself short ... My story chronicles my journey from slavery to freedom.

('Personal Story' from Wired In to Recovery website)

NO to addiction and YES to freedom, say no to drugs!!

(Campaign slogan, Radio Marataizes, Brazil, 2009)

The Partnership for Drug Freedom in America supports your natural human right to *freely choose* any food, drink, herb, spice, medicine, sacrament, fiber or other nourishment from the bountiful harvest of planet Earth.

(Partnership for Drug Freedom in America website, 2009)

Introduction

The project that I have been pursuing in this book has proved to be even more complex and stranger than I ever envisaged. I have found myself in some unfamiliar corners of scholarship that at times appeared to be a long distance away from the world of drugs – from behavioural economics to histories of insurance to accounts of global governance. This has made the process of writing the book quite a taxing (and lengthy!) one but it has also led me to think more about the nature of the drug question as a 'problem space'. What does it tell us that we need to look in such a diverse set of literatures and from such a range of perspectives?

It is tempting to describe it as an 'interdisciplinary' field of study. Up to a point, that is certainly true, but I have certain reservations about the idea of interdisciplinarity which has in any case become something of an academic cliché. As I noted in Chapter 6, Braithwaite (2000) has described the new regulatory scholarship that he has spearheaded as sweeping across the disciplines and leading to a paradigmatic shift in the social sciences. We might see the regulation perspective then as interdisciplinarity writ large. A similar view might be taken about the governmentality analytic. But as Braithwaite has gone on to argue, 'paradigmatic change is not about razing the work and the methodological rigour of disciplines; it is about reconfiguring the invaluable endeavours pursued within them so they can feed into more fertile modes of theory-driven organization' (Braithwaite, 2005b: 347). In other words, we need the discipline of the disciplines to ensure the highest levels of conceptual and methodological rigour but, in investigating any given problem, we should scan across them for the best intellectual tools and resources for the job. This resonates with Ian Hacking's (2004) argument that his own work is most accurately characterized in terms of collaborating disciplines rather than interdisciplinarity. For him, the endeavour should not be to break down disciplinary boundaries but rather to respect the distinctive contributions each can make and to draw on those where relevant to particular problems or projects.

This leads me to a couple of related reflections. First, pursued in the types of ways suggested by Hacking and Braithwaite, the study of the drug question can potentially make an important contribution to the reconfiguring of the social sciences in the early twenty-first century. In this sense, to consider it as a very specialist and narrow field of study is to miss a rather large trick! Second, and related to this point, attempts to set up a sub-discipline of 'addiction studies' may therefore not be very helpful in the long run. The intellectual project needs to be broader in its vision. These two points, if correct, present us with a formidable challenge – we need to couple mastery of the specialist detail with an understanding of the bigger picture. One way to read this book is as a modest contribution to this rather daunting project. I hope that others will go on to build on this in the future.

I am not sure that the drugs question is necessarily unique or even particularly distinctive in this respect. To take the example of crime, another issue that I know a little about, in my view the most insightful and interesting work in this field in recent years demonstrates exactly this kind of breadth of vision and imagination. The late Richard Ericson's last book *Crime in an Insecure World* (Ericson, 2007) or Ian Loader and Neil Walker's (2007) *Civilizing Security* are outstanding examples of work which is 'criminological', in the sense that it has a strong focus on crime, but which melds together social theory, political science and socio-legal scholarship. Perhaps then Braithwaite is right and the investigation of most contemporary social issues is likely to require us to sweep across the disciplines. This is a big question for today's social scientists.

In the next section, I will briefly trace the overall arc of the book's central narrative. I will then return to my core theme, the relationship between drugs and freedom, revisit its main contours and characteristics and reflect on its significance. Following on from this, I return to the short dictionary of misunderstood words that I began in Chapter 2, as a way of pulling together some important insights and themes from previous chapters. In conclusion,

I attempt to make sense of my project as a whole and consider how it might contribute to the future development of different and more constructive ways of imagining and governing what we currently call the 'drug problem'.

Drugs and liberalism

The story I have told in preceding chapters begins from the premise that the point of emergence for a genealogy of the contemporary drug problem can be traced back to the industrial revolution in the late eighteenth century. Robin Room puts it like this:

> The addiction concept came into currency about two centuries ago as a way of understanding a contradiction in the emerging world system of globalization, industrialization and commercialization. On the one hand, the new means of production and transportation demanded a sobriety for most people and much of the time which had not been required in traditional village and tribal societies. On the other hand, industrialization and improved transportation meant that a wider range of goods were made generally available, and that the health of the economy depended on the commodities being purchased and consumed.
>
> (Room, 2006: 286)

Room nails a fundamental point here but, as should be clear by now, in my view this is not the whole story. As I have argued throughout the book, it is the centrality of *freedom* to the problematic of liberal government that has made addiction a 'peculiarly liberal affliction' (O'Malley, 2004: 155) and which has moved it to centre stage within politics and government over the past 200 years. I will return to the question of freedom later but here I want to summarize my account of this 200-year history.

The narrative I presented in Chapters 3, 4 and 5 suggested that it is best understood in three broad phases.

The *first phase*, which I covered in Chapter 3 and which lasted roughly from the 1780s to the 1860s, saw a period of accommodation and adjustment to the newly industrial society. In regulatory terms, it involved a transition from a police economy to a new liberal one characterized by the notion of *laissez-faire*. For much of this period, controls on the production, sale, possession and consumption of therapeutic and psychoactive substances were minimal or non-existent. It was only towards the end of this phase that some of these substances began to be seen as problematic. The passing of the Pharmacy Act in 1868 introduced the first controls of any significance, primarily applying to opium and opium-based products and certain poisons (see Box 3.1 in Chapter 3), although these controls operated at the point of sale only and were limited in scope and impact. I argued that the 1868 legislation constituted a significant 'event' in my genealogy in at least three respects. First, it marked the formal beginning of the conception of opium and opiates as a 'problem'. This 'problem framework' has become, of course, an almost unquestioned feature of our contemporary perspective. Second, it was the starting point of the idea that medical professionals were the appropriate gatekeepers and dispensers of opium and opium-based products. Again, doctors and pharmacists remain lynchpins today in the control and management of users of these drugs. Third, it marked the beginning of the idea that legislative regulation of drug supply could be an effective way of dealing with the 'problem'. Arguably, this fixation on the supply side has become more and more significant, particularly in the latter decades of the twentieth century.

The *second phase*, covered in Chapter 4 and which lasted from the 1870s to the 1960s, saw the transition from classical to welfare liberalism, leading eventually to the construction of the welfare state. It was during this period that the 'great regulatory divide' was created, establishing a global prohibition system for the new category of 'dangerous drugs'. The passage of the Dangerous Drugs Act in 1920 marked the beginning of prohibition in Britain, following the international agreement made the previous year as part of the Versailles peace treaty. This 'event' was another key moment in the genealogy. First, and perhaps most significantly, it marked the starting point of the concept of 'dangerous drugs' as a separate and particular category of psychoactive substances. In this sense, it is the origin of the contemporary 'drug problem'. Second, it signified the beginning of the deployment of a framework of criminal law for the regulation of this new category of 'dangerous drugs'. This was quite a step forward from merely seeing them within a 'problem framework'. Today, it is for many people a 'self-evident' feature of any drug-control system. Third, it extended the primacy and dominance of medical professionals in the governance of the problem. Doctors, in particular, were placed at the heart of the 'British System' constructed in the 1920s, a system which only began to be dismantled at the tail end of the 1960s.

The *third phase*, covered in Chapter 5 and lasting from the 1970s to the present, involved the unravelling of welfarist politics and the emergence of neo-liberalism. It has seen a growing emphasis on managing the risks posed by drug users, to both themselves and others, in line with the wider 'rise of risk' across politics and government. This risk-based approach has focused variously on potential drug-related harms to health, safety and security. I argued that the Drugs Act 2005 was a key moment or 'event' in this phase, as it crystallized and extended this approach, notably in its enactment of coercive criminal justice measures, but also in the creation of new offences such as 'aggravated' drug dealing for those selling drugs in or around school premises.

So, the imagination and governance of the 'drug problem' has changed as liberal governance more broadly has mutated over the past 200 years. This 'liberal affliction' has been closely bound up with the story of liberalism itself. Binding them together is the notion of freedom, to which I now turn.

Drugs and freedom

The question of freedom – and the related ideas of responsibility, free will, choice and autonomy – has been at the heart of this book. In Chapter 2, I charted the basic conceptual contours of the drugs–freedom relation and then in Chapters 3, 4 and 5 I attempted to develop this further. I want now to try to bring this all together and capture the overall significance of this connection. In the context of my genealogy, I think that there are three important dimensions of the relation that can be distinguished and I will briefly address these in turn.

Economic freedom: free trade and the circulation of commodities

In his *Security, Territory, Population* course of lectures at the Collège de France in 1978, Foucault (2007: 48–49) identified the possibility of circulation, of people and things, as one component of modern freedom within liberal government. It was, for example, a central tenet of Adam Smith's 1776 masterpiece *The Wealth of Nations* that economic prosperity depended on sweeping away the regulatory restrictions of the police economy and supporting free trade. The Beer Act of 1830, which I discussed in Chapter 3, was an attempt to liberalize the beer trade in exactly this kind of way (Mason, 2001). Restrictions on the exchange and circulation of psychoactive or therapeutic substances as commodities therefore constituted restrictions on liberal freedom and required special justification.

John Stuart Mill's famous essay *On Liberty* published in 1859 directly addressed questions of temperance and prohibition which were gathering momentum at that time (Boire, 2002). He attacked the Maine Law of 1851 which was one of the first attempts to implement the prohibition of alcohol in the United States. Mill's objection was not just that the Maine Law constituted a restriction on free trade but that it also infringed on the private sphere of the individual's body over which he or she was properly sovereign. For Mill, private pleasure was not an appropriate domain of government. The liberal subject, or *Homo economicus*, was entitled to do whatever they wished, provided that their actions caused no significant harm to others.

This idea of economic freedom – of being free to buy, sell and exchange commodities within a market economy – has been an important strand of the drug–freedom relation throughout the past 200 years, as has Mill's related notion of the freedom to pursue private pleasures. But, more than this, and as *On Liberty* illustrates, the ongoing discourse about this dimension of freedom has been shaped along the way by debate about how psychoactive and therapeutic substances should be regulated. The Beer Act, for instance, was at the forefront of a growing antipathy towards monopolies and a growing appreciation of the benefits of free trade, as the parliamentary debates about the legislation made clear (Mason, 2001: 111). The fact that the working poor were the 'chief beneficiaries' of this deregulation of licensing (Mason, 2001: 109) helped enormously to cement the cause of free trade in the public and political arenas. In a certain sense, the 24,000 beer shops that appeared in the first six months after the Act came into force (Mason, 2001) were a national network of sites or spaces where the new liberal civilization was being assembled. That many contemporary commentators – from Mayhew (1849–52/1985) in his *London Labour and London Poor* to Engels (1844/1987) in *The Condition of the Working Class in England* – viewed the legislation as 'anti-civilizing' by contributing to the further emiseration of the poor points towards one of the enduring paradoxes here: (economic) freedom can lead to the destruction of freedom (as autonomy). This remains one of the central tensions within governance strategies in this field. A contemporary British example of this, with very strong echoes of the Beer Act, is the Licensing Act 2003 which introduced flexible opening hours for pubs and clubs (so-called '24-hour drinking'). The purpose was the liberalization of the drinking trade, in order to boost the functioning of night-time economies, but critics feared an increase in alcohol-related problems (the actual impact appears to have been minimal in either direction – see Hough et al., 2008).

Social freedom: citizenship and free will

The capacity of human beings for autonomous action has not always been unquestioned within liberal governance. The model of addiction as disease, which reached a peak in the late nineteenth century, was founded on the idea that addicts suffered impaired wills such that they were unable to act freely. In this, they were just one particular category of people who lacked full capacity to be autonomous and responsible citizens, alongside the feeble-minded, the mentally vulnerable, juvenile delinquents and habitual offenders. The role of government was to intervene to restore damaged wills so that individuals could take up their full responsibilities as social citizens.

The addiction concept went to the heart of the matter by highlighting the significance of the faculty of the will. As a 'disease of the will', addiction weakened an individual's capacity to act as a responsible liberal subject. Dr Thomas Clouston, for example, writing in the *Edinburgh Medical Journal* about addictions to alcohol, morphine, chloral and cocaine, referred to 'diseased cravings and paralysed control' (Clouston, 1890), whilst Levinstein's classic account of addiction in his *The Morbid Craving for Morphia* described 'the uncontrollable desire of a person to use morphia as a stimulant and a tonic' (1878: 3). Treatment regimes were often focused on methods for re-training or re-educating the will (e.g. Jennings, 1901).

There was a paradox here too. The disease model of addiction was a hybrid concept in which freedom and responsibility were never fully relinquished. After all, the first decision to try morphine or gin or opium was always a 'free' one (provided the individual's mental capacity was not already impaired for some other reason). Addiction was a disease which was 'individually oriented, where the addict was responsible, through volition, for his own condition ... [and] failure to achieve a cure was a failure of self control, not medical science' (Berridge, 1979: 77). Again, this tension has run through the governance of the drug problem ever since. For example, the UK Drug Policy Commission's recent consensus statement on 'recovery' emphasizes the importance of 'voluntarily-sustained control over substance use' which it defines as 'comfortable and sustained freedom from compulsion to use' (UKDPC, 2008). Recovery then is seen as a re-assertion of the will over the compulsion of addiction. This echoes Jellinek's identification of 'loss of control' as the hallmark of addiction in his classic *The Disease Concept of Alcoholism* (Jellinek, 1960).

Consumer freedom: choice and autonomy

As Bauman (1988) and others have observed, freedom today has largely come to mean consumer freedom. Individual freedom centres now on the ability to choose, buy and consume the commodities one desires. Consumer choices are an increasingly significant part of the way in which we construct our identities, as in Giddens' (1991) notion of 'narratives of the self'. Citizens have become consumers whose 'activity is to be understood in terms of the activation of the rights of the consumer in the marketplace' (Rose, 1999: 165).

Drug-taking can be understood as one sphere of consumer activity which fulfils this role of identity formation through consumer choice, especially amongst young people (Miles, 2000; Jones, 2004). Indeed, to the extent that in a consumer society hedonism and instant gratification are encouraged and valorized, the consumption of psychoactive substances (whether legal or illegal) fits perfectly with the consumer ethic, a point to which I will return later. Addictive behaviour, on the other hand, represents a form of 'disordered consumption' (Reith, 2004), in which the addict is unable to exercise properly their freedom of choice. Their personal agency or autonomy is undermined in such a way as to threaten their freedom as a consumer.

Again, this notion of addiction as 'disordered consumption' contains some tensions. Drug consumption is a choice of action but can become a forced act. The nature of volition or of the will becomes central here. At the point at which the will becomes compromised or weakened, choice shifts to compulsion and consumption becomes disordered. Yet, as I discussed in Chapter 5, paradoxically certain governmental strategies towards 'disordered consumption' actually rely on addicts' ability to exercise choice in a rational way. For example, the 'Tough Choices' project I described in that chapter utilizes the leverage of the criminal justice system to cajole and encourage individuals to 'choose' to engage with drug treatment, on the assumption that they are (more or less) rational calculators. As Reith (2004) observes, the notions of 'loss of control' or 'compulsive' behaviour are highly problematic in a neo-liberal consumer society.

Drugs and freedom: the semantic river

Readers may recall my reference in Chapter 2 to Kundera's image of the ever-changing river of meanings, a river in which all previous meanings also resonate like a 'parade of echoes'. This remains, in my view, a helpful way of capturing the complexity of meanings associated with the drug–freedom relation. There is no single connection that we can identify and point to. Nor does the relation remain static. It is continually changing and shifting. The relation is, in other words, dialectical, dynamic and interactive. Most significantly of all, if we listen carefully enough to this semantic river, we can hear that 'parade of echoes' of past drug–freedom connections loud and clear.

As we have seen, freedom is not a universal attribute of the human experience with a fixed meaning. Although it has a pre-modern history, it has been particularly valorized with the emergence of liberalism just over 200 years ago. But since then freedom has mutated as liberal governance itself has undergone transitions. If my central thesis or claim is correct, the ways in which we think about drugs and addiction have been fundamental elements which have underpinned the 'forms of life and reason' (Rose, 1990: 378) that have made up this history of liberalism and of its most cherished ideal, freedom. The two are intimately connected and bound up together. The arguments in this book then have a much wider significance than might otherwise be thought, speaking to fundamental questions of the nature of contemporary politics, government and personhood. Just as Foucault revealed in *Histoire de la Folie* that madness has formed the perpetual 'other side' of reason, I have attempted to show that addiction has done so for freedom. And all the time haunting this duality has been the image of the slave which we find deep both in the pre-modern roots of freedom and in the etymology of addiction. It is not coincidental that today we express the ideas of being a 'slave to consumerism' or of being 'enslaved by addiction' using the same servile imagery. The semantic river we step in in the early twenty-first century flows all the way back to Antiquity.

A short dictionary of misunderstood words (concluded)

Several key themes and ideas have run through this book and I want to bring together a selection of the most important in this section, with a focus on challenging some 'taken-for-granted' concepts.

Addiction and modern capitalism

As we have seen, the addiction concept is around 200 years old – not much more and certainly no less. Prior to this, taking the example of alcohol, the 'assumption was that people drank and got drunk because they wanted to, and not because they "had" to' (Levine, 1978: 144). I have argued that the birth of the concept is rooted in the emergence of modern industrial capitalism in the late eighteenth century. It is a capitalist concept in a twin sense: first, because of this historical connection with the emergence of modern capitalism; second, because, like modern capitalism, it is based on the notion of repeated consumption of commodities.

What are the implications of this idea? First of all, it points towards the importance of viewing the matter through an economic lens. As previous chapters have shown, questions of trade are fundamental to the story. The Opium Wars between Britain and China in the middle of the nineteenth century, for example, were essentially trade wars, with Britain seeking to use its military supremacy to force China to keep open its borders for the importation of opium from British India. It is partly for this reason that empire and imperial interests also feature so strongly in drug histories (see Mills, 2003; Mills and Barton, 2007). Related to this is the increasing significance to the narrative of globalizing forces, and their impact on global flows of capital and commodities (see Seddon, 2008a). As Pearson puts it, drugs like heroin are a 'currency in a vast economic system … which stretches around the world' (Pearson, 1987: 117). Understanding drugs as commodities flowing and circulating within a global economy is essential to grasping the nature of the contemporary drug problem. A nuanced account of the global–local dynamic is also at the heart of some of the most insightful studies of local drug problems (e.g. Auld et al., 1984, 1986; Pearson, 1987; Pearson and Patel, 1998; see also Seddon, 2006).

A second implication is that we might expect transformations in capitalism to be related to changes in the addiction concept and our understandings of drugs. This, in a sense, is just a different way of putting my overarching thesis that the changing governance of drugs is connected with mutations in liberal governance more broadly. The point is nicely illustrated when we look at the contemporary drug situation. As discussed above, there is a broad consensus that in recent decades capitalism has shifted from being organized around production to a new consumerist phase. This transition has had a major impact on how we view drug consumption. I have already covered aspects of consumer freedom above and here focus on consumerism as economic activity. The first reference that I can find to the relevance of the rise of consumer capitalism to the drug question is in a prescient article by Dorn (1975) from over 30 years ago in which he linked the growing prevalence of recreational drug use amongst young people to this new consumerism:

This quite recent change of economic priority or emphasis requires a new social character orientated to immediate and repeated gratification through consumption ... It is hypothesized that the consumer character is a potential candidate for psychoactive drug use: drugs (legal and illegal) are, in many ways, ideal consumer products. Drugs are non-reuseable, unlike consumer durables and therefore lend themselves to repeat purchase. By their very nature, they are valued for the social and personal attributes (attractive, understanding, compassionate, experienced, exciting, etc.) they confer on the user, rather than for any non-social utility value.

(Dorn, 1975: 60)

Since this novel contribution by Dorn, this idea has become commonplace, especially over the past ten years. For example, the landmark book by Howard Parker and colleagues (Parker et al., 1998: 21–31) on the 'normalization' of drug-taking amongst young people in the late twentieth century situates its analysis directly in this context of the new primacy of consumption in late-modern capitalist society (see also van Ree, 2002).

This brings to the surface an interesting conundrum. Despite the valorization of consumerism, there are certain types of economic activity and commodity consumption that we do not favour and in so doing we create important boundaries between categories of people. Bauman identifies the nub of the matter:

In a society organized around consumer freedom everybody is defined by his or her consumption. Insiders are wholesome persons because they exercise their market freedom. Outsiders are nothing else but flawed consumers. They may claim compassion, but they have nothing to boast about and no title to respect; after all, they failed where so many others succeeded, and they must still prove that cruel fate, rather than corrupt character, bears responsibility for the failure. Outsiders are also a threat and a nuisance. They are seen as a constraint on the insiders' freedom; they weigh heavily on the insiders' choice, taxing the contents of the insiders' pockets. They are a public menace, as their clamourings for help forebode new restrictions on all those who can do without help.

(Bauman, 1988: 93)

This reveals why Parker's normalization thesis has proved to be so profoundly controversial in some quarters. By suggesting that the consumption of certain substances – primarily those used as part of leisure activities, such as cannabis, ecstasy and so on – has become 'normalized' they are in effect making the claim that these consumers are 'insiders' in Bauman's terms. The moral and political opprobrium now attaches primarily to consumers of heroin and crack-cocaine, who are certainly viewed as 'flawed' and as a 'public menace' posing a burden on 'insiders'. As I discussed in Chapter 5, these flawed consumers have come to be described not so much as 'addicts' but more as 'problem drug users', a term which implies that other drug users are primarily not problematic.

At the time of writing this chapter in spring 2009, much of the world is still engulfed in the banking and financial crisis which some commentators have viewed as a crisis of capitalism more broadly. Looking to the future, admittedly somewhat speculatively, it might be anticipated that any trans-formation of capitalism that results from this crisis will have an impact on the drug situation. Should this involve a rolling back of rampant debt-fuelled consumerism, perhaps we will also see a shrinking of global drug consumption or at least major changes in patterns of consumption. Perhaps. But, as always, the only thing certain about the future is its unpredictability.

Drugs and regulation

The category of 'drugs', in the sense that we understand it today, is even more recent than the idea of addiction – around 100 years old. As I dis-cussed in Chapter 4, it was in effect constructed at the beginning of the twentieth century as part of the building of the drug-prohibition regime in order to provide an overarching term for this new category of prohibited psychoactive substances. Recalling Braithwaite and Drahos's (2000) analysis discussed in earlier chapters, 'drugs' was the label created when a new reg-ulatory branch was constructed. It is, in this sense, largely a regulatory con-cept (like 'prescription' or 'over-the-counter' medicines). It certainly has little intrinsic descriptive character relating to the substance itself. The principal conceptual difference between, say, alcohol and heroin is that they are regu-lated under completely separate regimes, rather than that they are substances of a fundamentally different kind from each other.

But it would be a rather reductive view to see the category of 'drugs' solely in terms of regulation. At the same time, it is also, as Ruggiero (1999) puts it, an 'evaluative' concept, carrying with it a set of moral judgements – about the nature of the substances that come under its umbrella and about the character of the people that consume them. This evaluative power should not be underestimated – to describe a person as a heroin user summons an array of powerful affective responses, from fear to loathing to pity. Yet there is a circularity here – these judgements are largely, if not totally, shaped by regulatory status. This is partly because the regulatory regime for 'drugs' is set within a criminal law framework which carries with it the idea that breaches involve moral wrongdoing. I think though that there is more to it than this. As we have seen in Chapters 2 and 3, in general terms, an asso-ciation between 'over-indulgence' and sin or vice pre-dates the establishment of this regime, indeed pre-dates the addiction concept. What the 'great regulatory divide' accomplished at the beginning of the twentieth century was to focus moral opprobrium on a particular sub-set of substances, that is those falling within the new category of 'dangerous drugs'. This opprobrium has never been evenly distributed, however, and at different times over the past 90 years, different groups have been under the microscope of societal disapproval. In the 1920s, for example, this moral discourse was profoundly gendered and racialized, as the 'cocaine girls' in the West End of London and the Chinese opium smokers in the East of the city came under public and media scrutiny (Kohn, 1992; Seddon, 2008b).

So to label a substance a 'drug' is to make a regulatory claim in part. It also at the same time invites a (related) moral or political judgement. Beyond this, the category conveys little else. It is not a term, for example, which describes any particular pharmacological or chemical character of the substances to which it refers. In this sense, if we wish to contest the contemporary drug-control regime, we also need to contest the very term 'drugs'. Attempts at radical policy reform which fail to do this are fatally flawed as they implicitly accept the very premise they seek to critique and overturn. It is for this reason that the R&D agenda I set out in Chapter 6 began from the point drawn from Braithwaite and Drahos (2000) that our existing drug-control system is just one branch created out of a wider regulatory tree covering all therapeutic and psychoactive substances. To accept and work with the notion of 'drugs' is, to a certain extent, to accept the existing system of regulatory branches.

In developing new regulatory approaches, we must be aware that the new categories we invent will also be regulatory, even if they are also designed to map on to categories based on other criteria (e.g. 'harmfulness'). We cannot escape the regulatory nature of the categories and concepts through which we understand the world. The ways in which we 'imagine' problems are bound up with the ways in which we govern them.

Prohibition and welfarism

As I explored in Chapter 4, one of the jarring realizations that emerges from my genealogy is that the drug-prohibition regime is rooted in the transition from classical to welfare liberalism at the turn of the twentieth century, a transition which led eventually to the establishment of the welfare state (Garland, 1985). The idea of a connection between welfarism and drug prohibition is perhaps not a comfortable one for some. The creation of the welfare state is often seen as a landmark of progressive politics (see Hennessy, 1992), whilst prohibition has come to be viewed as the very opposite. To see the two as closely related destabilizes our sense of contemporary politics, in which pro-prohibition 'drug warriors' are seen as reactionary right-wingers whilst supporters of the welfare state are considered as staunch left-wingers.

Why, though, has prohibition persisted even after the unravelling of welfarist politics in the 1970s? Surely we would expect it to have unravelled as well? I think the answer here lies in the idea of interventionism. This was one of the core elements of welfarism – it is for this reason that Braithwaite (2008) prefers the term the 'provider state' era. Prohibition can be understood partly as an instance of this new interventionism. For many commentators, neo-liberalism is associated with an opposite impulse, that is with deregulation and the rolling back of the state. Braithwaite argues, however, that in practice neo-liberalism has been accompanied by an extension and expansion of regulation – hence, he prefers the label 'regulatory capitalism'. So despite the 'myth of deregulation' (Braithwaite, 2008), interventionism is alive and well. This then helps to explain the persistence of prohibition after the demise of welfarism.

Public health

Drug-policy campaigners often call for policy to be re-oriented towards public health, as a more progressive and constructive approach than the criminalizing strategy of prohibition. The broad thrust of the call is that we should be more concerned about helping sick people, preventing the spread of disease and enhancing well-being, rather than punishing individuals for supposed moral transgressions. On the face of it, who could argue against that? But the genealogy I have traced here makes me a little queasy about this. As I discussed in Chapter 3, it was the growing public-health movement in the mid-nineteenth century that contributed to the development of the first regulatory controls in the 1868 legislation and it was these controls that then paved the way for prohibition. So, to a certain extent, prohibition itself has deep roots in public health.

Campaigners might counter that the regulatory approach of the Pharmacy Act was quite different from later prohibition. It was concerned with restricting access to powerful poisons in order to minimize deaths, accidental or otherwise. From this perspective, the call is for a return not to the pharmaceutical regulation of the 1868 regime but rather to the public-health focus of the 'British System', in which doctors were empowered to treat heroin addiction as a manifestation of a disease rather than as a vice. This view lies behind the repeated calls by some campaigners for heroin maintenance trials. But again, as I showed in Chapter 3 (see also Seddon, 2007b), things are not quite what they seem here either. The 'British System' was built on the foundation of a strategic liaison between the penal and welfare realms – penal–welfarism in Garland's (1985) terminology – rather than a clear division between the two.

More recently, the British response to the threat of HIV in the mid- to late 1980s has been seen as an exemplary public-health approach to the drug problem. Critics of the criminal justice turn in drug policy typically call for a return to the public health and harm reduction emphasis of the HIV era (e.g. Stimson, 2000). Yet, as I discussed in Chapter 5, at a strategic level there is considerable continuity between the two, as they share a focus on managing and controlling the risks posed to individuals and communities by 'problem drug users'.

The idea then of a public-health approach as a progressive alternative to a criminalizing penal one is problematic, as the two strategies are so closely intertwined within the genealogy I have described in this book. It is difficult to sustain the idea that they are polar opposites or stark policy alternatives. I do not mean by this that it is impossible, or undesirable, to emphasize or prioritize health concerns within a regulatory regime in this field. My point is rather that within the history of the present, these two lines are inextricably linked and, consequently, cannot be readily or easily disentangled. So simply to call for a 'public-health drug policy' is to ignore this ambiguous and mixed lineage. Again, the implication is that only a genuinely radical root-and-branch demolition of the existing framework of assumptions, categories and understandings could deliver a properly health-focused governance regime. I would argue, though, perhaps controversially, that even if the entire existing regime were to be swept away, it is not clear to me that health or public health would or should necessarily emerge as the sole or primary animating principle of any new approach. Other principles might stake an equal or greater claim to primacy, such as social justice, human rights, well-being or human security. Public-health advocates would need very sharp elbows to emerge triumphant from that competition.

Conclusion

So where does all this take us? At one level, one of my central critical purposes has simply been to disturb the self-evidence of how we see the matter today. As Bauman wisely observes, understanding this is an important step towards freeing up the possibilities for doing things differently in the future:

> The human condition is not pre-empted by its past. Human history is not predetermined by its past stages. The fact that something has been the case, even for a very long time, is not a proof that it will continue to be so. Each moment of history is a junction of tracks leading towards a number of futures. Being at the crossroads is the way human society exists. What appears in retrospect an 'inevitable' development began in its time as stepping onto one road among many stretching ahead.
>
> (Bauman, 1988: 89)

This resonates with the Foucauldian critical ethos of shaking the 'false self-evidence' of the present (see Foucault, 1991b) which has informed this book. So fundamental ideas like 'addiction', or the very category of 'drugs', have been pulled apart and their 'universal' or 'timeless' status unravelled. But the purpose has not simply been academic or intellectual game-playing. In

Chapter 6, I tried to sketch out a research and development agenda that might contribute to the opening up of new roads that may lead to better futures. This R&D agenda offers a framework within which NGOs, social movements, public intellectuals and others can collaborate and work together to develop new ideas and programmes for action. It will require some boldness, imagination and courage but I am optimistic about our ability to find better ways of doing things.

The importance of this cannot be overstated. Some readers may perhaps feel that I have not said enough in previous chapters about the pain and suffering and injustice associated with the drug problem. In fact, I do not seek to deny or downplay these at all. Indeed, they have motivated and animated my research in this field over the past 15 years, for 10 years in the NGO sector and then latterly in academia. It is for this reason that I have felt a strong obligation in this book not just to question and challenge what we think 'know' but also to say something about where we should go in the future (and how we might get there). And, of course, the right to challenge how we are governed is fundamental to us as human beings in the liberal age, as Nikolas Rose argues in these powerful concluding words in his book *Powers of Freedom*:

> We may not share an essence, a soul, an identity or any other fixed attributes with others. But there is one status that we do share, and this is our status as subjects of government. That is to say, like so many others, we are inhabitants of regimes that act upon our own conduct in the proclaimed interest of our individual and collective well-being. To the extent that we are governed in our own name, we have a right to contest the evils that are done to us in the name of government … In showing us that what we take to be solid and inevitable is less so than we believe, genealogies of power and freedom also show us that we do not know what human beings are capable of, and that it has been, and is, possible for even the most unlikely subjects, in the most unpropitious circumstances, to act upon their limits in the name of no principle but that of their own life. Above all, such analyses seek to open, but not to close, the space within which human beings, being the kinds of creatures they have become, can exercise their political responsibilities.
>
> (Rose, 1999: 284)

It is in this spirit that I hope that this book – despite its undoubted inadequacies, omissions and other shortcomings – can help us to 'contest the evils that are done to us in the name of government' and make a small contribution to creating a better future.

Appendix I

Pharmacy Act 1868 (selected extracts)

An Act to regulate the Sale of Poisons, and alter and amend the Pharmacy Act, 1852.

[...]

1. From and after the Thirty-first Day of *December* One thousand eight hundred and sixty-eight it shall be unlawful for any Person to sell or keep open Shop for retailing, dispensing, or compounding Poisons, or to assume or use the Title 'Chemist and Druggist' or Chemist or Druggist, or Pharmacist, or Dispensing Chemist or Druggist, in any Part of *Great Britain*, unless such Person shall be a Pharmaceutical Chemist, or a Chemist and Druggist within the Meaning of this Act, and be registered under this Act, and conform to such Regulations as to the keeping, dispensing, and selling of such poisons as may from Time to Time be prescribed by the Pharmaceutical Society with the Consent of the Privy Council.

2. The several Articles named or described in the Schedule (A) shall be deemed to be Poisons within the Meaning of the Act ...

[...]

10. It shall be the Duty of the Registrar to make and keep a correct Register, in accordance with the Provisions of this Act, of all Persons who shall be entitled to be registered under this Act, and to erase the Names of all registered Persons who shall have died, and from Time to Time to make the necessary Alterations in the Addresses of the Persons registered under this Act: to enable the Registrar duly to fulfil the Duties imposed upon him, it shall be lawful for the Registrar to write a Letter to any registered Person, addressed to him according to his Address on the Register, to inquire whether he has ceased to carry on Business or has changed his Residence, such Letter to be forwarded by Post as a Registered Letter, according to the Post Office Regulations for the Time being, and if no Answer shall be returned to such Letter within the Period of Six Months from the sending of the Letter, a

Second, of similar Purport, shall be sent in like Manner, and if no Answer be given thereto within Three Months from the Date thereof it shall be lawful to erase the Name of such Person from the Register: Provided always, that the same may be restored by Direction of the Council of the Pharmaceutical Society should they think fit to make an Order to that Effect.

11. Every Registrar of Deaths in *Great Britain*, on receiving Notice of the Death of any Pharmaceutical Chemist, or Chemist and Druggist, shall forthwith transmit by Post to the Registrar under the Pharmacy Act a Certificate under his own Hand of such Death, with the Particulars of the Time and Place of Death, and on the Receipt of such Certificate the said Registrar under the Pharmacy Act shall erase the Name of such deceased Pharmaceutical Chemist, or Chemist and Druggist, from the Register ...

[...]

15. From and after the Thirty-first Day of *December* One thousand eight hundred and sixty-eight any Person who shall sell or keep an open Shop for the retailing, dispensing, or compounding Poisons, or who shall take, use or exhibit the Name or Title of Chemist and Druggist, or Chemist or Druggist, not being a duly registered Pharmaceutical Chemist, or Chemist and Druggist, or who shall take, use or exhibit the Name or Title Pharmaceutical Chemist, Pharmaceutist, or Pharmacist, not being a Pharmaceutical Chemist, or shall fail to conform with any Regulation as to the keeping or selling of Poisons made in pursuance of this Act, or who shall compound any Medicines of the British Pharmacopeia except according to the Formularies of the said Pharmacopeia, shall for every such Offence be liable to pay a Penalty or Sum of Five Pounds, and the same may be sued for, recovered, and dealt with in the Manner provided by the Pharmacy Act for the Recovery of Penalties under that Act ...

16. Nothing herein-before contained shall extend to or interfere with the Business of any legally qualified Apothecary or of any Member of the Royal College of Veterinary Surgeons of *Great Britain*, nor with the making or dealing in Patent Medicines, nor with the Business of wholesale Dealers in supplying Poisons in the ordinary Course of wholesale Dealing ...

17. It shall be unlawful to sell any Poison, either by Wholesale or by Retail, unless the Box, Bottle, Vessel, Wrapper, or Cover in which such Poison is contained be distinctly labeled with the Name of the Article and the Word Poison, and with the Name and Address of the Seller of the Poison; and it shall be unlawful to sell any Poison of those which are in the First Part of Schedule (A) to this Act, or may hereafter be added thereto under Section Two of this Act, to any Person unknown to the Seller, unless introduced by

some Person known to the Seller; and on every Sale of any such Article the Seller shall, before Delivery, make or cause to be made an Entry in a Book to be kept for that Purpose stating, in the Form set forth in Schedule (F) to this Act, the Date of the Sale, the Name and Address of the Purchaser, the Name and Quantity of the Article sold, and the Purpose for which it is stated by the Purchaser to be required, to which Entry the Signature of the Purchaser and of the Person, if any, who introduced him shall be affixed; and any Person selling Poison otherwise than is herein provided shall, upon a summary Conviction before Two Justices of the peace in *England* or the Sheriff in *Scotland*, be liable to a Penalty not exceeding Five Pounds for the First Offence, and to a Penalty not exceeding Ten Pounds for the Second or any subsequent Offence ... but the Provisions of this Section, which are solely applicable to Poisons in the First Part of the Schedule (A) to this Act, or which require that the Label shall contain the Name and Address of the Seller, shall not apply to Articles to be exported from *Great Britain* by wholesale Dealers, nor to Sales by wholesale to retail Dealers in the ordinary Course of wholesale Dealing, nor shall any of the Provisions of this Section apply to any Medicine supplied by a legally qualified Apothecary to his Patient, nor apply to any Article when forming Part of the Ingredients of any Medicine dispensed by a Person registered under this Act; provided such Medicine be labelled in the Manner aforesaid, with the Name and Address of the Seller, and the Ingredients thereof be entered, with the Name of the Person to whom it is sold or delivered, nothing in this Act contained shall repeal or affect any of the Provisions of an Act of the Session holden in the Fourteenth and Fifteenth Years in the Reign of Her present Majesty, intituled *An Act to regulated the Sale of Arsenic.*

[...]

24. The Provisions of the Act of the Twenty-third and Twenty-fourth of *Victoria*, Chapter Eight-four, intituled *An Act for preventing the Adulteration of Articles of Food or Drink*, shall extend to all Articles usually taken or sold as Medicines, and every Adulteration of any such Article shall be deemed an Admixture injurious to Health; and any Person registered under this Act who sells any such Article adulterated shall, unless the contrary be proved, be deemed to have Knowledge of such Adulteration.

25. On and after the passing of this Act all Powers vested by the Pharmacy Act in One of Her Majesty's Principal Secretaries of State shall be vested in the Privy Council, and the Seventh Section of the Public Health Act, 1858, shall apply to all Proceedings and Acts of the Privy Council herein authorized.

26. The Privy Council may direct the Name of any Person who is convicted of any Offence against this Act which in their Opinion renders him unfit to

be on the Register under this Act to be erased from such Register, and it
shall be the Duty of the Registrar to erase the same accordingly.

[...]

Schedules

Schedule (A)

Part I

Arsenic and its Preparations
Cyanides of Potassium and all metallic Cyanides
Strychnine and all poisonous vegetable Alkaloids and their Salts
Aconite and its Preparations
Emetic Tartar
Corrosive Sublimate
Cantharides
Savin and its Oil
Ergot of Rye and its Preparations.

Part 2

Oxalic Acid
Chloroform
Belladonna and its Preparations
Essential Oil of Almonds unless deprived of its Prussic Acid
Opium and all Preparations of Opium or of Poppies.

Schedule (F)

Date	Name of Purchaser	Name and Quantity of Poison sold	Purpose for which it is required	Signature of Purchaser	Signature of Person introducing Purchaser

Appendix 2

Dangerous Drugs Act 1920 (selected extracts)

An Act to regulate the Importation, Exportation, Manufacture, Sale and Use of Opium and other Dangerous Drugs.

[...]

Part I

Raw opium

1. It shall not be lawful for any person to import or bring into the United Kingdom any raw opium except under licence and into approved ports.

2. (1) It shall not be lawful for any person to export from the United Kingdom any raw opium except under licence and from approved ports and except in packages marked in the prescribed manner with an indication of the contents thereof ...

3. Provision may be made by regulations for controlling or restricting the production, possession, sale and distribution of raw opium, and in particular, but without prejudice to the generality of the foregoing power, for prohibiting the production, possession, sale or distribution of raw opium except by persons licensed or otherwise authorised in that behalf.

Part II

Prepared opium

4. It shall not be lawful for any person to import or bring into, or to export from, the United Kingdom any prepared opium.

5. If any person –

(a) manufactures, sells or otherwise deals in prepared opium; or

(b) has in his possession any prepared opium; or

(c) being the occupier of any premises permits those premises to be used for the purpose of the preparation of opium for smoking or the sale or smoking of prepared opium; or

(d) is concerned in the management of any premises used for any such purpose as aforesaid; or

(e) has in his possession any pipes or other utensils for use in connection with the smoking of opium or any utensils used in connection with the preparation of opium for smoking; or

(f) smokes or otherwise uses prepared opium, or frequents any place used for the purpose of opium smoking;

he shall be guilty of an offence against this Act.

Part III

Cocaine, morphine, &c

6. It shall not be lawful to import or bring into, or to export from the United Kingdom any drug to which this Part of this Act applies except under licence.

7. (1) For the purpose of preventing the improper use of the drugs to which this Part of this Act applies, provision may be made by regulations for controlling the manufacture, sale, possession and distribution of those drugs, and in particular, but without prejudice to the generality of the foregoing power, for –

(a) prohibiting the manufacture of any drug to which this Part of this Act applies except on premises licensed for the purpose and subject to any conditions specified in the licence; and

(b) prohibiting the manufacture, sale or distribution of any such drug except by persons licensed or otherwise authorised under the regulations and subject to any conditions specified in the licence or authority; and

(c) regulating the issue by medical practitioners of prescriptions containing any such drug and the dispensing of any such prescriptions; and

(d) requiring persons engaged in the manufacture, sale or distribution of any such drug to keep such books and furnish such information either in writing or otherwise as may be prescribed.

(2) The regulations under this section shall provide for authorising any person who lawfully keeps open shop for the retailing of poisons in accordance with the provisions of the Pharmacy Act, 1868, as amended by the Poisons and Pharmacy Act, 1908,–

(a) to manufacture at the shop in the ordinary course of his retail business any preparation, admixture, or extract of any drug to which this Part of this Act applies; or

(b) to carry on at the shop the business of retailing, dispensing, or compounding any such drug;

Subject to the power of the Secretary of State to withdraw the authorisation in the case of a person who has been convicted of an offence against this Act or of an offence under the enactments relating to the customs as applied by this Act, and who cannot, in the opinion of the Secretary of State, properly be allowed to carry on the business of manufacturing or selling or distributing, as the case may be, any such drug:

Provided that the Secretary of State shall, before withdrawing the authorisation in the case of any such person consult the Council of the Pharmaceutical Society of Great Britain.

(3) Nothing in any regulations made under this section shall be taken to authorise the sale, or the keeping of an open shop for the retailing, dispensing, or compounding of, poisons by any person who is not qualified in that behalf under, or otherwise in accordance with, the provisions of the Pharmacy Act, 1868, as amended by the Poisons and Pharmacy Act, 1908, or to be in derogation of the provisions of the Pharmacy Act, 1868, as so amended, for prohibiting, restricting, or regulating the sale of poisons.

8. (1) The drugs to which this Part of this Act applies are morphine, cocaine, ecgonine, and diamorphine (commonly known as heroin), and their respective salts, and medicinal opium, and any preparation, admixture, extract, or other substance containing not less than one-fifth per cent of morphine or one-tenth per cent of cocaine, ecgonine or diamorphine ...

(2) If it appears to His Majesty that any new derivative of morphine or cocaine or of any salts of morphine or cocaine or any other alkaloid of opium or any other drug of whatever kind is or is likely to be productive, if improperly used, of ill effects substantially of the same character or nature as or analogous to those produced by morphine or cocaine, His Majesty may by Order in Council declare that this Part of this Act shall apply to that new derivative or alkaloid or other drug in the same manner as it applies to the drugs mentioned in subsection (1) of this section.

Part IV

General

[...]

10. (1) Any constable or other person authorised in that behalf by any general or special order of a Secretary of State shall, for the purposes of the execution of this Act, have power to enter the premises of any person carrying on the business of a producer, manufacturer, seller or distributor of any drugs to which this Act applies, and to demand the production of and to inspect any books relating to dealings in any such drugs and to inspect any stocks of any such drugs.

(2) If any person wilfully delays or obstructs any person in the exercise of his powers under this section or fails to produce or conceals or attempts to conceal any such books or stocks as aforesaid, he shall be of an offence against this Act.

[...]

12. Licences or authorities for the purposes of this Act may be issued or granted by a Secretary of State and may be issued or granted on such terms and subject to such conditions (including in the case of a licence the payment of a fee) as the Secretary of State thinks proper.

13. (1) If any person acts in contravention of or fails to comply with any regulation made under this Act, or acts in contravention of or fails to comply with the conditions of any licence issued or authority granted under or in pursuance of this Act, he shall be guilty of an offence against this Act.

(2) Any person guilty of an offence against this Act shall be liable on summary conviction to a fine not exceeding two hundred pounds or to imprisonment with or without hard labour for a term not exceeding six months or to both such fine and imprisonment, and in the case of a second or subsequent conviction to a fine not exceeding five hundred pounds, or to imprisonment with or without hard labour for a term not exceeding two years, or to both such fine and imprisonment, and the court dealing with the case may, in addition to any other punishment, order the goods in respect of which the offence was committed to be forfeited ...

14. Any constable may arrest without warrant any person who has committed, or attempted to commit, or is reasonably suspected by the constable of having committed or attempted to commit, an offence against this Act, if

he has reasonable ground for believing that that person will abscond unless arrested, or if the name and address of that person are unknown to and cannot be ascertained by him.

[...]

17. (1) This Act may be cited as the Dangerous Drugs Act, 1920.

(2) This Act shall come into operation on the first day of September, nineteen hundred and twenty.

Appendix 3

Drugs Act 2005 (selected extracts)

An Act to make provision in connection with controlled drugs and for the making of orders to supplement anti-social behaviour orders in cases where behaviour is affected by drug misuse or other prescribed factors.

Part 1

Supply of controlled drugs

1 Aggravated supply of controlled drug

(1) After section 4 of the Misuse of Drugs Act 1971 (c. 38) (restriction on production and supply of controlled drugs) insert –

4A Aggravation of offence of supply of controlled drug

(1) This section applies if –

(a) a court is considering the seriousness of an offence under section 4(3) of this Act, and

(b) at the time the offence was committed the offender had attained the age of 18.

(2) If either of the following conditions is met the court –

(a) must treat the fact that the condition is met as an aggravating factor (that is to say, a factor that increases the seriousness of the offence), and

(b) must state in open court that the offence is so aggravated.

(3) The first condition is that the offence was committed on or in the vicinity of school premises at a relevant time.

(4) The second condition is that in connection with the commission of the offence the offender used a courier who, at the time the offence was committed, was under the age of 18.

(5)   In subsection (3), a relevant time is –

(a) any time when the school premises are in use by persons under the age of 18;

(b) one hour before the start and one hour after the end of any such time.

(6)   For the purposes of subsection (4), a person uses a courier in connection with an offence under section 4(3) of this Act if he causes or permits another person (the courier) –

(a) to deliver a controlled drug to a third person, or

(b) to deliver a drug related consideration to himself or a third person.

(7)   For the purposes of subsection (6), a drug related consideration is a consideration of any description which –

(a) is obtained in connection with the supply of a controlled drug, or

(b) is intended to be used in connection with obtaining a controlled drug.

(8)   In this section –

'school premises' means land used for the purposes of a school excluding any land occupied solely as a dwelling by a person employed at the school ...

Part 2

Police powers relating to drugs

[...]

5 X-rays and ultrasound scans: England and Wales

(1)   After section 55 (intimate searches) of the Police and Criminal Evidence Act 1984 (c. 60) insert –

55A X-rays and ultrasound scans

(1)   If an officer of at least the rank of inspector has reasonable grounds for believing that a person who has been arrested for an offence and is in police detention –

(a) may have swallowed a Class A drug, and

(b) was in possession of it with the appropriate criminal intent before his arrest, the officer may authorise that an x-ray is taken of the person or an ultrasound scan is carried out on the person (or both).

(2)   An x-ray must not be taken of a person and an ultrasound scan must not be carried out on him unless the appropriate consent has been given in writing.

(3)   If it is proposed that an x-ray is taken or an ultrasound scan is carried out, an appropriate officer must inform the person who is to be subject to it –

   (a)   of the giving of the authorisation for it, and
   (b)   of the grounds for giving the authorisation.

(4)   An x-ray may be taken or an ultrasound scan carried out only by a suitably qualified person and only at –

   (a)   a hospital,
   (b)   a registered medical practitioner's surgery, or
   (c)   some other place used for medical purposes.

(5)   The custody record of the person must also state –

   (a)   the authorisation by virtue of which the x-ray was taken or the ultrasound scan was carried out,
   (b)   the grounds for giving the authorisation, and
   (c)   the fact that the appropriate consent was given.

(6)   The information required to be recorded by subsection (5) must be recorded as soon as practicable after the x-ray has been taken or ultrasound scan carried out (as the case may be).

(7)   Every annual report –

   (a)   under section 22 of the Police Act 1996, or
   (b)   made by the Commissioner of Police of the Metropolis, must contain information about x-rays which have been taken and ultrasound scans which have been carried out under this section in the area to which the report relates during the period to which it relates.

(8)   The information about such x-rays and ultrasound scans must be presented separately and must include –

   (a)   the total number of x-rays;
   (b)   the total number of ultrasound scans;
   (c)   the results of the x-rays;
   (d)   the results of the ultrasound scans.

(9)   If the appropriate consent to an x-ray or ultrasound scan of any person is refused without good cause, in any proceedings against that person for an offence –

   (a)   the court, in determining whether there is a case to answer,

(b) a judge, in deciding whether to grant an application made by the accused under paragraph 2 of Schedule 3 to the Crime and Disorder Act 1998 (applications for dismissal), and

(c) the court or jury, in determining whether that person is guilty of the offence charged, may draw such inferences from the refusal as appear proper.

[...]

7 Testing for presence of Class A drugs

(1) Section 63B of the Police and Criminal Evidence Act 1984 (c. 60) ('PACE') (testing for presence of Class A drugs) is amended in accordance with subsections (2) to (12).

(2) In subsection (1) for 'the following conditions are met' substitute ' –

(a) either the arrest condition or the charge condition is met;

(b) both the age condition and the request condition are met; and

(c) the notification condition is met in relation to the arrest condition, the charge condition or the age condition (as the case may be).'

(3) After subsection (1) insert –

'(1A) The arrest condition is that the person concerned has been arrested for an offence but has not been charged with that offence and either–

(a) the offence is a trigger offence; or

(b) a police officer of at least the rank of inspector has reasonable grounds for suspecting that the misuse by that person of a specified Class A drug caused or contributed to the offence and has authorised the sample to be taken.'

(4) In subsection (2), for 'The first condition is' substitute 'The charge condition is either'.

(5) For subsection (3) substitute –

'(3) The age condition is –

(a) if the arrest condition is met, that the person concerned has attained the age of 18;

(b) if the charge condition is met, that he has attained the age of 14.'

(6) In subsection (4), for 'third' substitute 'request'.

(7) After subsection (4) insert –

'(4A) The notification condition is that –

(a) the relevant chief officer has been notified by the Secretary of State that appropriate arrangements have been made for the police area as a whole, or for the particular police station, in which the person is in police detention, and

(b) the notice has not been withdrawn.

(4B) For the purposes of subsection (4A) above, appropriate arrangements are arrangements for the taking of samples under this section from whichever of the following is specified in the notification –

(a) persons in respect of whom the arrest condition is met;
(b) persons in respect of whom the charge condition is met;
(c) persons who have not attained the age of 18.'

[...]

(9)   After subsection (5A) insert –

'(5B) If a sample is taken under this section from a person in respect of whom the arrest condition is met no other sample may be taken from him under this section during the same continuous period of detention but –

(a) if the charge condition is also met in respect of him at any time during that period, the sample must be treated as a sample taken by virtue of the fact that the charge condition is met;
(b) the fact that the sample is to be so treated must be recorded in the person's custody record.

(5C) Despite subsection (1)(a) above, a sample may be taken from a person under this section if –

(a) he was arrested for an offence (the first offence),
(b) the arrest condition is met but the charge condition is not met,
(c) before a sample is taken by virtue of subsection (1) above he would (but for his arrest as mentioned in paragraph (d) below) be required to be released from police detention,
(d) he continues to be in police detention by virtue of his having been arrested for an offence not falling within subsection (1A) above, and
(e) the sample is taken before the end of the period of 24 hours starting with the time when his detention by virtue of his arrest for the first offence began.

(5D) A sample must not be taken from a person under this section if he is detained in a police station unless he has been brought before the custody officer' ...

[...]

Part 3

Assessment of misuse of drugs

9 *Initial assessment following testing for presence of Class A drugs*

(1) This section applies if –

   (a) a sample is taken under section 63B of PACE (testing for presence of Class A drug) from a person detained at a police station,

   (b) an analysis of the sample reveals that a specified Class A drug may be present in the person's body,

   (c) the age condition is met, and

   (d) the notification condition is met.

(2) A police officer may, at any time before the person is released from detention at the police station, require him to attend an initial assessment and remain for its duration.

(3) An initial assessment is an appointment with a suitably qualified person (an 'initial assessor') –

   (a) for the purpose of establishing whether the person is dependent upon or has a propensity to misuse any specified Class A drug,

   (b) if the initial assessor thinks that he has such a dependency or propensity, for the purpose of establishing whether he might benefit from further assessment, or from assistance or treatment (or both), in connection with the dependency or propensity, and

   (c) if the initial assessor thinks that he might benefit from such assistance or treatment (or both), for the purpose of providing him with advice, including an explanation of the types of assistance or treatment (or both) which are available.

(4) The age condition is met if the person has attained the age of 18 or such different age as the Secretary of State may by order made by statutory instrument specify for the purposes of this section.

(5) In relation to a person ('A') who has attained the age of 18, the notification condition is met if –

   (a) the relevant chief officer has been notified by the Secretary of State that arrangements for conducting initial assessments for persons who have attained the age of 18 have been made for persons from whom samples have been taken (under section 63B of PACE) at the police station in which A is detained, and

   (b) the notice has not been withdrawn.

(6) In relation to a person ('C') who is of an age which is less than 18, the notification condition is met if –

(a) the relevant chief officer has been notified by the Secretary of State that arrangements for conducting initial assessments for persons of that age have been made for persons from whom samples have been taken (under section 63B of PACE) at the police station in which C is detained, and
(b) the notice has not been withdrawn.

(7) In subsections (5) and (6), 'relevant chief officer' means the chief officer of police of the police force for the police area in which the police station is situated.

10 Follow-up assessment

(1) This section applies if –

(a) a police officer requires a person to attend an initial assessment and remain for its duration under section 9(2),
(b) the age condition is met, and
(c) the notification condition is met.

(2) The police officer must, at the same time as he imposes the requirement under section 9(2) –

(a) require the person to attend a follow-up assessment and remain for its duration, and
(b) inform him that the requirement ceases to have effect if he is informed at the initial assessment that he is no longer required to attend the follow-up assessment.

(3) A follow-up assessment is an appointment with a suitably qualified person (a 'follow-up assessor') –

(a) for any of the purposes of the initial assessment which were not fulfilled at the initial assessment, and
(b) if the follow-up assessor thinks it appropriate, for the purpose of drawing up a care plan.

(4) A care plan is a plan which sets out the nature of the assistance or treatment (or both) which may be most appropriate for the person in connection with any dependency upon, or any propensity to misuse, a specified Class A drug which the follow-up assessor thinks that he has
...

[...]

11 Requirements under sections 9 and 10: supplemental

(1) This section applies if a person is required to attend an initial assessment and remain for its duration by virtue of section 9(2).

(2)   A police officer must –

   (a) inform the person of the time when, and the place at which, the initial assessment is to take place, and
   (b) explain that this information will be confirmed in writing.

(3)   A police officer must warn the person that he may be liable to prosecution if he fails without good cause to attend the initial assessment and remain for its duration.

(4)   If the person is also required to attend a follow-up assessment and remain for its duration by virtue of section 10(2), a police officer must also warn the person that he may be liable to prosecution if he fails without good cause to attend the follow-up assessment and remain for its duration.

(5)   A police officer must give the person notice in writing which –

   (a) confirms that he is required to attend and remain for the duration of an initial assessment or both an initial assessment and a follow-up assessment (as the case may be),
   (b) confirms the information given in pursuance of subsection (2), and
   (c) repeats the warning given in pursuance of subsection (3) and any warning given in pursuance of subsection (4).

(6)   The duties imposed by subsections (2) to (5) must be discharged before the person is released from detention at the police station.

(7)   A record must be made, as part of the person's custody record, of –

   (a) the requirement imposed on him by virtue of section 9(2),
   (b) any requirement imposed on him by virtue of section 10(2),
   (c) the information and explanation given to him in pursuance of subsection (2) above,
   (d) the warning given to him in pursuance of subsection (3) above and any warning given to him in pursuance of subsection (4) above, and
   (e) the notice given to him in pursuance of subsection (5) above.

(8)   If a person is given a notice in pursuance of subsection (5), a police officer or a suitably qualified person may give the person a further notice in writing which –

   (a) informs the person of any change to the time when, or to the place at which, the initial assessment is to take place, and
   (b) repeats the warning given in pursuance of subsection (3) and any warning given in pursuance of subsection (4).

12 Attendance at initial assessment

(1)   This section applies if a person is required to attend an initial assessment and remain for its duration by virtue of section 9(2).

(2) The initial assessor must inform a police officer or a police support officer if the person –

(a) fails to attend the initial assessment at the specified time and place, or

(b) attends the assessment at the specified time and place but fails to remain for its duration.

(3) A person is guilty of an offence if without good cause –

(a) he fails to attend an initial assessment at the specified time and place, or

(b) he attends the assessment at the specified time and place but fails to remain for its duration.

(4) A person who is guilty of an offence under subsection (3) is liable on summary conviction to imprisonment for a term not exceeding 51 weeks, or to a fine not exceeding level 4 on the standard scale, or to both.

(5) If a person fails to attend an initial assessment at the specified time and place, any requirement imposed on him by virtue of section 10(2) ceases to have effect ...

13 Arrangements for follow-up assessment

(1) This section applies if –

(a) a person attends an initial assessment in pursuance of section 9(2), and

(b) he is required to attend a follow-up assessment and remain for its duration by virtue of section 10(2).

(2) If the initial assessor thinks that a follow-up assessment is not appropriate, he must inform the person concerned that he is no longer required to attend the follow-up assessment.

(3) The requirement imposed by virtue of section 10(2) ceases to have effect if the person is informed as mentioned in subsection (2).

(4) If the initial assessor thinks that a follow-up assessment is appropriate, the assessor must –

(a) inform the person of the time when, and the place at which, the follow-up assessment is to take place, and

(b) explain that this information will be confirmed in writing.

(5) The assessor must also warn the person that, if he fails without good cause to attend the follow-up assessment and remain for its duration, he may be liable to prosecution.

(6) The initial assessor must also give the person notice in writing which –

(a) confirms that he is required to attend and remain for the duration of the follow-up assessment,

(b) confirms the information given in pursuance of subsection (4), and

(c) repeats the warning given in pursuance of subsection (5).

(7) The duties mentioned in subsections (2) and (4) to (6) must be discharged before the conclusion of the initial assessment.

(8) If a person is given a notice in pursuance of subsection (6), the initial assessor or another suitably qualified person may give the person a further notice in writing which –

(a) informs the person of any change to the time when, or to the place at which, the follow-up assessment is to take place, and

(b) repeats the warning mentioned in subsection (5).

14 Attendance at follow-up assessment

(1) This section applies if a person is required to attend a follow-up assessment and remain for its duration by virtue of section 10(2).

(2) The follow-up assessor must inform a police officer or a police support officer if the person –

(a) fails to attend the follow-up assessment at the specified time and place, or

(b) attends the assessment at the specified time and place but fails to remain for its duration.

(3) A person is guilty of an offence if without good cause –

(a) he fails to attend a follow-up assessment at the specified time and place, or

(b) he attends the assessment at the specified time and place but fails to remain for its duration.

(4) A person who is guilty of an offence under subsection (3) is liable on summary conviction to imprisonment for a term not exceeding 51 weeks, or to a fine not exceeding level 4 on the standard scale, or to both …

15 Disclosure of information about assessments

(1) An initial assessor may disclose information obtained as a result of an initial assessment to any of the following –

(a) a person who is involved in the conduct of the assessment;

(b) a person who is or may be involved in the conduct of any follow-up assessment.

(2) A follow-up assessor may disclose information obtained as a result of a follow-up assessment to a person who is involved in the conduct of the assessment.

(3) Subject to subsections (1) and (2), information obtained as a result of an initial or a follow-up assessment may not be disclosed by any person without the written consent of the person to whom the assessment relates ...

16 Samples submitted for further analysis

(1) A requirement imposed on a person by virtue of section 9(2) or 10(2) ceases to have effect if at any time before he has fully complied with the requirement –

  (a) a police officer makes arrangements for a further analysis of the sample taken from him as mentioned in section 9(1)(a), and

  (b) the analysis does not reveal that a specified Class A drug was present in the person's body.

(2) If a requirement ceases to have effect by virtue of subsection (1), a police officer must so inform the person concerned ...

[...]

Part 4

Miscellaneous and general

20 Anti-social behaviour orders: intervention orders

(1) After section 1F of the Crime and Disorder Act 1998 (c. 37) (inserted by section 142(1) of the Serious Organised Crime and Police Act 2005 (c. 15)) insert –

"1G Intervention orders

(1) This section applies if, in relation to a person who has attained the age of 18, a relevant authority –

  (a) makes an application for an anti-social behaviour order or an order under section 1B above (the behaviour order),

  (b) has obtained from an appropriately qualified person a report relating to the effect on the person's behaviour of the misuse of controlled drugs or of such other factors as the Secretary of State by order prescribes, and

  (c) has engaged in consultation with such persons as the Secretary of State by order prescribes for the purpose of ascertaining that, if the report recommends that an order under this section is made, appropriate activities will be available.

(2) The relevant authority may make an application to the court which is considering the application for the behaviour order for an order under this section (an intervention order).

(3) If the court –

(a) makes the behaviour order, and
(b) is satisfied that the relevant conditions are met, it may also make an intervention order.

(4) The relevant conditions are –

(a) that an intervention order is desirable in the interests of preventing a repetition of the behaviour which led to the behaviour order being made (trigger behaviour);
(b) that appropriate activities relating to the trigger behaviour or its cause are available for the defendant;
(c) that the defendant is not (at the time the intervention order is made) subject to another intervention order or to any other treatment relating to the trigger behaviour or its cause (whether on a voluntary basis or by virtue of a requirement imposed in pursuance of any enactment);
(d) that the court has been notified by the Secretary of State that arrangements for implementing intervention orders are available in the area in which it appears that the defendant resides or will reside and the notice has not been withdrawn.

(5) An intervention order is an order which –

(a) requires the defendant to comply, for a period not exceeding six months, with such requirements as are specified in the order, and
(b) requires the defendant to comply with any directions given by a person authorised to do so under the order with a view to the implementation of the requirements under paragraph (a) above.

(6) An intervention order or directions given under the order may require the defendant –

(a) to participate in the activities specified in the requirement or directions at a time or times so specified;
(b) to present himself to a person or persons so specified at a time or times so specified.

(7) Requirements included in, or directions given under, an intervention order must, as far as practicable, be such as to avoid –

(a) any conflict with the defendant's religious beliefs, and

(b) any interference with the times (if any) at which he normally works or attends an educational establishment.

(8) If the defendant fails to comply with a requirement included in or a direction given under an intervention order, the person responsible for the provision or supervision of appropriate activities under the order must inform the relevant authority of that fact.

[...]"

References

Advisory Council on the Misuse of Drugs (ACMD) (1982) *Treatment and Rehabilitation.* London: HMSO.

——(1988) *AIDS and Drug Misuse. Part 1.* London: HMSO.

——(1989) *AIDS and Drug Misuse. Part 2.* London: HMSO.

——(1991) *Drug Misusers and the Criminal Justice System: Part I: Community Resources and the Probation Service.* London: HMSO.

——(1993) *AIDS and Drug Misuse – Update.* London: HMSO.

——(1994) *Drug Misusers and the Criminal Justice System: Part II: Police, Drug Misusers and the Community.* London: HMSO.

Albut, T.C. (1870) 'On the abuse of hypodermic injections of morphia' *The Practitioner* 5 329–30.

Allen, L., Trace, M. and Klein, A. (2004) *Decriminalisation of drugs in Portugal: a current overview.* Briefing Paper 6. Beckley Foundation Drug Policy Programme.

Ashton, J. and Seymour, H. (1988) *The New Public Health: The Liverpool Experience.* Milton Keynes: Open University Press.

Ashton, M. (2006) 'The Rolleston legacy' *Drug and Alcohol Findings* 15 4–5.

Auld, J., Dorn, N. and South, N. (1984) 'Heroin now: bringing it all back home' *Youth & Policy* No. 9 Summer 1–7.

——(1986) 'Irregular work, irregular pleasures: heroin in the 1980s' in: R. Matthews and J. Young (eds) *Confronting Crime.* London: Sage, pp 166–187.

Ayres, I. and Braithwaite, J. (1992) *Responsive Regulation: Transcending the Deregulation Debate.* Oxford: Oxford University Press.

Baker, T. (2000) 'Insurance and the law'. University of Pennsylvania Law School Working Paper. Available at SSRN: http://ssrn.com/abstract=242026 or DOI: 10.2139/ssrn.242026

——(2002) 'Risk, Insurance, and the Social Construction of Responsibility' in: T. Baker and J. Simon (eds) *Embracing Risk: The Changing Culture of Insurance and Responsibility.* Chicago: University of Chicago Press, pp. 33–51.

Bartrip, P. (1992) 'A "Pennurth of Arsenic for Rat Poison": The Arsenic Act, 1851 and the Prevention of Secret Poisoning' *Medical History* 36 53–69.

Bauman, Z. (1988) *Freedom.* Milton Keynes: Open University Press.

Beck, U. (1992) *The Risk Society: Towards a New Modernity.* London: Sage.

Becker, G. and Murphy, G. (1988) 'A theory of rational addiction' *Journal of Political Economy* 96 675–700.

Beeching, J. (1975) *The Chinese Opium Wars.* New York: Harcourt Brace.

Berridge, V. (1977a) 'Fenland opium eating in the nineteenth century' *British Journal of Addiction* 72 275–84.

——(1977b) 'Opium eating and life insurance' *British Journal of Addiction* 72 371–77.

——(1978) 'War conditions and narcotics control: the passing of Defence of the Realm Act Regulation 40B' *Journal of Social Policy* 7(3) 285–304.

——(1979) 'Morality and medical science: concepts of narcotic addiction in Britain' *Annals of Science* 36 67–85.

——(1980) 'The making of the Rolleston report, 1908–26' *Journal of Drug Issues* 10(1) 7–28.

——(1982) 'Opiate use in England, 1800–1926' *Annals of the New York Academy of Sciences* 398(1) 1–11.

——(1984) 'Drugs and social policy: the establishment of drug control in Britain, 1900–1930' *British Journal of Addiction* 79 17–29.

——(1991) 'AIDS and British drug policy: history repeats itself ... ?' in: D. Whynes and P. Bean (eds) *Policing and Prescribing: the British System of Drug Control*. London: Macmillan, pp. 176–98.

——(1996a) 'Drug policy: should the law take a back seat?' *The Lancet* 347 301–5.

——(1996b) *AIDS in the UK: The Making of Policy, 1981–1994*. Oxford: Oxford University Press.

——(1999) *Opium and the People: Opiate Use and Drug Control Policy in Nineteenth and Early Twentieth Century England*. Revised Edition. London: Free Association.

——(2001) 'Illicit drugs and internationalism: the forgotten dimension' *Medical History* 45 282–88.

——(2004a) 'Punishment or treatment? Inebriety, drink and drugs, 1860–2004' *The Lancet* 364 4–5.

——(2004b) 'Why alcohol is legal and other drugs are not' *History Today* May 18–20.

——(2005a) 'The "British System" and its history: myth and reality' in: J. Strand and M. Gossop (eds) *Heroin Addiction and the British System. Volume 1: Origins and Evolution*. London: Routledge, pp. 7–16.

——(2005b) *Temperance: Its History and Impact on Current and Future Alcohol Policy*. York: Joseph Rowntree Foundation.

Berridge, V. and Edwards, G. (1981) *Opium and the People: Opiate Use in Nineteenth-Century England*. London: Allen Lane.

Bewley, T. (1965) 'Heroin addiction in the United Kingdom, 1954–64' *British Medical Journal* 2 1284–86.

——(1966) 'Recent changes in the pattern of drug abuse in the United Kingdon' *Bulletin on Narcotics* 18 1–9.

——(2005) 'The drugs problem of the 1960s: A new type of problem' in: J. Strand and M. Gossop (eds) *Heroin Addiction and the British System. Volume 1: Origins and Evolution*. London: Routledge, pp. 43–52.

Bewley-Taylor, D. (1999) *The United States and International Drug Control, 1909–1997*. London: Continuum.

Biermann, F. and Pattberg, P. (2008) 'Global environmental governance: taking stock, moving forward' *Annual Review of Environment and Resources* 33 277–94.

Black, J. (2001) 'Decentring regulation: understanding the role of regulation and self-regulation in a "post-regulatory' world" *Current Legal Problems* 54 103–47.

——(2002) 'Critical reflections on regulation' *Australian Journal of Legal Philosophy* 27 1–36.

Bland, L. (2005) 'White women and men of colour: miscegenation fears in Britain after the Great War' *Gender & History* 17(1) 29–61.

Boire, R.G. (2002) 'John Stuart Mill and the liberty of inebriation' *The Independent Review* 7(2) 253–58.

Bolton, D. (1976) 'The development of alkaloid manufacture in Edinburgh, 1832–1932' *Chemistry and Industry* September 4 702.

Braithwaite, J. (1985) *To Punish or Persuade: Enforcement of Coal Mine Safety*. Albany, NY: State University of New York Press.

——(2000) 'The new regulatory state and the transformation of criminology' in: D. Garland and R. Sparks (eds) *Criminology and Social Theory*. Oxford: Oxford University Press.

——(2002) *Restorative Justice and Responsive Regulation*. New York: Oxford University Press.

——(2003) 'What's wrong with the sociology of punishment?' *Theoretical Criminology* 7(1) 5–28.

——(2005a) *Markets in Vice, Markets in Virtue*. New York and Sydney: Oxford and Federation Press.

——(2005b) 'For public social science' *British Journal of Sociology* 56(3) 345–53.

——(2006) 'Peacemaking networks and restorative justice' in: J. Fleming and J. Wood (eds) *Fighting Crime Together: The Challenges of Policing and Security Networks*. Sydney: University of New South Wales Press, pp. 195–217.

——(2008) *Regulatory Capitalism: How it Works, Ideas to Make it Work Better*. Cheltenham: Edward Elgar.

Braithwaite, J. and Drahos, P. (2000) *Global Business Regulation*. Cambridge: Cambridge University Press.

Braithwaite, J. and Pettit, P. (1990) *Not Just Deserts: A Republican Theory of Criminal Justice*. Oxford: Oxford University Press.

Braithwaite, V. (ed.) (2003) *Taxing Democracy: Understanding Tax Avoidance and Evasion*. London: Ashgate.

Braithwaite, V. and Braithwaite, J. (2006) 'Democratic sentiment and cyclical markets in vice' *British Journal of Criminology* 46 1110–27.

Brand, J.L. (1965) *Doctors and the State: The British Medical Profession and Government Action in Public Health, 1870–1912*. Baltimore: Johns Hopkins Press.

Brown, J.B. (1973) 'Politics of the poppy: the society for the suppression of the opium trade, 1874–1916' *Journal of Contemporary History* 8 97–111.

Bruun, K. (1970) 'Alkoholihaitat mahdollisimman vähäisiksi (The minimization of alcohol damage)' *Alkoholipolitiikka* 35 185–91.

Bull, M. (2008) *Governing the Heroin Trade: From Treaties to Treatment*. Aldershot: Ashgate.

Burchell, G. (1991) 'Peculiar interests: civil society and governing "the system of natural liberty"' in: G. Burchell, C. Gordon and P. Miller (eds) *The Foucault Effect: Studies in Governmentality*. Chicago: University of Chicago Press, pp. 119–50.

Burris, S. (2004) 'Governance, microgovernance and health' *Temple Law Review* 77 335–60.

Burris, S., Drahos, P. and Shearing, C. (2005) 'Nodal governance' *Australian Journal of Legal Philosophy* 30 30–58.

Burris, S., Kempa, M. and Shearing, C. (2008) 'Changes in governance: a cross-disciplinary review of current scholarship' *Akron Law Review* 41 1–66.

Buxton, J. (2006) *The Political Economy of Narcotics: Production, Consumption and Global Markets*. London: Zed Books.

Bynum, W.F. (1968) 'Chronic alcoholism in the first half of the 19th century' *Bulletin of the History of Medicine* 42(2) 160–85.

Cahalan, D. (1970) *Problem Drinkers: A National Survey*. San Francisco: Jossey-Bass.

Campbell, T.D. (1977) 'Adam Smith and natural liberty' *Political Studies* 25(4) 523–34.

Cartwright, J. and Shearing, C. (2004) 'Building peace in the Cape' *Safer Society* Winter 20–22.

Castel, R. (1994) '"Problematization" as a mode of reading history' in: J. Goldstein (ed) *Foucault and the Writing of History*. Oxford: Basil Blackwell.

Castells, M. (1996) *The Information Age. Volume 1: The Rise of the Network Society*. Oxford: Blackwell.

——(1997) *The Information Age. Volume 2: The Power of Identity*. Oxford: Blackwell.

——(1998) *The Information Age. Volume 3: The End of Millennium*. Oxford: Blackwell.

——(2000) 'Materials for an exploratory theory of the network society' *British Journal of Sociology* 51(1) 5–24.

Chadwick, E. (1842) *Report from the Poor Law Commissioners on an Inquiry into the Sanitary Conditions of the Labouring Population of Great Britain*. London: HMSO.

Cherney, A., O'Reilly, J. and Grabosky, P. (2005) *The Governance of Illicit Synthetic Drugs*. Hobart: NDLERF.

——(2006) 'Networks and meta-regulation: strategies aimed at governing illicit synthetic drugs' *Policing and Society* 16(4) 370–85.

Christison, R. (1832) 'On the effects of opium eating on health and longevity' *Edinburgh Medical and Surgical Journal* 37 123–35.

——(1854) 'An investigation of the deaths in the Standard Assurance Company' *Journal of the Institute of Actuaries* 4 76–78.

Clark, G. (1999) *Betting on Lives: The Culture of Life Insurance in England, 1695–1775*. Manchester: Manchester University Press.

——(2002) 'Embracing fatality through life insurance in eighteenth-century England' in: T. Baker and J. Simon (eds) *Embracing Risk: The Changing Culture of Insurance and Responsibility*. Chicago: University of Chicago Press, pp. 80–96.

Clark, W.B. (1966) 'Operational definition of drinking problems and associated prevalence rates' *Quarterly Journal of Studies on Alcohol* 27(4) 648–68.

Clouston, T. (1890) 'Diseased cravings and paralysed control' *Edinburgh Medical Journal* 35 508–21, 689–705, 793–809, 985–96.

——(1914) 'Some of the psychological and clinical aspects of alcohol' *British Journal of Inebriety* 11 105–31.

Cohen, P. (2003) 'The drug prohibition church and the adventure of reformation' *International Journal of Drug Policy* 14 213–15.

Cohen, S. (1985) *Visions of Social Control*. Cambridge: Polity Press.

Collins, W. (1916) 'The ethics and law of drug and alcohol addiction' *British Journal of Inebriety* 13 141.

Connell, P. (1958) *Amphetamine Psychosis*. Maudsley Monographs No. 5. Oxford: Oxford University Press.

Conway, S. (1990) 'Bentham and the nineteenth-century revolution in government' in: R. Bellamy (ed.) *Victorian Liberalism: Nineteenth-century Political Thought and Practice*. London: Routledge, pp. 71–90.

Costa, A.M. (2007) 'Free drugs or drug free?' Speech at the Drug Policy Alliance Conference, New Orleans. Available at: http://www.unodc.org/unodc/en/frontpage/free-drugs-or-drugs-free.html (accessed 12/03/08).

Courtwright, D. (2001) *Forces of Habit: Drugs and the Making of the Modern World*. Cambridge, MA and London: Harvard University Press.

——(2004) 'Drug wars: policy hots and historical cools' *Bulletin of the History of Medicine* 78 440–50.

——(2005) 'Mr ATOD's wild ride: what do alcohol, tobacco and other drugs have in common?' *The Social History of Alcohol and Drugs* 20 105–24.

Crawford, A. (2006) 'Networked governance and the post-regulatory state? Steering, rowing and anchoring the provision of policing and security' *Theoretical Criminology* 10(4) 449–79.

Curtis, B. (2002) 'Foucault on governmentality and population: the impossible discovery' *Canadian Journal of Sociology* 27(4) 505–33.

Davies, J.B. (1992) *The Myth of Addiction: An Application of the Psychological Theory of Attribution to Illicit Drug Use*. Reading: Harwood Academic Publishers.

de Alarcon, R. (1969) 'The spread of heroin abuse in a community' *Bulletin on Narcotics* 21 17–22.

Dean, M. (1994) *Critical and Effective Histories: Foucault's Methods and Historical Sociology*. London: Routledge.

——(1999) 'Risk, calculable and incalculable' in: D. Lupton (ed.) *Risk and Sociocultural Theory: New Directions and Perspectives*. Cambridge: Cambridge University Press.

Department for Work and Pensions (DWP) (2008) *No One Written Off: Reforming Welfare to Reward Responsibility*. London: DWP.

Dikotter, F., Laamann, L.P. and Xun, Z. (2004) *Narcotic Culture: A History of Drugs in China*. London: C. Hurst & Co.

Dingwerth, K. and Pattberg, P. (2006) 'Global governance as a perspective on world politics' *Global Governance* 12 185–203.

Dodsworth, F. (2008) 'The idea of police in eighteenth-century England: discipline, reformation, superintendence, c. 1780–1800' *Journal of the History of Ideas* 69(4) 583–604.

Doll, R. and Hill, A.B. (1950) 'Smoking and carcinoma of the lung' *British Medical Journal* 2 (4682) 739–48.

Doll, R. and Hill, A.B. (1964) 'Mortality in relation to smoking: ten years' observations of British doctors' *British Medical Journal* 1399–1410, 1460–67.

Donzelot, J. (1984) *L'invention du social*. Paris: Vrin.

Dorf, M. and Sabel, C. (1998) 'A constitution of democratic experimentalism' *Columbia Law Review* 98 267–473.

Dorn, N. (1975) 'Functions and varieties of explanation of recreational drug use' *British Journal of Addiction* 70 57–63.

——(1994) 'Three faces of police referral: welfare, justice and business perspectives on multi-agency work with drug arrestees' *Policing and Society* 4 13–34.

——(ed.) (1999) *Regulating European Drug Problems: Administrative Measures and Civil Law in the Control of Drug Trafficking, Nuisance and Use*. The Hague: Kluwer Law International.

Dorn, N. and South, N. (1987) 'Introduction' in N. Dorn and N. South (eds) *A Land Fit for Heroin?* Basingstoke: Palgrave Macmillan.

Dorn, N. and White, S. (1999) 'Drug trafficking, nuisance and use: opportunities for a regulatory space' in: N. Dorn (ed.) *Regulating European Drug Problems: Administrative Measures and Civil Law in the Control of Drug Trafficking, Nuisance and Use*. The Hague: Kluwer Law International, pp. 263–90.

Douglas, M. (1986) *Risk Acceptability*. New York: Basic Books.

——(1992) *Risk and Blame: Essays in Cultural Theory*. London: Routledge.

Douglas, M. and Wildavsky, A. (1982) *Risk and Culture: An Essay on the Selection of Technological and Environmental Dangers*. Berkeley: University of California Press.

Duke, K. (2006) 'Out of crime and into treatment?: The criminalization of contemporary drug policy since *Tackling Drugs Together*' *Drugs: Education, Prevention and Policy* 13(5) 409–15.

Dupont, B. (2006) 'Delivering security through networks: studying the relations landscape of security managers in an urban setting' *Law & Legal Change* 45 165–84.

Dupont, B. and Wood, J. (2006) 'Urban security from nodes to networks: on the value of connecting disciplines' *Canadian Journal of Law and Society* 22(2) 95–112.

Duryea, L.C. and Hirsh, J. (1948) 'Problem drinking: a challenge to psychiatry' *Mental Hygiene* 32(2) 246–52.

Dyzenhaus, D. (2008) *Accountability and the Concept of (Global) Administrative Law*. IILJ Working Paper 2008/7 (Global Administrative Law Series). New York: Institute for International Law and Justice, New York University Law School.

Edwards, G. and Gross, M. (1976) 'Alcohol dependence: provisional description of a clinical syndrome' *British Medical Journal* 1 1058–61.

Edwards, J. (1754/1957) *Freedom of the Will*. Edited by P. Ramsey. Yale: Yale University Press.

Elden, S. (2003) 'Plague, panopticon, police' *Surveillance & Society* 1(3) 240–53.

Engels, F. (1844/1987) *The Condition of the Working Class in England*. London: Penguin.

Erickson, C. and Wilcox, R. (2006) 'Please, not "addiction" in DSM-V' *American Journal of Psychiatry* 163(11) 2015–16.

Ericson, R.V. (2007) *Crime in an Insecure World*. Cambridge: Polity Press.

Ericson, R.V. and Carriere, K. (1994) 'The fragmentation of criminology' in: D. Nelken (ed.) *The Futures of Criminology*. London: Sage, pp. 89–109.

Ericson, R.V. and Haggerty, K. (1997) *Policing the Risk Society*. Toronto: University of Toronto Press.

Ewald, F. (1991) 'Insurance and risk' in: G. Burchell, C. Gordon and P. Miller (eds) *The Foucault Effect: Studies in Governmentality*. Chicago: University of Chicago Press, pp. 197–210.

——(2002) 'The return of Descartes' malicious demon: an outline of a philosophy of precaution' in: T. Baker and J. Simon (eds) *Embracing Risk: The Changing Culture of Insurance and Responsibility*. Chicago: University of Chicago Press.

Fainsinger, R., Thai, V., Frank, G. and Fergusson, J. (2006) 'What's in a word? Addiction versus dependence in DSM-V' *American Journal of Psychiatry* 163(11) 2014–15.

Fay, P. (1975) *The Opium War, 1840–1842*. Chapel Hill: University of North Carolina.

Ferejohn, J. (2007) *Accountability in a Global Context*. IILJ Working Paper 2007/5 (Global Administrative Law Series). New York: Institute for International Law and Justice, New York University Law School.

Ferentzy, P. (2001) 'From sin to disease: differences and similarities between past and current conceptions of chronic drunkenness' *Contemporary Drug Problems* 28 363–90.

Foucault, M. (1973) *The Birth of the Clinic: An Archaeology of Medical Perception*. London: Tavistock.

——(1974) 'Prisons et asiles dans le méchanisme du pouvoir' in: *Dits et Ecrits*. Paris: Gallimard, pp. 523–24.

——(1977) *Disipline and Punish: The Birth of the Prison*. London: Allen Lane.

——(1979) *Omnes et Singulatim: Towards a Criticism of 'Political Reason'*. The Tanner Lectures on Human Values. Delivered at Stanford University, October 10 and 16 1979. Available at: http://www.tannerlectures.utah.edu/lectures/documents/foucault81.pdf (accessed 06/06/09).

——(1980a) 'Truth and power' in: C. Gordon (ed.) *Power/Knowledge: Selected Interviews and Other Writings, 1972–1977*. New York: Pantheon Books, pp. 109–33

——(1980b) 'The politics of health in the eighteenth century' in: C. Gordon (ed.) *Power/Knowledge: Selected Interviews and Other Writings, 1972–1977*. New York: Pantheon Books, pp. 166–82

——(1983) 'Structuralism and post-structuralism: An interview with Michel Foucault' *Telos* 55 195–211.

——(1984) 'Nietzsche, genealogy, history' in: P. Rabinow (ed.) *The Foucault Reader*. New York: Pantheon Books, pp. 76–100.

——(1991a) 'Governmentality' in: G. Burchell, C. Gordon and P. Miller (eds) *The Foucault Effect: Studies in Governmentality*. Chicago: University of Chicago Press, pp. 87–104.

——(1991b) 'Questions of method' in: G. Burchell, C. Gordon and P. Miller (eds) *The Foucault Effect: Studies in Governmentality*. Chicago: University of Chicago Press, pp. 73–86.

——(2007) *Security, Territory, Population: Lectures at the Collège de France, 1977–1978*. Basingstoke: Palgrave Macmillan.

——(2008) *The Birth of Biopolitics: Lectures at the Collège de France, 1978–1979*. Basingstoke: Palgrave Macmillan.

Fraser, N. and Gordon, D. (1994) 'A genealogy of *dependency*: tracing a keyword of the US welfare state' *Signs: Journal of Women in Culture and Society* 19(2) 309–36.

Friedman, M. and Friedman, R. (1980) *Free to Choose: A Personal Statement*. San Diego: Harcourt.

Froestad, J. and Shearing, C. (2007) 'The Zwelethemba Model: practising human rights through dispute resolution' in: S. Parmentier and E. Weitekamp (eds) *Crime and Human Rights*. Oxford: Elsevier.

Garland, D. (1981) 'The birth of the welfare sanction' *British Journal of Law and Society* 8(1) 29–45.

——(1985) *Punishment and Welfare: A History of Penal Strategies*. Aldershot: Gower.

——(1990) *Punishment and Modern Society: A Study in Social Theory*. Oxford: Clarendon Press.

——(2001) *The Culture of Control: Crime and Social Order in Contemporary Society*. Oxford: Oxford University Press.

——(2003) 'The rise of risk' in: R. Ericson and A. Doyle (eds) *Risk and Morality*. Toronto: University of Toronto Press.

Garside, R. (2003) 'Nine words that shook the criminal justice world' *Safer Society* 16 2–4.

Giddens, A. (1990) *The Consequences of Modernity*. Cambridge: Polity Press.

——(1991) *Modernity and Self-Identity: Self and Society in the Late Modern Age*. Cambridge: Polity Press.

Goldstein, J. (ed.) (1994) *Foucault and the Writing of History*. Oxford: Blackwell.

Gordon, C. (1991) 'Governmental rationality: an introduction' in: G. Burchell, C. Gordon and P. Miller (eds) *The Foucault Effect: Studies in Governmentality*. Chicago: University of Chicago Press, pp. 1–52.

Gossop, M., Keaney, F., Sharma, P. and Jackson, M. (2005) 'The unique role of diamorphine in British medical practice: a survey of general practitioners and hospital doctors' *European Addiction Research* 11 76–82.

Habermas, J. (1986) 'Taking aim at the heart of the present' in: D.C. Hoy (ed.) *Foucault: A Critical Reader*. Oxford: Blackwell, pp. 103–08.

——(1987) *The Philosophical Discourse of Modernity*. Cambridge, MA: MIT Press.

Hacking, I. (1982) 'Biopower and the avalanche of printed numbers' *Humanities in Society* 5 279–95.

——(1990) *The Taming of Chance*. Cambridge: Cambridge University Press.

——(1991) 'How should we do the history of statistics?' in: G. Burchell, C. Gordon and P. Miller (eds) *The Foucault Effect: Studies in Governmentality*. Chicago: University of Chicago Press, pp. 181–96.

——(2004) 'The complacent disciplinarian' http://www.interdisciplines.org/interdisciplinarity/ papers/7

Hale, T. (2008) 'Transparency, accountability and global governance' *Global Governance* 14(1) 73–94.

Hall, S., Critchley, C., Jefferson, T., Clarke, J. and Roberts, B. (1978) *Policing the Crisis*. London: Macmillan.

Hamacher, W. (1986) "Disgregation of the will': Nietzsche on the individual and individuality' in: T. Heller, M. Sosna, C. Brooke-Rose and D. Wellbery (eds) *Reconstructing Individualism: Autonomy, Individuality and the Self in Western Thought*. Stanford: Stanford University Press, pp. 106–39.

Hammersley, R. (2008) *Drugs and Crime: Theories and Practices*. Cambridge: Polity Press.

Harding, C. and Wilkin, L. (1988) "The dream of a benevolent mind': the late Victorian response to inebriety' *Criminal Justice History* 9 189–207.

Harding, G. (1988) *Opium Addiction, Morality and Medicine: From Moral Illness to Pathological Disease*. London: Macmillan.

Harrison, B. (1994) *Drink and the Victorians*. 2nd edition. Keele: Keele University Press.

Harvey, D. (2007) *A Brief History of Neoliberalism*. Oxford: Oxford University Press.

Haworth, A. and Acuda, W. (1998) 'Sub-Saharan Africa' in: M. Grant (ed.) *Alcohol and Emerging Markets*. Washington: International Center for Alcohol Policies, pp. 19–90.

Hayek, F. (1944) *The Road to Serfdom*. Chicago: University of Chicago Press.

——(1960) *The Constitution of Liberty*. Chicago: University of Chicago Press.

——(1973–79) *Law, Legislation and Liberty*. Three volumes. Chicago: University of Chicago Press.

Heather, N. and Vuchinich, R. (2003) 'Concluding comments' in: R. Vuchinich and N. Heather (eds) *Choice, Behavioural Economics and Addiction*. Oxford: Pergamon Press, pp. 409–26.

Heather, N., Wodak, A., Nadelmann, E. and O'Hare, P. (eds) (1993) *Psychoactive Drugs and Harm Reduction: From Faith to Science*. London: Whurr.

Held, D., McGrew, A., Goldblatt, D. and Perraton, J. (1999) *Global Transformations: Politics, Economics and Culture*. Cambridge: Polity Press.

Hennessy, P. (1992) *Never Again: Britain 1945–1951*. London: Jonathan Cape.

Hennock, E.P. (2000) 'The urban sanitary movement in England and Germany, 1838–1914' *Continuity and Change* 15(2) 269–96.

Hindess, B. (2001) 'The liberal government of unfreedom' *Alternatives* 26 93–111.

Hirsh, J. (1949) *The Problem Drinker*. New York: Duell, Sloan & Pierce.

Hobsbawm, E. (1962) *The Age of Revolution, 1789–1848*. London: Penguin.

Holloway, S.W.F. (1966) 'The Apothecaries Act, 1815: a reinterpretation' *Medical History* 10 107–29, 221–36.

——(1995) 'The regulation of the supply of drugs in Britain before 1868' in: R. Porter and M. Teich (eds) *Drugs and Narcotics in History*. Cambridge: Cambridge University Press, pp. 77–96.

Hölstrom, R. (2006) 'The fruits of fear' *Druglink* Sept./Oct. 10–12.

Holt, E. (1964) *The Opium Wars in China*. New York: Putnam & Co.

Home Office (2006) *DIP – Tough Choices Project FAQs*. June 9 version. London: Home Office.

Hough, M., Hunter, G., Jacobson, J. and Cossalter, S. (2008) *The Impact of the Licensing Act 2003 on Levels of Crime and Disorder: An Evaluation*. Home Office Research Report 04. London: Home Office.

Hucklesby, A., Eastwood, C., Seddon, T. and Spriggs, A. (2007) *The Evaluation of the Restriction on Bail Pilots: Implementation Lessons from the First Six Months*. Home Office online report 36/05. London: Home Office.

Hughes, C. and Stevens, A. (2007) *The Effects of Decriminalisation of Drug Use in Portugal*. Briefing Paper 14. Beckley Foundation Drug Policy Programme.

Hunt, N. and Stevens, A. (2004) 'Whose harm? Harm reduction and the shift to coercion in UK drug policy' *Social Policy & Society* 3(4) 333–42.

Hutchinson, S. (2006) 'Countering catastrophic criminology: reform, punishment and the modern liberal compromise' *Punishment & Society* 8(4) 443–67.

Inglis, B. (1976) *The Opium War*. Philadelphia: Coronet.

Innes, M. (2006) 'Land, freedom and the making of the medieval West' *Transactions of the Royal Historical Society* 16 39–74.

Jackson, F. (1998) *From Metaphysics to Ethics: A Defence of Conceptual Analysis*. Oxford: Oxford University Press.

Jayne, M., Holloway, S. and Valentine, G. (2006) 'Drunk and disorderly: alcohol, urban life and public space' *Progress in Human Geography* 30(4) 451–68.

Jellinek, E. (1960) *The Disease Concept of Alcoholism*. New Haven: Hillhouse.

Jennings, O. (1901) 'On the physiological cure of the morphia habit' *The Lancet* 2 360.

Johnson, B. (1975) 'Righteousness before revenue: the forgotten moral crusade against the Indo-China opium trade' *Journal of Drug Issues* 5 304–26.

Johnstone, G. (1996) 'From vice to disease? The concepts of dipsomania and inebriety, 1860–1908' *Social & Legal Studies* 5 37–56.

Jones, M. (2004) 'Anxiety and containment in the risk society: theorising young people and drug prevention policy' *International Journal of Drug Policy* 15 367–76.

Kelly, M. (ed) (1994) *Critique and Power: Recasting the Foucault/Habermas Debate*. Cambridge, MA: MIT Press.

Keynes, J.M. (1920) *The Economic Consequences of the Peace*. New York: Harcourt Brace.

Kingsbury, B. (2009) 'The concept of "law" in global administrative law' *European Journal of International Law* 20(1) 23–57.

Kingsbury, B., Krisch, N. and Stewart, R. (2005) 'The emergence of global administrative law' *Law and Contemporary Problems* 68(3) 15–61.

Knemeyer, F.-L. (1980) 'Polizei' *Economy and Society* 9 172–96.

Knupfer, G. (1967) 'The epidemiology of problem drinking' *American Journal of Public Health* 57(6) 973–86.

Kohn, M. (1992) *Dope Girls: The Birth of the British Drug Underground*. London: Granta.

Krisch, N. (2006) 'The pluralism of global administrative law' *European Journal of International Law* 17(1) 247–78.

Krisch, N. and Kingsbury, B. (2006) 'Introduction: global governance and global administrative law in the international legal order' *European Journal of International Law* 17(1) 1–13.

Kundera, M. (1984) *The Unbearable Lightness of Being*. London: Faber & Faber.

Lawrence, S.C. (1991) 'Private enterprise and public interests: medical education and the Apothecaries Act, 1780–1825' in: R. French and A. Wear (eds) *British Medicine in an Age of Reform*. London: Routledge, pp. 45–83.

Levi-Faur, D. (2005) 'The global diffusion of regulatory capitalism' *Annals of the American Academy of Political and Social Science* 598(1) 12–32.

Levine, H. (1978) 'The discovery of addiction: changing conceptions of habitual drunkenness in America' *Journal of Studies on Alcohol* 39(1) 143–74.

——(1993) 'Temperance cultures: concerns about alcohol problems in Nordic and English-speaking cultures' in: M. Lader, G. Edwards and C. Drummond (eds) *The Nature of Alcohol and Drug-Related Problems*. New York: Oxford University Press, pp. 16–36.

Levine, H. and Reinarman, C. (1991) 'From prohibition to regulation: lessons from alcohol policy for drug policy' *The Milbank Quarterly* 69(3) 461–94.

Levinstein, E. (1878) *The Morbid Craving for Morphia*. London: Smith, Elder & Co.

Lister, S., Seddon, T., Wincup, E., Barrett, S. and Traynor, P. (2008) *Street Policing of Problem Drug Users*. York: Joseph Rowntree Foundation.

Little, R. (1850) 'On the habitual use of opium' *Monthly Journal of Medical Science* 10 524–38.

Loader, I. and Sparks, R. (2004) 'For an historical sociology of crime policy in England and Wales since 1968' *Critical Review of International Social and Political Philosophy* 7(2) 5–32.

Loader, I. and Walker, N. (2007) *Civilizing Security*. Cambridge: Cambridge University Press.

Lowes, P.D. (1966) *The Genesis of International Narcotics Control*. Geneva: Libraire Droz.

McCormick, M. (1969) 'First representations of the gamma alcoholic in the English novel' *Quarterly Journal of Studies on Alcohol* 30 957–80.

McDermott, P. (2005) 'The great Mersey experiment: the birth of harm reduction' in: J. Strang and M. Gossop (eds) *Heroin Addiction and the British System. Vol. 1: Origins and Evolution*. London: Routledge, pp. 139–56.

MacDonagh, O. (1958) 'The nineteenth-century revolution in government: a reappraisal' *Historical Journal* 1 52–67.

MacGregor, S., Ettorre, E., Coomber, R., Crosier, A. and Lodge, H. (1991) *Drug Services in England and the Impact of the Central Funding Initiative*. Research Monograph 1. London: ISDD.

MacLeod, R. (1967) 'The edge of hope: social policy and chronic alcoholism 1870–1900' *Journal of the History of Medicine* July 215–45.

——(ed.) (2003) *Government and Expertise: Specialists, Administrators and Professionals, 1860–1919*. Cambridge: Cambridge University Press.

Manderson, D. (2005) 'Possessed: drug policy, witchcraft and belief' *Cultural Studies* 19(1) 35–62.

Marlowe, D.B., Merikle, E.P., Kirby, K.C., Festinger, D. and McLellan, A.T. (2001) 'Multi-dimensional assessment of perceived treatment-entry pressures among substance abusers' *Psychology of Addictive Behavior* 15 97–108.

Marlowe, D.B., Kirby, K., Bonieskie, L., Glass, D., Dodds, L., Husband, S., Platt, J. and Festinger, D. (1996) 'Assessment of coercive and noncoercive pressures to enter drug abuse treatment' *Drug and Alcohol Dependence* 42 77–84.

Marshall, T.H. (1950) *Citizenship and Social Class and Other Essays*. Cambridge: Cambridge University Press.

Mart, G.R. (1832) 'Effects of the practice of opium eating' *The Lancet* 712–13.

Mason, N. (2001) '"The sovereign people are in a beastly state": the Beer Act of 1830 and Victorian discourse on working-class drunkenness' *Victorian Literature and Culture* 109–27.

Matthews, L. (1962) *History of Pharmacy in Britain*. Edinburgh and London: E&S Livingstone.

May, T., Warburton, H., Turnbull, P.J. and Hough, M. (2002) *Times They are A-Changing: Policing of Cannabis*. York: Joseph Rowntree Foundation.

May, T., Duffy, M., Warburton, H. and Hough, M. (2007) *Policing Cannabis as a Class C Drug: An Arresting Change?* York: Joseph Rowntree Foundation.

Mayhew, H. (1849–52/1985) *London Labour and the London Poor*. London: Penguin.

Measham, F. and Brain, K. (2005) '"Binge" drinking, British alcohol policy and the new culture of intoxication' *Crime Media Culture* 1(3) 262–83.

Miles, S. (2000) *Youth Lifestyles in a Changing World*. Buckingham: Open University Press.

Mill, J.S. (1859/2002) *On Liberty*. Mineola, NY: Dover.

Miller, S. (2006) 'Language and addiction' *American Journal of Psychiatry* 163(11) 2015.

Miller, P. and Rose, N. (1997) 'Mobilising the consumer: assembling the subject of consumption' *Theory, Culture and Society* 14(1) 1–36.

Mills, J. (2003) *Cannabis Britannica: Empire, Trade and Prohibition, 1800–1928*. Oxford: Oxford University Press.

——(2005) 'Morality, society and the science of intoxication: a response to David Courtwright's 'Mr ATOD's wild ride: what do alcohol, tobacco and other drugs have in common?'' *Social History of Alcohol and Drugs* 20 133–37.

Mills, J. and Barton, P. (eds) (2007) *Drugs and Empires: Essays in Modern Imperialism and Intoxication, c. 1500–c. 1930*. Basingstoke: Palgrave Macmillan.

Ministry of Health (1926) *Report of the Departmental Committee on Morphine and Heroin Addiction*. 'The Rolleston Report'. London: Ministry of Health.

——(1961) *Drug Addiction. Report of the Interdepartmental Committee*. 'The First Brain Report'. London: HMSO.

——(1965) *Drug Addiction. Second Report of the Interdepartmental Committee*. 'The Second Brain Report'. London: HMSO.

Mold, A. and Berridge, V. (2007) 'Crisis and opportunity in drug policy: changing the direction of British drug services in the 1980s' *Journal of Policy History* 19(1) 29–48.

Nadelmann, E. (1990) 'Global prohibition regimes: the evolution of norms in international society' *International Organization* 44(4) 479–526.

Newburn, T. and Sparks, R. (eds) (2004) *Criminal Justice and Political Cultures: National and International Dimensions of Crime Control*. Cullompton, Devon: Willan.

Newcombe, R. (1987) 'High time for harm reduction' *Druglink* 2(1) 10–11.

Nutt, D. (2009) 'Equasy – an overlooked addiction with implications for the current debate on drug harms' *Journal of Psychopharmacology* 23(1) 3–5.

Nutt, D., King, L., Saulsbury, W. and Blakemore, C. (2007) 'Developing a rational scale for assessing the risks of drugs of potential misuse' *The Lancet* 369 1047–53.

Nye, R. (1984) *Crime, Madness and Politics in Modern France: The Medical Concept of National Decline*. Princeton: Princeton University Press.

O'Brien, C., Volkow, N. and Li, T.-K. (2006) 'Dr O'Brien replies' *American Journal of Psychiatry* 163(11) 2016–17.

Ogus, A. (1994) *Regulation: Legal Form and Economic Theory*. Oxford: Hart.

O'Hare, P., Newcombe, R., Matthews, A., Buning, E. and Drucker, E. (eds) (1992) *The Reduction of Drug-related Harm*. London: Routledge.

O'Malley, P. (1992) 'Risk, power and crime prevention' *Economy and Society* 21(3) 252–75.

——(1998) 'Imagining insurance: risk, thrift and industrial life insurance in Britain' *Connecticut Insurance Law Journal* 5(2) 675–705.

——(1999) 'Consuming risks: harm minimization and the government of "drug-users"' in: R. Smandych (ed.) *Governable Places: Readings in Governmentality and Crime Control*. Aldershot: Dartmouth, pp. 191–214.

——(2004) *Risk, Uncertainty and Government*. Abingdon: Routledge-Cavendish.

——(2008) 'Experiments in risk and criminal justice' *Theoretical Criminology* 12(4) 451–69.

O'Malley, P. and Valverde, M. (2004) 'Pleasure, freedom and drugs: the uses of "pleasure" in liberal governance of drug and alcohol consumption' *Sociology* 38(1) 25–42.

Osborne, D. and Gaebler, T. (1992) *Reinventing Government*. New York: Addison-Wesley.

Osborne, T. (1993) 'On liberalism, neo-liberalism and the 'liberal profession' of medicine' *Economy and Society* 22(3) 345–56.

Pan, L. (1975) *Alcohol in Colonial Africa*. Helsinki: Finnish Foundation for Alcohol Studies.

Parker, H. (2000) 'How young Britons obtain their drugs: drug transactions at the point of consumption' in: M. Natarajan and M. Hough (eds) *Illegal Drug Markets: From Research to Prevention Policy*. New York: Criminal Justice Press, pp. 59–81.

Parker, H. and Newcombe, R. (1987) 'Heroin use and acquisitive crime in an English community' *British Journal of Sociology* 38(3) 331–50.

Parker, H., Bakx, K. and Newcombe, R. (1988) *Living with Heroin: The Impact of a Drugs 'Epidemic' on an English Community*. Milton Keynes: Open University Press.

Parker, H., Aldridge, J. and Measham, F. (1998) *Illegal Leisure: The Normalization of Adolescent Recreational Drug Use*. London: Routledge.

Parssinen, T. (1983) *Secret Passions, Secret Remedies: Narcotic Drugs in British Society 1820–1930*. Manchester: Manchester University Press.

Parssinen, T. and Kerner, K. (1980) 'Development of the disease model of drug addiction in Britain, 1870–1926' *Medical History* 24 275–96.

——(1981) 'An historical fable for our time: the illicit traffic in morphine in the early twentieth century' *Journal of Drug Issues* Winter 45–60.

Pasquino, P. (1991) 'Theatrum politicum: the genealogy of capital – police and the state of prosperity' in: G. Burchell, C. Gordon and P. Miller (eds) *The Foucault Effect: Studies in Governmentality*. Chicago: University of Chicago Press, pp. 105–18.

Patterson, O. (1991) *Freedom. Volume 1: Freedom in the Making of Western Culture*. London: I.B. Tauris & Co.

Pearson, G. (1987) *The New Heroin Users*. Oxford: Blackwell.

——(2001) 'Drugs and poverty' in: S. Chen and E. Skidelsky (eds) *High Time for Reform: Drug Policy for the 21st Century*. London: Social Market Foundation.

Pearson, G. and Patel, K. (1998) 'Drugs, deprivation and ethnicity: outreach among Asian drug users in a northern English city' *Journal of Drug Issues* 28(1) 199–224.

Pearson, G., Gilman, M. and McIver, S. (1986) *Young People and Heroin: An Examination of Heroin Use in the North of England*. London: Health Education Council.

Peele, S. (1985) *The Meaning of Addiction*. San Francisco: Jossey-Bass.

Pick, D. (1993) *Faces of Degeneration: A European Disorder, c. 1848–c. 1918*. Cambridge: Cambridge University Press.

Pohlenz, M. (1966) *Freedom in Greek Life and Thought: The History of an Ideal*. Dordrecht: D. Reidel.

Polanyi, K. (1944) *The Great Transformation: The Political and Economic Origins of Our Time*. Boston: Beacon Press.

Porter, D. (1994) 'Introduction' in: D. Porter (ed.) *The History of Public Health and the Modern State*. Amsterdam: Rodopi, pp. 1–44.

——(1999) *Health, Civilization and the State: A History of Public Health from Ancient to Modern Times*. London: Routledge.

Porter, R. (1985) 'The drinking man's disease: the "pre-history" of alcoholism in Georgian Britain' *British Journal of Addiction* 80 385–96.

——(1993) *Disease, Medicine and Society in England, 1550–1860*. Second edition. Basingstoke: Macmillan.

——(1996) 'The history of the "drugs problem"' *Criminal Justice Matters* 24 3–5.

——(2003) 'Introduction' in: R. Porter and D. Wright (eds) *The Confinement of the Insane: International Perspectives, 1800–1965*. Cambridge: Cambridge University Press, pp. 1–19.

Raaflaub, K. (2004) *The Discovery of Freedom in Ancient Greece*. Second edition. Chicago: University of Chicago Press.

Rabinow, P. and Rose, N. (2006) 'Biopower today' *BioSocieties* 1(2) 195–217.

Radzinowicz, L. and Hood, R. (1986) *History of English Criminal Law and its Administration. Volume 5: The Emergence of Penal Policy*. London: Stevens.

Read, J. (2009) 'A genealogy of Homo-economicus: neoliberalism and the production of subjectivity' *Foucault Studies* 6 25–36.

Redfield, M. (1997) 'Introduction' *Diacritics* 27(3) 3–7.

Reichman, N. (1986) 'Managing crime risks: towards an insurance based model of social control' *Research in Law, Deviance and Social Control* 8 151–72.

Reinarman, C. (2005) 'Addiction as accomplishment: the discursive construction of disease' *Addiction Research and Theory* 13(4) 307–20.

Reith, G. (2004) 'Consumption and its discontents: addiction, identity and the problems of freedom' *British Journal of Sociology* 55(2) 283–300.

Riley, J. and Marden, C. (1947) 'The social pattern of alcoholic drinking' *Quarterly Journal of Studies on Alcohol* 8 265–73.

Roberts, D. (1960) *Victorian Origins of the Welfare State*. Yale: Yale University Press.

Robertson, R. (2005) 'The arrival of HIV' in: J. Strang and M. Gossop (eds) *Heroin Addiction and the British System. Vol. 1: Origins and Evolution*. London: Routledge, pp. 123–38.

Roe, G. (2005) 'Harm reduction as paradigm: is better than bad good enough? The origins of harm reduction' *Critical Public Health* 15(3) 243–50.

Rolles, S., Kushlick, D. and Jay, M. (2006) *After the War on Drugs: Options for Control*. Bristol: Transform Drug Policy Foundation.

Room, R. (1975) 'Minimizing alcohol problems' in: M. Chafetz (ed.) *Proceedings of the Fourth Annual Alcoholism Conference of the National Institute on Alcohol Abuse and Alcoholism: Research, Treatment and Prevention*. DHEW Publication No. (ADM) 76–284. Washington, DC: US Government Printing Office, pp. 379–93.

——(1984) 'Alcohol control and public health' *Annual Review of Public Health* 5 293–317.

——(2004) 'Alcohol and harm reduction, then and now' *Critical Public Health* 14(4) 329–44.

——(2006) 'Addiction concepts and international control' *Social History of Alcohol and Drugs* 20 276–89.

Rose, N. (1985) *The Psychological Complex: Psychology, Politics and Society in England, 1869–1939*. London: Routledge & Kegan Paul.

——(1990) 'Of madness itself: *Histoire de la Folie* and the object of psychiatric history' *History of the Human Sciences* 3(3) 373–80.

——(1996) 'Governing "advanced" liberal democracies' in: A. Barry, T. Osborne and N. Rose (eds) *Foucault and Political Reason*. London: UCL Press, pp. 37–64.

——(1999) *Powers of Freedom: Reframing Political Thought*. Cambridge: Cambridge University Press.

——(2000) 'Government and control' in: D. Garland and R. Sparks (eds) *Criminology and Social Theory*. Clarendon Studies in Criminology. Oxford: Oxford University Press, pp. 183–208.

——(2003) 'Neurochemical selves' *Society* November/December 46–59.

——(2006) *The Politics of Life Itself: Biomedicine, Power and Subjectivity in the Twenty-first Century*. Princeton: Princeton University Press.

——(2007) 'Molecular biopolitics, somatic ethics and the spirit of biocapital' *Social Theory & Health* 5 3–29.

Rose, N. and Miller, P. (1992) 'Political power beyond the state: problematics of government' *British Journal of Sociology* 43(2) 173–205.

Rose, N., O'Malley, P. and Valverde, M. (2006) 'Governmentality' *Annual Review of Law and Social Science* 2 83–104.

Rosen, G. (1958) *A History of Public Health*. New York: MD Publications.

Rosenau, J. (1995) 'Governance in the twenty-first century' *Global Governance* 1 13–43.

Ruggiero, V. (1999) 'Drugs as a password and the law as a drug: discussing the legalisation of illicit substances' in: N. South (ed.) *Drugs: Cultures, Controls and Everyday Life*. London: Sage, pp. 123–38.

Rutgers, M. (1998) 'Paradigm lost: crisis as identity of the study of public administration' *International Review of Administrative Sciences* 64 553.

Sachs, J. (1999) 'Twentieth-century political economy: a brief history of global capitalism' *Oxford Review of Economic Policy* 15(4) 90–101.

——(2000) 'Globalization and patterns of economic development' *Review of World Economics* 136(4) 579–600.

Savary, J.-F., Hallam, C. and Bewley-Taylor, D. (2009) *The Swiss Four Pillars Policy: An Evolution from Local Experimentation to Federal Law*. Briefing Paper 18. Beckley Foundation Drug Policy Programme

Schivelbusch, W. (1992) *Tastes of Paradise: A Social History of Spices, Stimulants and Intoxicants*. New York: Pantheon.

Scott, I. (1998) 'A hundred-year habit' *History Today* June 6–8.

Seddon, T. (2000) 'Explaining the drug–crime link: theoretical, policy and research issues' *Journal of Social Policy* 29(1) 95–107.

——(2005) 'Searching for the next (techno-)fix: drug testing in the criminal justice system' *Criminal Justice Matters* 58 16–17.

——(2006) 'Drugs, crime and social exclusion: social context and social theory in British drugs-crime research' *British Journal of Criminology* 46 680–703.

——(2007a) 'Drugs and freedom' *Addiction Research & Theory* 15(4) 333–42.

——(2007b) 'The regulation of heroin: drug policy and social change in early twentieth century Britain' *International Journal of the Sociology of Law* 35(3) 143–56.

——(2007c) 'Coerced drug treatment in the criminal justice system: conceptual, ethical and criminological issues' *Criminology & Criminal Justice* 7(3) 269–86.

——(2008a) 'Drugs, the informal economy and globalization' *International Journal of Social Economics* 35(10) 717–28.

——(2008b) 'Women, harm reduction and history: gender perspectives on the emergence of the "British System" of drug control' *International Journal of Drug Policy* 19(2) 99–105.

Seddon, T., Ralphs, R. and Williams, L. (2008) 'Risk, security and the "criminalization" of British drug policy' *British Journal of Criminology* 48(6) 818–34.

Sedgwick, E. (1994) 'Epidemics of the will' in: E. Sedgwick (ed.) *Tendencies*. London: Routledge, pp. 129–40.

Shearing, C. (2001) 'Punishment and the changing face of governance' *Punishment and Society* 3(2) 203–20.

Shearing, C. and Wood, J. (2003) 'Governing security for common goods' *International Journal of the Sociology of Law* 31 205–25.

Sherratt, A. (1995) 'Introduction: peculiar substances' in: J. Goodman, P. Lovejoy and A. Sherratt (eds) *Consuming Habits: Drugs in History and Anthropology*. London: Routledge, pp. 1–10.

Sidgwick, H. (1874) *The Method of Ethics*. London: Macmillan.

Simon, J. (1987) 'The emergence of a risk society: insurance, law and the state' *Socialist Review* 95 61–89.

——(1988) 'The ideological effects of actuarial practices' *Law and Society Review* 22 771–800.

Singleton, N. (2008) 'The role of drug testing in the criminal justice system' *Drugs and Alcohol Today* 8(3) 4–8.

Skodbo, S., Brown, G., Deacon, S., Cooper, A., Hall, A., Millar, T., Smith, J. and Whitham, K. (2007) *The Drug Interventions Programme (DIP): Addressing Drug Use and Offending through 'Tough Choices'*. Home Office Research Report 02. London: Home Office.

Smart, C. (1984) 'Social policy and drug addiction: a critical study of policy development' *British Journal of Addiction* 79 31–39.

——(1992) 'Disruptive bodies and unruly sex: the regulation of reproduction and sexuality in the nineteenth century' in: C. Smart (ed.) *Regulating Womanhood: Historical Essays on Marriage, Motherhood and Sexuality*. London: Routledge.

Smith, A. (1776) *An Inquiry into the Nature and Causes of the Wealth of Nations*. Two volumes. London: Strahan and Cadell.

——(1978) *Lectures on Jurisprudence*. Edited by R. Meek, D. Raphael and P. Stein. Oxford: Oxford University Press.

Sneader, W. (1998) 'The discovery of heroin' *The Lancet* 352 1697–99.

Sparks, R. (1997) 'Recent social theory and the study of crime and punishment' in: M. Maguire, R. Morgan and R. Reiner (eds) *The Oxford Handbook of Criminology*. Second edition. Oxford: Clarendon Press, pp. 409–36.

——(2001) 'Degrees of estrangement: the cultural theory of risk and comparative penology' *Theoretical Criminology* 5(2) 159–76.

Spear, H.B. (1969) 'The growth of heroin addiction in the United Kingdom' *British Journal of Addiction* 64 245–55.

——(2002) *Heroin addiction care and control: the British System 1916–1984*. London: DrugScope.

Stein, S.D. (1985) *International Diplomacy, State Administrators and Narcotics Control: The Origins of a Social Problem*. Aldershot: Gower.

Stevens, A. (2007) 'When two dark figures collide: evidence and discourse on drug-related crime' *Critical Social Policy* 27(1) 77–99.

Stevens, A., McSweeney, T., van Ooyen, M. and Uchtenhagen, A. (2005) 'On coercion' *International Journal of Drug Policy* 16 207–9.

Stimson, G. (2000) '"Blair declares war": the unhealthy state of British drug policy' *International Journal of Drug Policy* 11 259–64.

Stimson, G. and Lart, R. (1991) 'HIV, drugs, and public health in England: new words, old tunes' *International Journal of the Addictions* 26(12) 1263–77.

Stimson, G. and Oppenheimer, E. (1982) *Heroin Addiction: Treatment and Control in Britain*. London: Tavistock.

Stimson, G., Alldritt, L., Dolan, K., Donoghoe, M. and Lart, R. (1988) *Injecting Equipment Exchange Schemes, Final Report*. London: Goldsmiths College.

Strang, J. and Stimson, G. (eds) (1990) *AIDS and Drug Misuse*. London: Routledge.

Studlar, D. (2008) 'US tobacco control: public health, political economy, or morality policy?' *Review of Policy Research* 25(5) 393–410.

Thompson, G. (2000) 'Economic globalization?' in: D. Held (ed.) *A Globalizing World? Culture, Economics, Politics*. London: Routledge, pp. 85–126.

Trocki, C. (1999) *Opium, Empire and the Global Political Economy: A Study of the Asian Opium Trade 1750–1950*. London: Routledge.

United Kingdom Drug Policy Commision (UKDPC) (2008) *Recovery Consensus Statement: A Vision for Recovery*. London: UKDPC.

Vaissade, L. and Legleye, S. (2009) 'Capture–recapture estimates of the local prevalence of problem drug use in six French cities' *European Journal of Public Health* 19(1) 32–37.

Valverde, M. (1998) *Diseases of the Will: Alcohol and the Dilemmas of Freedom*. Cambridge: Cambridge University Press.

——(2003) 'Police science, British style: pub licensing and knowledges of urban disorder' *Economy and Society* 32(2) 234–52.

van Duyne, P. (2003) 'Organizing cigarette smuggling and policy making, ending up in smoke' *Crime, Law and Social Change* 39 285–317.

van Ree, E. (2002) 'Drugs, the democratic civilising process and the consumer society' *International Journal of Drug Policy* 13 349–53.

Vincent-Jones, P. (2002) 'Value and purpose in government: central–local relations in regulatory perspective' *Journal of Law & Society* 29(1) 27–55.

Voruz, V. (2005) 'The politics of *The Culture of Control*: undoing genealogy' *Economy and Society* 34(1) 154–72.

Vuchinich, R. and Heather, N. (eds) (2003) *Choice, Behavioural Economics and Addiction*. Oxford: Pergamon Press.

Waley, A. (1958) *The Opium War through Chinese Eyes*. Stanford: Stanford University Press.

Warner, J. (1994) ''Resolv'd to drink no more': addiction as a preindustrial construct' *Journal of Studies on Alcohol* 55 685–91.

White, W. (1998) *Slaying the Dragon – The History of Addiction Treatment and Recovery in America*. Bloomington: Lighthouse Training Institute.

Wiener, M.J. (1990) *Reconstructing the Criminal: Culture, Law and Policy in England, 1830–1914*. Cambridge: Cambridge University Press.

Wood, J. and Shearing, C. (2007) *Imagining Security*. Cullompton, Devon: Willan.

World Health Organization (WHO) (1964) *Thirteenth Report of the Expert Committee on Addiction-producing Drugs*. WHO Technical Report Series, No. 273. Geneva: WHO.

Zimmer, L. (1997) 'The ascendancy and decline of worldwide cannabis prohibition' in: L. Böllinger (ed.) *Cannabis Science: From Prohibition to Human Right*. Frankfurt am Main: Peter Lang.

Index